D1478408

PREVIOUS PAGE: 7TH HOLE
SHINNECOCK HILLS.
(L.C. Lambrecht)

RIGHT: 18TH HOLE BETHPAGE
BLACK. *(L.C. Lambrecht)*

Copyright © 2002 Sleeping Bear Press

All rights reserved. No part of this book may be
reproduced in any manner without the express written
consent of the publisher, except in the case of brief
excerpts in critical reviews and articles. All inquiries
should be addressed to:

Sleeping Bear Press
310 North Main Street
P.O. Box 20
Chelsea, MI 48118
www.sleepingbearpress.com

Printed and bound in Canada

10 9 8 7 6 5 4 3 2 1

Library of Congress Cataloging-in-Publication Data

Quirin, William L. America's linksland : a century of
Long Island golf / by William Quirin.
 p. cm.
ISBN 1-58536-087-2
 1. Golf—New York (State)—Long Island—History—20th
century. I. Title.
GV982.N7 Q57 2002
796.352'09747'21—dc21
2002001131

AMERICA'S

A Century of Long Island Golf

LINKSLAND

William Quirin

Photography by L. C. Lambrecht

Sleeping Bear Press

To all the golfers of Long Island

Acknowledgments

First and foremost, I want to thank the Metropolitan Golf Association (and its Executive Director, Jay Mottola), for providing me with the platform to facilitate the research that has produced this book, as well as the Association's 100th anniversary book, *Golf Clubs of the MGA*. Also I want to express my gratitude to the many MGA committeemen and club members who gave so freely of their time and knowledge.

Secondly, the ever-helpful Patti Moran of the United States Golf Association staff, who gave of her time endlessly and always with a smile on her face.

A special thanks goes to Larry Lambrecht for the wonderful photography that portrays the Black Course so dramatically for the 2002 U.S. Open, and to Bradley Klein for his recollections of Long Island as it was during our youth.

A tip of the hat goes to my daughter, Kristin, who makes her photographic debut in dad's book.

Also, the following: Joe Donahue of the Long Island Golf Association; Dave Catalano of Bethpage State Park; Joan Marcello of the Long Island Classic; George Bahto, Dave Senft, Jack Pascal, Billy Edwards, Jim Tingley, Bob Capazzi; Garden City Golf Club, The Creek Club, The Maidstone Club; the Long Island Studies Institute at Hofstra University; and Daniel Wexler, for the use of several photographs from his book, *The Missing Links*.

PREVIOUS PAGE (OPPOSITE DEDICATION):
9TH GREEN, SHINNECOCK HILLS CLUBHOUSE
(*L.C. Lambrecht*)

OPPOSITE PAGE: 18TH HOLE PIPING ROCK.
(*L.C. Lambrecht*)

Foreword

For a young golfer, there was no better place in the world to grow up than Long Island. I grew up in the southeast corner of Queens County, near JFK Airport, but also within a five-mile bicycle ride of the golf-rich Five Towns area of Nassau County. There, as a youthful caddie in the late 1960s, I had the run on Mondays of some classic private layouts—Seawane, Woodmere, Rockaway Hunting Club, and Inwood, scene of Bobby Jones's historic triumph in the 1923 U.S. Open—as well as the upscale municipal layout at Lawrence. I liked earning money as a bagtoter, but my real motivation for carrying those heavy bags was that it qualified me for golf at facilities that I'd never otherwise had access to.

Traveling the island by car or on the Long Island Railroad, I sometimes got the impression that there was nothing but golf there to gawk at. Nowadays, when my commercial airline flights take a path across the island on the way to—or from—Connecticut, where I live, I stare down from the window and try to spot as many of the layouts as I can. It makes for an intriguing form of "plane spotting" that is, I suspect, common among experienced golf travelers.

The two farthest ends of Long Island, 94 miles apart, are occupied, appropriately enough, by daily-fee golf courses. On the western-most tip sits Brooklyn's Dyker Beach GC, one of only two courses serving the 2.4 million people of New York City's most populous borough. Due east, at the extreme end of Suffolk County's south fork, is Montauk Downs GC. Between them can be found some of the world's most historic golf ground—home to over 160 golf courses, including the sites of seven U.S. Amateurs, six U.S. Opens, five PGA's, four Women's Amateurs, and three Walker Cups. How appropriate it is, then, for historian Bill Quirin to chronicle the story of golf on this diverse island. For all the attention on the private retreats, such as Shinnecock Hills and National Golf Links of America, there are also some storied public tracts that have generated their share of lore. The world will discover one of these in the form of Bethpage State Park's Black Course, home of the 2002 U.S. Open. My only regret about the event is they won't make the pros spend all night before their rounds camping out in the parking lot waiting for a tee time.

Bradley S. Klein
Editor of *Golfweek Superintendent News*
Author of *Rough Meditations* (1997)
Discovering Donald Ross: The Architect and His Golf Courses (2001)

Opposite page: 8th hole Atlantic.
(L.C. Lambrecht)

Prologue

Golf in the United States: date of birth, 1888 at St. Andrew's in Yonkers, New York. Or so traditionalists tell us. Or perhaps the first American golf course was in Kentucky, or in Vermont, or in Pennsylvania. Perhaps the first golf shots struck in this country took place at the Meadow Brook Hunt Club, somewhere in the vicinity of today's Nassau Coliseum.

Whatever the facts may be, it is true that golf's first tourist attraction was the original course at Shinnecock Hills in Southampton, where pilgrims arrived to survey the first great American golf course laid out with the aid of a British expert.

Shinnecock Hills has been in and out of the golfing spotlight since then, hosting the second-ever U.S. Open (and the far more important U.S. Amateur) in 1896, then emerging from a veil of secrecy and exclusivity to host the U.S. Open once again in 1986 and 1995, with a fourth on the horizon for 2004.

No sooner had Shinnecock Hills enjoyed its first moment of glory than Garden City stepped in. Its course was instantly recognized as an American landmark, and major championships were held regularly on its hallowed links. Nassau soon followed suit, and the two clubs produced the two men, Walter Travis of Garden City and Jerry Travers of Nassau, who would become golf's first great rivalry. They would fill their trophy cases with numerous national amateur championships, even a U.S. Open title and a British Amateur crown.

At this point you meet Charles Blair Macdonald, who came to Long Island from Canada by way of Scotland and Chicago. Macdonald didn't think the early American courses were on a par with the best in Great Britain, and set out to raise the bar. He did so on Long Island, first with the National Golf Links in Southampton, then a decade later at Lido. For almost two decades, these two Long Island courses were considered among the three best in the country.

During the Roarin' Twenties, Nassau County's north shore—the Gold Coast, as it was called—was the setting for the glittering parties that gave the era its everlasting glamour. The south shore was the stage for one of the great moments in golf history, Bobby Jones's terrific shot to the 18th green at Inwood that won him his first major championship, the U.S. Open. In between, on the old Hempstead Plain, arose the "Sports Center of America," as the Salisbury Country Club came to be known. With five 18-hole golf courses, Salisbury had no peer.

In that same era, Macdonald, the National Golf Links, and Garden City all played key roles in the inception of the first international competition between the United States and Great Britain. The first two Walker Cups played in this country

OPPOSITE PAGE: 8TH HOLE, MAIDSTONE CLUB. (*L.C. Lambrecht*)

(13

were contested on Long Island, at National and Garden City, with Macdonald influential in creating the matches and bringing them to National.

The Depression and war years, of course, were difficult on Long Islanders and Long Island golf clubs, several of which closed their doors forever. The era did have a few high points, though. There were a few national championships held on Long Island during that difficult period of history, perhaps the most notable being the 1932 U.S. Open at the old Fresh Meadow course in Flushing. For it was there that Gene Sarazen staged one of golf's first great "charges" from behind, playing the last 28 holes in exactly 100 strokes.

It was also during the Depression that the magnificent Bethpage State Park complex in Farmingdale was created, giving Long Islanders perhaps the finest public facility in the country, four outstanding courses, including the legendary Black Course which in 2002 will become the first truly public course to host the U.S. Open.

Immediately following the end of World War II, the face of Long Island began changing. The exodus of the masses from the city out into eastern Queens, Nassau County, and eventually into Suffolk County, rippled through the golf community. So, too, did the construction of roads needed to support the suburban commute. Several clubs in Queens found their properties in demand for housing development, and either moved out to Nassau or closed their doors forever. Others found their property bisected by the new roads, and did the same.

As the population of the suburbs increased, the need for new golf courses, both private and public, became apparent, and a number of new facilities were built during the 1960s and 1970s. And then came the drought, with practically no additions to the Long Island golfscape during the 1970s and 1980s, a reflection in part of growing real estate values on Long Island.

The status quo has changed dramatically during the 1990s and into the twenty-first century, mostly in spacious Suffolk County. Several new exclusive private clubs have come into being, a few deserving of entry into the national rankings of the elite among American courses. In addition, upscale public courses, offering golfers the experience of country club life "for a day," are proliferating at a rapid rate, significantly enhancing Long Island's publinxers options.

Long Island golf today is state-of-the-art and top-of-the-line. Current rankings issued by the two leading golf magazines of the day prove the point. Five Long Island courses are ranked among the country's top 50. Eleven of New York State's top 20 courses can be found on Long Island. With two U.S. Opens coming in the next three years, attracting thousands of golfing "pilgrims" to the Open sites and

OPPOSITE PAGE: 15TH HOLE, THE CREEK.
(L.C. Lambrecht)

nearby courses as well, those rankings can only improve.

Long Island has been a major player in American golf almost from the sport's inception in this country. Major championships have been a regular visitor to its shores, starting with the 1896 U.S. Open and Amateur at Shinnecock Hills. That heritage can only be enhanced when the Open is played at Bethpage Black in 2002 and once again at Shinnecock Hills in 2004.

1

A Brief History of Long Island

16) Shortly after the turn of the twentieth century, when Charles Blair Macdonald sought the perfect location on which to build his "ideal American course" he chose Long Island. Why? Most certainly, it was the dramatic variety in its terrain.

The great Canadian glaciers shaped the hills and finger bays of Long Island's North Shore and the rich plains of the South Shore. The ice caps, one thousand feet tall (skyscraper height), started coming down from Canada 2.4 million years ago, expanding and receding across North America several times. Long Island was glaciated twice, the second time some 22,000 years ago. The glaciers changed the landscape drastically, obliterating millions of years of geological development.

The second ice cap stopped mid-Island, thereby forming a hilly moraine (Long Island's central spine), together with the fertile Hempstead Plain just to its south. The receding glaciers also formed separate moraines on the North Shore, as well as kettle holes like Lake Ronkonkoma and Lake Success.

The Hempstead Plain was flat and treeless, with tall grasses and wildflowers. It was the first prairie in America, and ultimately Long Island's first tourist attraction. It encompassed 60,000 acres, extending from the eastern border of Queens almost to Suffolk County, bordered by the present-day Hempstead Turnpike and Northern State Parkway, and was 16 miles long and 4 miles wide. Racetracks, military bases, and airfields were built there, along with villages such as Garden City and Levittown. The Plains are now dotted with several great golf courses, Garden City Golf Club being the

Golf Digest's **Current National Rankings**

#5 Shinnecock Hills
#16 National Golf Links
#27 Garden City Golf Club
#42 Maidstone
#46 Bethpage Black
#100 Atlantic

Golf Digest ranked 11 Long Island courses among its top 25 in New York State. Also included on that list were Piping Rock, Meadow Brook, The Creek, and Deepdale.

THE MANHANSETT MANOR HOUSE ON
SHELTER ISLAND, LONG ISLAND'S FIRST
GREAT RESORT. *(The Golf Guide 1899)*

Golf Magazine's **Current National Rankings**

#5 Shinnecock Hills (6)

#14 National Golf Links (23)

#27 Bethpage Black (45)

#33 Garden City Golf Club (57)

#39 Maidstone (65)

#78 The Creek

#93 Piping Rock

(World ranking, if any, in parentheses)

most notable.

The first Homo sapiens came to Long Island 12,000 years ago. These "native Americans" were nomadic hunters from Asia who came across the Bering Strait by means of a land bridge created when the glaciers absorbed much of the water from the oceans. They called Long Island "Sewanhackey," meaning "land of shells" (or wampum). The Seawane Club memorializes that seminal name.

The Europeans arrived early in the sixteenth century in the person of Verrazano in 1524, who sailed into New York harbor. Henry Hudson was the second, sailing up the river that now bears his name in 1609. In 1614 Adrian Block became the first European to see Long Island and the Sound, and claimed the island for the Netherlands. Hempstead was the first Dutch settlement, established in 1643.

The first Englishman to make his home on Long Island was Lion Gardiner, circa 1638-1639, on the island that now bears his name. Toward the end of the nineteenth century, the Manhansett Manor House on Shelter Island, overlooking Gardiner's Bay, rivaled Newport and Southampton as a summer destination for "the spoiled children of fortune," who arrived daily on steamers from New York and New London.

The English colonies at Southold and Southampton followed in 1640. John Underhill, founder of the Southold colony, eventually lived on an estate in Oyster Bay called Killingworth.

During the 1640s and 1650s, with the two nations at peace in Europe, the Dutch

(17

and British colonies coexisted on Long Island. Western Long Island was Dutch, eastern Long Island was English. The Treaty of Hartford in 1650 established a north-south line from Greenwich, Connecticut, passing just west of Oyster Bay that defined the boundary line. Bethpage Park is situated close to that boundary.

The peace ended in Europe in the mid 1650s, and a decade later, the English ordered the Dutch to leave Manhattan, which they did, peacefully. The English called their new colony Yorkshire after James, Duke of York, brother of King Charles II. Richard Nicholls became the first English governor of New York. In 1693, Long Island was named the Island of Nassau, honoring King William III, who descended from the German House of Nassau. Eventually, a county and a prominent country club would bear that name.

Long Island was divided during the Revolutionary War. Queens County, Jamaica, Hempstead, and Oyster Bay were loyalist, while North Hempstead and Suffolk County supported the patriots. The Battle of Long Island (in Brooklyn) was the first major military test for the Continental Army. Their defeat led to seven years of British occupation of Long Island. They may have been Long Island's first golfers.

As late as the 1830s, Long Islanders traveled by stage-coach. Long Island's first major road was Fulton Avenue, followed by North Country Road (Northern Blvd.), South Country Road (Montauk Highway), and Middle Country Road (Jericho Turnpike).

The Long Island Railroad opened in 1844 as part of a rail-sea shortcut to Boston. Travelers would take the train to Greenport, then a steamer across the Sound before boarding a second train to New England destinations. During the railroad-building boom of 1865–1875, many competitive lines existed, all eventually merged into the Long Island Railroad. Before the end of the century, golf

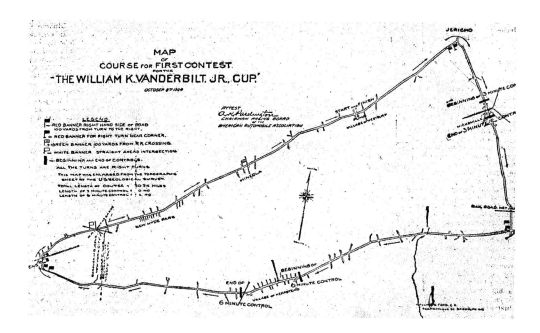

Opposite page: William K. Vanderbilt, Jr.
(*Golf Illustrated*)

Diagram of the route of the Vanderbilt
Cup race in 1904. (*New York Times*)

pilgrims would travel by railroad to Garden City or Southampton to view the first great American golf courses.

The only United States president to have lived on Long Island was Teddy Roosevelt, whose Sagamore Hill estate in Oyster Bay was the summer White House during 1902–1908. Although a member at the old Oyster Bay Golf Club, Roosevelt did not enjoy golf, asserting that it was not vigorous enough to suit his tastes. Scientist Albert Einstein summered on Nassau Point, and loved to sail in Little Peconic Bay, although there is no record he ever visited Shinnecock Hills or the National for a round of golf.

The first international automobile race held in the United States took place in Nassau County in 1904. It was the Vanderbilt Cup, and it was staged by one of Long Island's all-time leading sportsmen, William K. Vanderbilt Jr., later the patriarch of the Deepdale Golf Club. The race originally was contested on public roads like Jericho and Hempstead Turnpikes, which, of course, were closed for the occasion. The race started in Westbury, followed Jericho Turnpike to Queens Village, turned back eastward on Hempstead Turnpike all the way to Bethpage, went north to Jericho, then came back to the starting point and grandstand on Jericho Turnpike in Westbury.

Following a fatality in the 1906 race, the Vanderbilt Motor Parkway was built to host the race. It was a private road for autos only, the first to be built of concrete, and

OPPOSITE PAGE: THE 1906 VANDERBILT CUP RACE ON JERICHO TURNPIKE. *(Nassau County Museum at Long Island Studies Institute)*

ABOVE: DEAD MAN'S CURVE ON THE MOTOR PARKWAY. *(Nassau County Museum at Long Island Studies Institute)*

the first to use bridges and overpasses to eliminate intersections. It no sooner had been completed (in 1910) when auto racing was banned.

The Motor Parkway became a fenced-in limited-access toll road, 100 feet wide with a 20-foot roadway, connecting Flushing with Lake Ronkonkoma that became "the" place for a pleasant drive on a Sunday afternoon. The road ultimately became antiquated, superseded by the new Northern and Southern State Parkways, and was closed on Easter Day, 1938. Remnants of the Motor Parkway can be seen today cutting through the middle of the Wheatley Hills Golf Club's property. In its day the Motor Parkway provided easy access to a number of clubs, including Fresh Meadow, Glen Oaks, and Bethpage. Indeed, the road's western terminus was adjacent to the eastern flank of the old Fresh Meadow course in Flushing.

Glenn Curtiss flew the first air flight on Long Island in 1909, taking off from Mineola and flying for half an hour. Two decades later, in 1927, Charles Lindbergh began his solo flight to Europe from Roosevelt Field, heading in the direction of the Salisbury Country Club (now Eisenhower Park), narrowly missing the electrical wires along Merrick Avenue as he gained altitude. Roosevelt Field, once the largest airfield in the world, was closed in 1951, and the site became the largest shopping center in the world in 1956. The Old Westbury Golf Club (no relation to the present club) was situated between the airfield and the Motor Parkway to its west.

During the "Roaring Twenties," the social spotlight focused on the "Gold Coast" (Nassau County's north shore), where some 500 gilded mansions hosted the legendary parties of that era. The Piping Rock and Creek Clubs played a prominent social and sporting role during this era. The South Shore was not without its own "Glitter Alley," a.k.a. the "Great Light Way," a collection of roadhouses, nightclubs, and speakeasies along Merrick Road and Sunrise Highway. America's best-known bands and show biz personalities performed there.

Few men (if any) have had a more lasting or telling effect on Long Island than Robert Moses. He promoted the use of automobiles, of parks and parkways, expressways, bridges and tunnels, and ultimately ... traffic congestion. Lincoln Center, Shea Stadium, and the United Nations all bear his signature, as did the 1939 and 1964 World's Fairs in Flushing. He also reshaped the destiny of several of Long Island's golf clubs.

Moses conceived Jones Beach in 1926 (at the age of 37) from what had been an isolated, inaccessible sandbar. Jones Beach, Heckscher State Park, and the entire Southern State Parkway all were completed in 1929.

The original plan for the Northern State Parkway went through some of Long Island's most expensive estates, including Otto Kahn's in Woodbury and several in Old Westbury. Although the route eventually was changed, Moses made a number of prominent enemies in the process.

He also extended the Meadowbrook Parkway north to connect the Northern State Parkway with the Southern State Parkway in 1954, thereby making the South Shore beaches accessible to most Long Islanders. That enhancement, unfortunately, uprooted the Meadow Brook Hunt Club, its fabled polo fields and golf course.

If the Depression was not enough to set the 1930s apart as an unhappy decade in American history, the devastating hurricane of September 21, 1938, added a surprise exclamation point. The most violent hurricane of the century came practically without warning, and lasted just three hours in late afternoon. It left more than 50 dead, including 29 in Westhampton Beach alone. The storm's 125 mph winds and 15-foot waves left the area within one mile of the beach under six feet of water, and destroyed all but 26 of the 179 houses between Quiogue and Moriches. Total damage was estimated at $6.2 million (in 1938 dollars). Golf courses from Westhampton to Maidstone felt its wrath well into the following year.

The 15 years of economic depression followed by global conflict affected the lives of most Long Islanders. Several Long Island golf and country clubs suffered a fatal blow, closing their doors forever.

In the years following World War II, with more and more people living in the suburbs and owning automobiles, the parkways were jammed on weekends and during rush hours. In 1953 Moses came up with the idea of a six-lane 81-mile expressway through the center of the Island. Work on the Long Island Expressway started in 1954 and proceeded slowly, reaching Glen Cove Road late in 1958, the Nassau-Suffolk border by 1962, and Riverhead in 1972. The old Oakland and Deepdale golf courses stood in its path; Deepdale was able to move, Oakland was not so fortunate.

The final pieces of the puzzle were the Throggs Neck Bridge (1961) and Verrazzano Bridge (1964), which made travel to and from Long Island more reasonable. Soon, the professional golf tours visited, and eventually the U.S. Open returned.

OPPOSITE PAGE, TOP: AIRPLANE GOLF OVER THE OLD WESTBURY GOLF CLUB (ADJACENT TO ROOSEVELT FIELD) IN 1928. *(Golf Illustrated)*

OPPOSITE PAGE, BOTTOM: AN AERIAL VIEW OF ROOSEVELT FIELD. NOTE THE GOLF HOLES ON THE LEFT. *(Nassau County Museum at Long Island Studies Institute)*

BELOW: ROBERT MOSES. *(New York State Office of Parks, Recreation and Historic Preservation)*

BELOW RIGHT: CONSTRUCTION OF THE LONG ISLAND EXPRESSWAY NEAR ROUTE 110. *(Newsday)*

(23

2

Genesis at Shinnecock Hills

24)

During the winter of 1890–1891, a young Scottish golfer named Willie Dunn was in southern France building an 18-hole course at Biarritz, a favorite watering spot of the rich and famous. Coincidentally, three Americans from the exclusive Southampton colony on the eastern end of Long Island were enjoying their winter respite at Biarritz at the same time. William K. Vanderbilt, Duncan Cryder, and Edward S. Mead had heard about golf and its popularity in Britain, and asked Dunn if he might demonstrate the game for them.

Dunn took the trio to the now-famous "chasm hole," a 125-yarder across a deep ravine, and proceeded to hit several balls, all of them onto the green, some quite close to the hole. "This beats rifle shooting for distance and accuracy. It is a game I think would go in our country," exclaimed Vanderbilt. And so were planted the seeds that ultimately would result in one of America's greatest championship courses, Shinnecock Hills, Long Island's first and, perhaps, finest.

Later that year, the Southamptonites contacted the Montreal Golf Club, and received permission to "borrow" their professional, Willie Davis, for one month to lay out their golf course which, like the original Prestwick course in Scotland, consisted of just 12 holes. A local engineer named David Raynor was engaged to survey the land, and his son Seth, then 17, carried the rods and chains. This was Seth Raynor's only connection with golf until 1908 when he was retained by Charles Blair Macdonald to survey the property destined to become the National Golf Links.

OPPOSITE PAGE: THE OPENING HOLE AT SHINNECOCK HILLS FROM RIGHT OF THE TEE WITH THE FAIRWAY AND GREEN INVITING THE PLAYER FOR AN ADVENTUROUS START. (*L. C. Lambrecht*)

To build the Shinnecock course, Davis employed a crew of 150 Shinnecock Indians from the nearby reservation. The Shinnecocks had lived and hunted toward the end of Long Island as far back as the fifteenth century. The construction project was not without its difficulties, though, as the following later determined to be secondhand report from Dunn reveals:

"Except for several horse-drawn road scrapers, all the work was done by hand. The fairways were cleaned off and the natural grass left in. The rough was very rough, with clothes-ripping blueberry bushes, large boulders, and many small gullies. The place was dotted with Indian burial mounds and we left some of these intact as bunkers in front of the greens. We scraped out some of the mounds and made sand traps. It was here that the Indians buried their empty whiskey bottles, but we did not find this out until later when playing the course. One never knew when an explosion shot in a trap would bring out a couple of firewater flasks, or perhaps a bone or two."

26)

Nonetheless, the course was ready for play by June, and the club used a makeshift clubhouse that resembled a roadside hot dog stand. Other hazards on the golf course included a family of skunks known to take a leisurely stroll across a fairway, and bald eagles that would occasionally swoop down and pilfer a golf ball!

The Shinnecock Hills Golf Club was organized later that summer. Construction of a clubhouse was approved, and the club was incorporated, becoming the first such legal entity in this country.

The clubhouse was completed in June of 1892. Stanford White, the most fashionable architect of the day, designed it. A favorite in New York social circles, White's previous credits included Penn Station and the original Madison Square Garden, above which he lived in a "tower studio." White was destined to gain even more notoriety in death, a murder victim in 1906 during a theater performance at the Garden. The ensuing trial was one of the most sensational in the city's history.

Built in the shingled country house style of the region, the Shinnecock Hills clubhouse was the first building of its kind in the United States, and formed the nucleus of the present clubhouse. Aside from being the dominant landmark in the area, it also quickly became a focal point for the Southampton social set. The social status associated with membership in the club became so desirable that Shinnecock Hills soon was forced to establish a waiting list, the first of its kind in this country. The club also was noted for its lavish meals, particularly those served at

RIGHT: THE FIFTH HOLE, KNOWN AS "THE BASTION." *(Golf)*

BELOW: APPROACH TO THE HOME GREEN. *(Golf)*

lunchtime. Indeed, Shinnecock Hills was the prototype of the modern country club. (27

Golf quickly became a fad at Southampton, especially among the women. The men dressed for golf in red blazers with monogrammed brass buttons and either knickers or white flannel trousers, and the women wore long white dresses and fancy hats. The original 12-hole course soon became so crowded that another nine holes (the Red Course) were laid out in the valley north of the clubhouse, for the exclusive use of the ladies. Soon the 12-hole course was expanded to the 18-hole White Course.

The original Shinnecock Hills layout was thought to be a cut above other courses of that era. Laid out over rolling, treeless terrain, it featured a number of blind shots. The greens were quite small in size, although many were severely contoured. The railroad from New York—a 2 1/2 hour journey—adjoined the course and came into play on four holes on the front nine. It also carried many pilgrims from other clubs to the end of Long Island to study the first legitimate golf course in the United States. Yet the course measured just 4,423 yards, a weakness that was "exploited" during the 1896 U.S. Amateur and Open Championships.

The 1896 tournaments were the second to be held under the auspices of the fledgling U.S.G.A., of which Shinnecock Hills was a charter member. They were staged concurrently at the same site (a practice discontinued after 1897), with the Amateur of far greater stature. In 1896 they were contested in mid-July, during a

spell of extreme summer heat.

The Amateur marked the first of back-to-back titles captured by H.J. Whigham, a recent graduate of the Scottish links, and son-in-law of Charles Blair Macdonald. Whigham emerged victorious from a field of 80 contestants, of whom 16 qualified for the match play part of the tournament. He led all qualifiers with scores of 86 and 77.

The *New York Times'* coverage of the semifinal matches was quite sparse, discussing nothing more than the drives off the first tee and the final scores—there was no on-course reporting then. Nonetheless, the story tells us something of the flavor of the Shinnecock Hills course:

> *"The match play was begun by J.G. Thorp with a long straight drive from the first tee. The drive went to the right of the windmill and far out on the green. H.P. Toler followed with a long, low drive to the left of the mill, landing in a good position."It was twenty minutes later when H.J. Whigham and A.M. Coates followed. The delay was occasioned by the failure of Coates to be on hand on time. Whigham*

THE "CRATER" GREEN. *(Golf)*

OPPOSITE PAGE: H.J. WHIGHAM, WINNER OF THE 1896 U.S. AMATEUR. *(Golf)*

sent off a long drive, and the ball landed close to the roadway. Coates followed with
a good one to the left of the windmill."

Whigham and Thorp reached the 36-hole finals, and Whigham was the easy victor, 8&7. He used an unusual "wooden putter" to great effect, running his short approaches onto the greens rather than pitching them as his rivals did.

Charles Blair Macdonald, the defending champion, reportedly was suffering the effects of ptomaine poisoning (likely a nineteenth century colloquialism for "hangover") when Thorp eliminated him in the first round.

Driving and putting contests followed the Amateur Championship; it took a drive of 210 yards to win the former.

The Open was merely a one-day "add-on" to the Amateur in those days, and was won by James Foulis, professional at the Chicago Golf Club. Foulis's scores of 78-74=152 proved best by 3 strokes in the field of 28. The *New York Times* provided some background on the winner:

> *"Foulis certainly earned his honors by splendid play, and his score of 74 in the second round tied Whigham's record for the course made early in the week. Foulis learned the game at the famous St. Andrews links in Scotland, and has been two years in this country, having been imported by C.B. Macdonald, and he has been with the Chicago Golf Club ever since."*

Other contestants included Willie Davis, Willie Dunn, Amateur champion Whigham (who finished tied for fifth), and two Shinnecock Indians, John Shippen and Oscar Bunn, both 21 years old at the time, both former members of the work crew that built Shinnecock Hills five years earlier, and both caddies at the club.

Shippen, in contention until a disastrous 11 on the short par-4 13th hole, where his tee shot found a sandy road, eventually tied for fifth place. He later became the professional at nearby Maidstone. The son of a black minister and a Shinnecock mother, he is remembered as the first black man to compete in the Open Championship. Indeed, Shippen's entry led to a rebellion, the white professionals refusing to play until U.S.G.A. president Theodore Havemeyer threatened to conduct the tournament with just the two Shinnecocks competing. Shippen's first-round 78 left him tied for the lead, but without a playing companion. His original partner, an indignant Macdonald, stormed off the course after a morning round 83, and did not return! Such is the legend, but the *New York Times* report tells otherwise:

"Shippen beat Macdonald by 12 strokes in the first half, and the latter with-drew in the second half and simply kept Shippen's score."

It is interesting to note that the galleries at Shinnecock Hills for the 1896 Championships were predominantly female. According to the *New York Times*, regarding the attendance at the U.S. Open:

"... although there was not as much interest taken in the play as in the amateur event, there were equally as many persons present as during the preceding days. In the afternoon, when the second round was being played, there was a continuous string of carriages arriving at the clubhouse, and by 3 o'clock there were over 300 ladies on the links, many of whom followed the players over the greater part of the course. The gay costumes of the ladies and the scarlet-coated club members made a very pretty picture, scattered as they were, all over the hills."

30)

Shinnecock Hills was virtually the birthplace of women's golf in this country. Indeed, it was the enthusiasm of the women that led to the rapid growth of the club.

After the 1896 tournaments the Shinnecock Hills course was revised. Too many players broke 80, and there was talk the course wasn't of championship caliber. At first, it was lengthened to 5,369 yards, but in 1901, the Red Course was abandoned so that the White Course might be expanded to a championship test of over 6,000 yards. One final adjustment at the hands of Charles B. Macdonald and Seth Raynor, completed in 1916, included the creation of the present seventh hole and the basic routing of four other holes.

Shinnecock Hills' women won the first four U.S. Women's Amateur titles. Mrs. C.S. Brown won the first (unofficial) Amateur at Meadow Brook in 1895. And then came Beatrix Hoyt, America's first female teenage phenomenon. Miss Hoyt was the granddaughter of Salmen Chase, Secretary of the Treasury under Abraham Lincoln, and eventually Chief Justice of the Supreme Court. (Chase's likeness adorns the $10,000 bill.) Beatrix Hoyt won three consecutive U.S. Women's Amateurs (1896–1898) at ages 17-19, was the medalist five consecutive years (1896–1900), then abruptly retired from competitive golf at age 21 less than two months after losing on the 20th hole in the semifinals in 1900 at her home club.

The magazine *Golf* set the stage for the 1900 Women's Amateur at Shinnecock Hills:

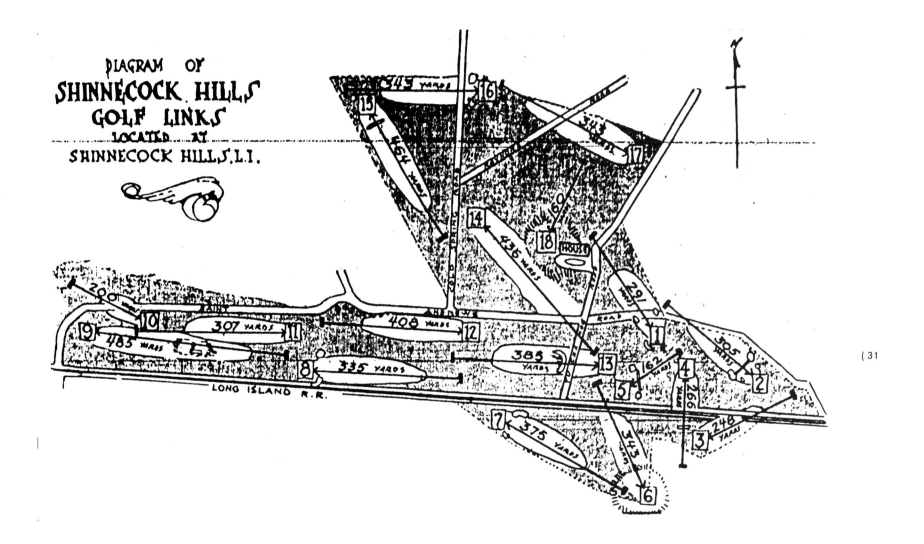

DIAGRAM OF THE SHINNECOCK HILLS
COURSE IN 1915. *(New York Telegram)*

"The weather was sultry for the first two days, but with the shift of the wind, the last half of the week was delightfully cool and pleasant, veritable picnic weather. The Green Committee had doubtless done their utmost to bring the course into shape, but the long-continued drought was too much for them. The putting greens were excellent, but the fair green was in about its poorest condition, patchy, hard, and filled with innumerable cups. The course was at its full stretch, and none of the tees had been put forward. The women desired to play under the exact conditions of masculine golfing prowess, and their wish was gratified."

Beatrix Hoyt won the medal with a score of 94, two strokes better than ultimate winner Frances Griscom of Merion. They were the only ones to break 100; Margaret Curtis of Essex County (outside Boston) was third at 101. Sixteen ladies qualified for match play.

Griscom and 16-year-old Curtis advanced to the finals in similar fashion. Both were dormie 2 in their semifinal matches against Eunice Terry and Beatrix Hoyt, respectively, and both allowed their opponents to win the last two holes. Griscom won on the 19th hole, Curtis on the 20th. *Golf* commented on Miss Hoyt's demise:

Below: Frances Griscom, 1900 U.S. Women's Amateur champion. *(Golf)*

Opposite page, top: Margaret Curtis playing from the railroad tracks crossing the sixth hole during 1900 Women's Amateur. *(Golf)*

Opposite page, bottom: Beatrix Hoyt winning her quarterfinal match. *(Golf)*

> *"The luck of the tournament was certainly not on Miss Hoyt's side. She had an extremely hard game with Mrs. Caleb Fox, which she won by 1-up, and then had to play in the semifinals with Miss Margaret Curtis, the surprise of the tournament. But it was in losing the twentieth hole that she had her hardest luck, for while both players drove into the bunker at the second green, Miss Curtis had the good fortune not to be penalized in the slightest degree by the bad shot as her ball stopped exactly opposite an opening in the bunker, through which she was able to lay it dead for the hole. But for this no doubt Miss Hoyt would be champion once more, for her ability to win a majority of matches with Miss Griscom is conceded."*

Curtis's ball lay in the sand, directly behind an opening between two mounds; Hoyt's ball was behind one of the mounds. Her choice of a cleek to execute the 80-yard shot was criticized by reporters on the scene.

According to the *New York Times*, the youthful Curtis had a jittery start in the finals:

> *"Miss Curtis failed to uphold her accurate driving reputation, and sliced her ball into high grass behind the stables. Her next two shots were short, while Miss Griscom got away a fine brassie , and from the road reached the green in three. She won the hole handily in 5, Miss Curtis needing two more. The latter appeared to no better advantage in driving from the second tee. She topped the ball, sending it into high grass, and plunked into the bunker on her third, failing to get over in four and just clearing the mound in five. This woeful lack of championship form was expressed in the sad countenances of the Bostonian fraternity. Miss Curtis's nerves steadied a bit on the next tee, and she made her first good drive."*

Curtis did, indeed, overcome her early nervousness, and had the match back to all even after five holes, only to have Griscom turn around and win the next four

holes to establish an insurmountable lead. Here are selected comments from the *New York Times'* coverage:

"The seventh green is 357 yards from the tee, and if a man makes it in the bogey figure of five, he will talk about it for the rest of the day. Miss Griscom did better, and made it in four from a sensational ten-foot putt. Miss Curtis was exactly as good, and only for the fact that the golfing fates do not generally allow two ten-foot putts on one green was she destined to lose. On the eighth Miss Griscom made the longest drive of the week at that point, dropping nearly fifty yards beyond the railroad track. Miss Curtis fell into the bank, and playing irregularly to the green lost in 8 to 6. Both showed thoroughbred form in playing the long ninth, 480 yards ... the Philadelphian played faultlessly, but her opponent had the advantage in distance, and was on top of the hill in three when, unfortunately, she overran several yards on her approach. She covered 500 yards in four shots. Miss Griscom excelled in her approach, stopping on the green, and won the hole in six."

Griscom ultimately won the match 6&4.

Golf's reporter, who used the pen name "Oldcastle," had some interesting comments about the American women golfers. He noted that Frances Griscom won the tournament with her excellent iron play, but about her driving, he said:

"In driving she uses a full swing, the club coming straight back over the shoulder, and as she does she turns around, apparently losing her balance in the act. She shows in this the general defect of her sex when the full swing is attempted. There is no follow through, though, strange to say, she was able usually to obtain good distance."

"Oldcastle" continued, first discussing Beatrix Hoyt's swing, then that of Margaret Curtis, in the process shedding some light on how the final match was won ... or lost:

"Miss Hoyt should be an object lesson to them in this respect. She has a short swing, three quarters at most, and though it is somewhat lacking in ease, yet clearly

she is in complete control of her club through the stroke, and so is able to follow through fairly well, and obtain both distance and direction. Unquestionably for general all-round play Miss Hoyt is still the leading player among the women, and so far as could be seen she was the one of those in the front rank who made use of her wrists as Travis does to get distance in driving. Now with Miss Margaret Curtis the case is altogether different. She has perhaps the easiest swing of any player in the country. It is full to the extreme, but she never twists off her feet or throws herself into an attitude suggestive of a contortionist, as so many do, and her club follows through in the most admirable manner. There is, besides, great power in her driving, and she obtains distance without apparent effort. This makes it surprising that she would have pressed so continually in the finals with Miss Griscom, because she can at all times beat the latter at the long game without an effort. As it was, she sliced and pulled constantly, getting in the long grass unnecessarily, without having sufficient mastery of her irons to enable her to make a good recovery. She is besides too impetuous. There is such a thing as too much deliberation, but there are times when some thought is necessary, and somehow she did not seem to realize this, frequently making every expensive mistakes through her undue haste."

J. H. Taylor, the immortal British professional and member of the famed "Triumvirate," was on hand and had some interesting comments:

"There was one phase of the contest that struck me as a great mistake–that is, the absolute childlike reliance that is placed on one's caddie."Coming to the play itself, I cannot say that I was very favorably impressed with the form shown. It seemed to me that only a few of the ladies had a correct swing. For example, one lady swung her club as though she was performing with a battle-axe."I am fully of the opinion that a team of American ladies would not have the slightest chance against the pick of our lady players."

Taylor pointed out that two-time American Amateur champion H.J. Whigham, a Scot, could not safely give more than four strokes per round to his sister Molly, who drove a ball measured at 235 yards at that season's British Women's Amateur.

Taylor also critically dissected Beatrix Hoyt's swing in none too favorable terms. That, and criticism she received for the manner in which she played the 20th hole of her semifinals match, may have been contributing factors in her decision to retire from competitive golf shortly thereafter.

THE INWARD NINTH HOLE WITH SHINNECOCK'S CLUBHOUSE IN THE BACKGROUND. *(L.C. Lambrecht)*

3

East End Neighbors

Although Shinnecock Hills had its "firsts," it also had its predecessors in the Hamptons. Shinnecock joined the good company of Maidstone (1891) in East Hampton, Westhampton (1890), and the oldest of them all, Quiogue (1887). All would soon follow Shinnecock into the golf world.

Maidstone actually has a legitimate claim as the first club in the Hamptons, being a successor club to the East Hampton Lawn Tennis Club, which had been organized in 1879. Maidstone was founded by the same group of people as a tennis and bathing club, indeed a family club, for the wealthy summer residents of East Hampton. They were a couple of generations removed from the summer colony of artists and writers, including John Howard Payne, who penned "Home Sweet Home" there in 1823.

Maidstone's first clubhouse was located out beyond today's third green, overlooking Hook Pond, the dunes, and the ocean. It featured 12 tennis courts, a baseball field, and bowling alleys. Members would arrive at the club by stagecoach, a bumpy one-hour ride over a dirt road from the nearest railroad station in Bridgehampton six miles away.

Maidstone expanded its early golf facilities to a full 18 holes in 1899. The course included seven holes "on the very margin of the waves," including two on the dunes just above the beach. These were located behind and to the east of the present clubhouse site.

Below: Maidstone's ninth hole. *(Maidstone Club)*

Opposite page: Maidstone's 14th hole, with ocean in background. *(Maidstone Club)*

Following a fire in 1922 that destroyed the original clubhouse, the club purchased a large plot of dunes land between Hook Pond and the ocean, and expanded to a pair of 18-hole courses (reduced to 27 holes by the hurricane of 1938). The club also built the present clubhouse overlooking the ocean and the new cabanas and pool.

Willie Park Jr., did the golf course work. His new holes on the dunesland were critically acclaimed. Bernard Darwin, the famed British writer, said that "the dunes holes (#6 through #10) were the finest stretch he had ever seen in America." Most memorable of these are two par 3s, the eighth and 14th, the former hidden from the beach by a tall dune, the latter playing straight at the ocean from a tee perched high atop a large dune. Also the ninth, one of the world's greatest par 4s, with the dunes separating the fairway from the beach to the right. The course is typically included among the "top 50" in the biannual ratings issued by the major golf magazines.

The terrain at Maidstone is relatively treeless, swept by the winds that typically blow from the southwest off the ocean. But the most vivid impression of golf at Maidstone is of the fearsome carries over marshland vegetation that the golfer faces on at least half the tees. A famous Scottish philosopher once said: "'Tis better to have golfed and foozled than never golfed at all." He might have whistled a different tune after a bad day off the tee at Maidstone.

(37

The Westhampton and Quiogue clubs were natural rivals, whether the issue be golf, baseball, or collegiate affiliation. The summer residents of Westhampton hailed primarily from Brooklyn, and many of them had attended Princeton. Quiogue attracted visitors from New York City, most of whom were graduates of Yale.

One of Westhampton's most storied families was the Homans. Sheppard Homans, a two-time football All-American at Princeton, was the father of Helen Homans, the national tennis champion of 1906, and grandfather of Eugene Homans, whom Bobby Jones defeated in the finals of the 1930 U.S. Amateur, the last leg of his Grand Slam.

Sailing and baseball were the passions of the early summer visitors. Large wagers were not uncommon on the ball games or the boat races. The baseball games between the two clubs were intense, often bitter.

Quiogue had a nine-hole course laid out in 1895. Later extended to 18 holes, the course was reduced to nine holes again by the devastating hurricane of 1938.

Westhampton's first course was on the Homans' property in Quiogue Point. Eventually, the club was able to secure property near the clubhouse, and build a new nine-hole course there.

While at Quiogue, a group of Westhampton members engaged in a rather noisy

mutation of baseball and golf. As many as nine would tee off simultaneously, then each player would rush to a ball; if his own, he would attempt to advance it toward the green; if an opponent's, back toward the tee. The first player to hole out his own ball was the winner. Needless to say, the game was not very popular with the club's greenkeeper!

In 1915, Westhampton obtained its present property, and engaged Seth Raynor to lay out an 18-hole golf course. The original clubhouse was moved across Moniebogue Bay to its new site during the winter chill.

Toward the end of the 1920s, reacting to an overabundance of golfers, the club decided to build a second 18-hole course at Oneck Point, about a quarter of a mile south of the existing course. The club hired Charlie Banks (a protégé of Raynor) to design "one of the finest golf courses on Long Island." The new course opened in 1930. The terrain sloped gently to the center, forming a slight valley through which a winding brook flowed southerly, connecting a chain of small lakes before emptying into the larger Oneck Lake. In 1933, that course was lost, a victim of the Depression.

ABOVE: SHEP AND GENE HOMANS (R) AT THE FATHER & SON TOURNAMENT AT GARDEN CITY GOLF CLUB IN 1930. (*Golf Illustrated*)

OPPOSITE PAGE: A VIEW OF MAIDSTONE'S NINTH AS IT APPEARS TODAY. (*L.C. Lambrecht*)

RIGHT: THE 14TH HOLE AT MAIDSTONE AS IT IS TODAY. NOTE HOW THE SAND AREAS IN FRONT OF THE GREEN HAVE CHANGED THROUGH THE YEARS. (*Maidstone Club*)

39)

4

The Hunt Set Takes Notice

Long Island's first golf rounds most likely were played at Shinnecock Hills, although the first golf shots struck on Long Island likely were played elsewhere. The sport may have been introduced first to the local hunt set, rather than the social set in the Hamptons. Meadow Brook may have been the first of Long Island's clubs to witness the new game.

One sparkling Sunday afternoon during the summer of 1888, Horace Hutchinson, the British Amateur champion of 1886–1887 and a pioneer golf writer, paid a visit to the Meadow Brook Hunt Club. (Or perhaps it was 1889 — Hutchinson's writings leave us with both possibilities.) Meadow Brook was located on the Hempstead Plain, land that is now partly in Garden City, Hempstead, Uniondale, and Westbury. Hutchinson appeared as the guest of member Robert Purdey. The purpose of his visit was to demonstrate the game called golf that had become so popular in Scotland and England.

Purdey took it upon himself to ensure that a large audience of members and other guests were on hand for the exhibition. Hutchinson appeared at the club dressed in a scarlet coat with green velvet collar, brass buttons, tight-fitting knickers, golfing hose, and high gaiters. He brought with him a putter and six clubs, "his baffy, long spoon, short spoon, lofter, field-iron, and his favorite Tom Morris driver." An improvised course was laid out, one which Horace himself thought the equal of the best inland links in England, and holes were cut in the soil with a carving knife.

THE EIGHTH AND NINTH HOLES AT MEADOW BROOK TODAY WITH THE CLUBHOUSE IN THE BACKGROUND. THOSE WERE THE 17TH AND 18TH HOLES FOR THE LONG ISLAND CLASSIC. *(L.C. Lambrecht)*

Hutchinson's performance did not capture the imagination of those members of the hunt set who attended. Nor did their own attempts at striking the ball win over many converts. Perhaps the most favorable comment Hutchinson heard that day was that golf might make "a good game for Sundays." Meadow Brook did, however, request that Hutchinson send them some clubs upon his return to England.

In such manner was golf presented to the membership at Meadow Brook, and "rejected" by them. The club's lack of interest was short-lived, however. By 1894, a nine-hole course had been completed. One authority called it the "best nine-hole course in the East."

Since the U.S.G.A. did not formally provide for a Women's championship in 1895, Meadow Brook decided to sponsor such an event late in the season, suggesting that the winner be entitled to call herself the champion of the United States. The tournament was scheduled for 18 holes at medal play on November 9. Neither rain nor fog deterred the 13 contestants, who played the nine-hole course once before lunch, then again in the afternoon.

Mrs. Charles S. Brown of Shinnecock Hills emerged a 2-stroke victor with a final total of 132 that included scores ranging from 3 to 14, with four holes in double figures. Needless to say, scores ran high that day, and this was attributed not just to the weather conditions, but as much to the fact that the women had to play from the men's tees over one of the longest courses in the country at that time. Many considered the course unsuited to test the skill of the players, who were accustomed to shorter courses, and it came as no surprise when a Shinnecock Hills lady, seasoned over that club's women's course, came out on top.

Two weeks before the Women's championship, Meadow Brook was the scene of a grudge match between member Winthrop Rutherford and Charles Sands, who had been unsuccessful earlier that year in the finals of the first United States Amateur championship. Sands had taken up golf just three months prior to that tournament, and many considered his performance a fluke. Rutherford was of that opinion, and remarked that Sands was not much of a player. An argument ensued, and that led to the match for a stake of $1,000. A sizable gallery attended, the local press was on hand, and reportedly large sums were wagered on the outcome. Sands won the match 3&2, taking 195 strokes for the 34 holes played. To add insult to injury, while the match was progressing, thieves dressed in red hunting coats (the attire of the men in the gallery) entered the clubhouse and stole money and jewels from the lockers. Rutherford was the big loser here, too, having left a watch and chain, a diamond ring, two diamond studs, cuff buttons, as well as more than $800

in cash in his locker.

Three years later, in 1899, Meadow Brook member Herbert M. Harriman won the U.S. Amateur title after becoming the very first M.G.A. Amateur champion. He was the first Long Island resident to win the national title. A relative newcomer to major competition, it was thought that his preparations over the tough Meadow Brook course set him up well for the challenges he faced in the championships.

The original Meadow Brook course was short-lived, however. The members simply were more interested in polo, and by 1905 the course was abandoned and eventually a new polo field was built on part of it. Interest was rekindled in 1915 when a new 18-hole course was built. It utilized Meadow Brook, "a beautiful little stream that winds through the links," to a great extent, placing 10 greens beside the brook. One par 3 of 120 yards called for a tee-to-green carry over water to an island green.

The Meadow Brook Hunt Club had been incorporated in Westbury in 1881 and leased land that sprawled from Merrick Avenue on the east to Mitchell Field, and from Old Country Road to Hempstead Turnpike for its frequent hunt meets. Meadow Brook's hunt breakfasts and dinner parties were held regularly at the Garden City Hotel.

It was neither fox hunting nor golf, however, that brought Meadow Brook its greatest fame. Rather, it was polo. Meadow Brook's first polo field was built in

(43

ABOVE: A GALLERY AT A MEADOW BROOK MATCH IN 1896. *(Golf Illustrated)*

OPPOSITE PAGE: HERBERT HARRIMAN DRIVING FROM THE FIRST TEE AT GARDEN CITY IN THE 1900 MET AMATEUR. *(Golf)*

RIGHT: THE ORIGINAL NINE-HOLE COURSE AT MEADOW BROOK. *(Golf)*

1884. Eventually, the club would have unmatched facilities, including eight fields, with the magnificent International Field, its grandstands painted in the club's robin's egg blue colors, reserved for only the most important matches. And these were commonplace at Meadow Brook, attracting the greatest players in the world for events such as the U.S. Open, Westchester Cup, and Cup of the Americas. The Meadow Brook team of Harry Payne Whitney, Devereux Milburn, Monty and Larry Waterbury, known as the "Big Four," was directly responsible for the United States winning the 1909, 1911, and 1913 competitions, thereby ending England's domination of the sport. Milburn, incidentally, was regarded by many as the

BELOW: MEADOW BROOK'S "FOUR HORSEMEN." FROM LEFT TO RIGHT: DEVEREUX MILBURN, H.P. WHITNEY, MONTY AND LARRY WATERBURY. *(The Creek)*

OPPOSITE PAGE: FOXHALL KEENE, THE GOLFER. *(Golf)*

greatest polo player ever produced in this country.

Meadow Brook was not the only prominent hunt club on Long Island. Indeed, the Rockaway Hunting Club in Cedarhurst has a legitimate claim as the oldest "club" in the country. Not a "country club," Rockaway catered to the horse set, featuring fox hunting and steeplechase racing. The club was founded in 1878 in Far Rockaway.

The move to the present location on Ocean Avenue in Cedarhurst took place in 1884. There the members built a clubhouse considered the largest and most luxurious on Long Island, two miles from the ocean, overlooking a polo field and steeplechase course, Reynolds Channel, and Long Beach Island.

During its 120-plus years' existence, Rockaway Hunting has played a leading role in several sports, perhaps the least of which was golf. Like Meadow Brook, the sport that brought Rockaway its greatest laurels was polo. The often-bitter rivalry with Meadow Brook started in 1885. By 1888 the two clubs were so far superior to all others that a handicap system was created. The Rockaway team won national championships in 1901 and 1902.

Certainly the greatest athlete in club history was Foxhall Keene, for eight years rated the #1 polo player in the country. James R. Keene, his father, once offered a $100,000 wager that no one could beat his son in a contest including 10 sports. There were no takers. During the late 1890s, Keene took a brief respite from polo and developed into one of just two scratch golfers in the Met district—the other being Walter Travis. Keene was a regular competitor in regional and national tournaments, but not with the success expected of him. He did compete in the 1897 U.S. Open, and advanced to the quarterfinals of the 1898 U.S. Amateur, where he was defeated by Travis.

Golf has been with the club since 1890 or 1891, although intermittently in the early years. With several holes crossing or playing alongside large bodies of water, and some severely undulating, multilevel greens, Rockaway Hunt today is a superb match course. *Golf* magazine rated the ninth hole, designed in 1926 by A.W. Tillinghast, among the 100 best in the country in 1986. Marshes and an elbow of Reynolds Channel must be carried off the tee. The hole curves gracefully to the right, with the Channel ever-present on that side from tee to green.

(45

5

Garden City: A Landmark Course

46)   Among Long Island's most prominent citizens of the nineteenth century was Alexander T. Stewart, who built the world's largest retail store in Manhattan, and owned more city real estate than anyone except William Astor. Stewart bought what remained of the Hempstead Plain in 1869, paying $395,328 for the 7,170 acres ($55 per acre), which extended from Floral Park to Bethpage, and immediately presented plans for the "model community" he named Garden City.

Progress came slowly to Garden City, though, and it was hoped that having an outstanding golf course in the village would entice substantial people to take up residence there, while attracting others as guests of the Garden City Hotel, which had been designed by Stanford White.

And so was born the Island Golf Links, a nine-hole public-subscription course for residents and hotel guests. The course was laid out on "rolling prairie country" to the northwest of the hotel, between Lake Cornelia and Old Country Road. The architect was Devereux Emmet, a neophyte as far as golf course design was concerned, but a player familiar with the best courses at home and abroad.

The Island Golf Links opened for play on May 29, 1897, and received high praise from the golf experts who played there. The course was expanded to a full 18 holes by the fall of the following year.

At the time the golf course was being expanded to 18 holes, there was a move underway to convert the facility into a private club, an idea that reached fruition on

OPPOSITE PAGE: ALEXANDER T. STEWART.
(Garden City Historical Society)

RIGHT: GARDEN CITY IN THE MID-1870S,
WITH THE HOTEL ON THE RIGHT. *(Garden
City Historical Society)*

BELOW: DIAGRAM OF THE ORIGINAL
COURSE. *(Garden City Golf Club)*

BELOW, RIGHT: DEVEREUX EMMET.
(Golf Illustrated)

(47

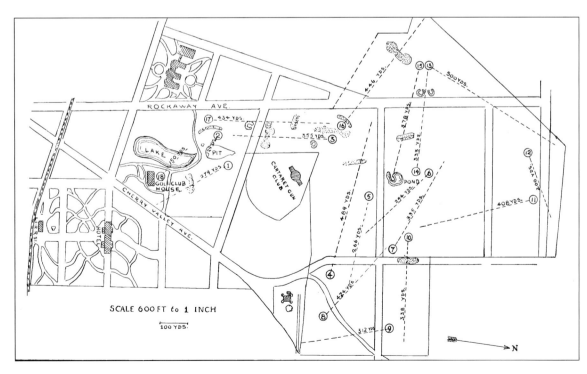

May 17, 1899 as the Garden City Golf Club.

As the reputation of the course grew, many of the leading players of the day joined the club, which listed four U.S. Amateur champions among its members within two years of its inception. Garden City was indeed the hub of golf in the New York area at that time.

Over the years, Garden City Golf has hosted numerous major events, including one U.S. Open, four U.S. Amateurs, one Metropolitan Open, six Metropolitan Amateurs, an Ike Championship, the inaugural New York State Amateur Championship, and a Walker Cup.

Herbert Harriman of Meadow Brook won the inaugural Met Amateur at Garden City in 1899, defeating Reginald Brooks, also of Meadow Brook, in the finals. The 36-hole match, which pitted Harriman's power against Brooks's finesse, was played on April 15. The match was close all the way, in fact all square after nine, 18, and 27 holes, with no more than one hole separating the players at any point until the 34th hole, which Harriman won to assume a 2-up lead. He won the match on the next hole, 2&1.

Others among the final 16 were Findlay Douglas, Walter Travis (eliminated by Harriman in the semifinals), Theodore Havemeyer (the first president of the U.S.G.A.), and H.B. Hollins (the first M.G.A. president, representing Suffolk County's Westbrook Golf Club).

Two national championships followed. For the United States Amateur of 1900, the "tee hazards" were extended out to 100 yards—previously, even a duffer could negotiate them. The course was set up to play at 6,070 yards for the tournament.

The qualifying scores ranged from a low of 166 to 187, with Walter Travis the medalist. The week proved to be a "tour de force" for Travis, who not only won the championship but also established a new course record (78). Only once, during his semifinal match, did Travis trail at any point of a match. *Golf* made note of Travis's game plan:

> *"He had previously figured out for himself the play best suited for his game for every single hole, and kept steadily to that plan of action, with but scant regard to what his opponent might be doing. He kept himself as free as possible from any kind of annoyance and distraction; the deliberation with which he walked and played was the index to his mental attitude. Finally, he played with his head, and used his brains, the latter ingredients being conspicuously absent in the work of some of his competitors."*

Travis met Findlay Douglas, the long-hitting Scot from St. Andrews, in the finals.

OPPOSITE PAGE: HERBERT HARRIMAN AND FINDLAY DOUGLAS AT THE 1900 U.S. AMATEUR. *(Golf)*

It was Douglas who had sent Travis to the sidelines in the previous two championships, but Travis was ready for him in 1900. According to *Golf*:

> *"It was in the final game with Douglas that Travis demonstrated the wonderful improvement he has made even in the last twelve months. On Travis' strength at the tee twelve months ago, Douglas would have out driven him every time from twenty-five to forty yards, the Garden City captain himself admitting that he was then rarely able to drive more than 170 yards. Nowadays he can get up to 200 quite easily. As it was, the amount by which Douglas out drove him was comparatively of no account, the results being determined by the approach play and the work on the greens." "Eight times Travis got into the sand hazards or in the long grass, and each time with his iron he laid himself dead for the hole. Such consistent work in surmounting difficulties surely cannot be called luck. It is good play, play of the highest order, in which the brain carefully reasons how defeat may be averted, and the hand trained by long and arduous practice, successfully executes the cleverly conceived plan of action. This Travis did to perfection, and though it was bad play on his part to have landed himself in so many difficulties, he redeemed himself by the skill with which he got out of them."*

The match ended in a violent thunderstorm, the remarkable account of which was recounted in *Golf*:

"The sensational part of the final round started in the drive-off from the sixteenth tee. The sky became black, the wind increased in volume as though about to become a tempest, and in a few moments the rain fell in torrents. But the play went on, while the gallery ran to cover. Here Travis had great luck. His third shot was a wretched one, and should have landed in the bunker which protects the sixteenth green, but the terrific wind caught the ball and not only carried it over the bunker but actually laid it within a few feet of the hole, while Douglas' good stroke was punished by being landed by the wind right in the bunker, causing the loss of the hole.
"At the seventeenth tee the players' difficulties increased, as did the storm. The bulky form of Harriman, who was now fore-caddying, was lost in the gloom, and the pinches of sand for teeing purposes washed away as soon as they were placed on the ground. Under these circumstances it is not to be wondered at that Travis topped his ball, but strange to say, Douglas, aided by the wind, made the best drive of the day— quite 250 yards—and on his second overdrove the hole, 429 yards. It was Douglas' hole easily, leaving Travis dormie 1. The home green was now a lake, several inches of water completely covering it, and both balls landed with a splash. The play on the green at the last hole will not soon be forgotten by those few who saw it. Devereux Emmet, the vice-president of the Garden City Club, stood near the hole with a broom trying to sweep the water away, and having the same success as Mrs. Partington had with the Atlantic Ocean. The water grew deeper every minute, but the game had to be finished. Putting was out of the question, for the ball would not roll an inch. Playing the odd, Douglas did not loft with sufficient strength, going only halfway to the hole, while Travis making a perfect shot under the circumstances, laid his ball dead with a flop in six inches of water, and so won the amateur championship of America by 2-up."

Such was the success of the 1900 U.S. Amateur that Garden City was quickly chosen to host a second national championship, the 1902 U.S. Open. The tournament was contested on October 10-11, 72 holes in two days. A field of 97, including 14 amateurs, competed over a course that was in great shape, with exceptionally fast greens. The U.S.G.A. drew some criticism, though, for placing the pins in some unfair positions, in the corners of the greens, near bunkers or rough grass.

The pin placements did not stop Laurence Auchterlonie from beating the previous U.S. Open record by six strokes. Auchterlonie, a Scot, carded rounds of 78-78-74-77=307 to lead amateur Travis (82-82-75-74=313) and professional Stewart Gardner (82-76-77-78=313), also of the host club, by six strokes. Travis's play on the

Opposite page: Laurence Auchterlonie, 1902 U.S. Open winner. *(Golf)*

Right: Willie Anderson driving from first tee in 1902 U.S. Open. *(Golf)*

The Travis Memorial

The memory of Walter Travis is honored at the club by means of an amateur match-play tournament bearing his name. The Travis Memorial is held in May, and attracts one the strongest fields of the season, combining the leading local players with several others of equal stature from around the country. It was inaugurated in 1902 as the Spring Invitational Tournament, and the name was changed in 1927 following Travis's death.

second day, when scores were generally lower despite the weather (misty in the morning, hard rain all afternoon), was the best of the tournament.

Auchterlonie led Gardner by just two strokes after the first day's play, then added three strokes to his lead in the third round. He sealed his victory with an eagle 2 at the first hole in the final round. Amazingly, the three leading contenders played the dangerous 18th hole in an aggregate one under par (a birdie by Travis).

Willie Anderson, who won the 1900, 1901, 1903, and 1904 Opens, finished tied for fifth place with Maidstone's John Shippen, while Shinnecock Hills' Charlie Thom was seventh. Noted architect Donald Ross was ninth.

Auchterlonie won a grand prize of $150 and a gold medal valued at $50 for his efforts.

The word that best describes the Garden City course is "natural." The holes are basically the same today as those first laid out in 1898 on a gently rolling treeless stretch of land featuring sandy soil and wild grasses, offering little protection from the winds sweeping in from the "nearby" ocean. The course was treeless, prompting Horace Hutchinson's evaluation "Rather ugly surroundings, but a fine test of golf." When the accomplished amateur Findlay Douglas, a Scot from St. Andrews, first saw the course before the turn of the century, he described it as the "nearest thing to St. Andrews" he had ever seen.

Within a decade, Garden City Golf was regarded as Walter Travis's course. The "Old Man's" stature as amateur champion gave him carte blanche to revise "his" course as he saw fit. Travis was not an advocate of cross bunkering, a prominent feature of the course. He did favor deeper greenside bunkers than Emmet had built,

(51

52)

OPPOSITE PAGE: DIAGRAM OF THE GARDEN CITY COURSE IN 1915. *(New York Telegram)*

ABOVE: THE TEE SHOT ON THE FIRST HOLE. *(Garden City Golf Club)*

and greens with more severe undulations than Emmet had created. Travis's signature, though, was his use—which some thought excessive—of deep pot bunkers to narrow fairways and protect greens. Travis was not considered an inventive architect, but rather a member of the penal school who did his best work tightening up existing courses.

Garden City's second hole is a short par 3 that demands a do-or-die carry over Garden City's infamous "bottomless pit," a by-product of the excavation that provided sand and gravel for the village's streets long before there was a golf course on the site. The following quote, taken from an article in the September 1899 issue of *Outing* magazine, describes the hole as it appeared then:

ABOVE LEFT: SIDE VIEW OF THE THIRD FAIRWAY. *(Garden City Golf Club)*

LEFT: THE "BOTTOMLESS PIT" ON THE SECOND HOLE. *(Garden City Golf Club)*

"The pride of the course, which often goeth before a ball, is the bottomless pit between the second tee and hole, an old gravel pit, forty feet deep and seventy-five yards wide, which has to be carried, or woe betide the hapless player."

Garden City's home hole is perhaps its most (in)famous, having been the stage for many disastrous finishes over the years. The one-shotter is played across Lake Cornelia, another by-product of the excavation, to a huge sloping green in front of the clubhouse—the upper right portion is used as a practice putting green. A small, eight-foot-deep pot bunker sits dead center in front of the green, flanked by a larger bunker at its right. A narrow sand pit encircles the back of the green, and to the left lies the deep "Travis bunker," which Travis himself added in 1906 to close in the left side of the hole. Working as a team, the frontal pot and the "Travis bunker" give the hole an "Eden" effect, Travis's rendition of the famous 11th hole at St. Andrews. For years, Garden City's home hole was one of the most discussed in the country.

(55

ABOVE: THE TREACHEROUS 18TH HOLE. (*Golf Illustrated*)

RIGHT: THE HILL (TRAVIS) BUNKER, LEFT OF THE 18TH GREEN. (*American Golfer*)

6

The North Shore Awakens

Three years after Garden City's U.S. Amateur, the national championship returned to Long Island, this time at the Nassau Country Club in Glen Cove. The tournament was held during the first five days of September.

There were dire predictions of an oversized field since all entrants were allowed to come to Nassau to compete at match play. Fortunately, only 145 opted to play, and 34 of them were chosen by lot to play in a preliminary round (and 111 drew byes) to fill out a field of 128. Findlay Douglas, the 1898 champion and a Nassau member, was among the 34 "selected" to play in the round; he won, but lost in the first round.

Among those competing were two-time champion Walter Travis (1900–1901); a Nassau Country Club teenager named Jerry Travers; golf course designer Devereux Emmet and future architect A. W. Tillinghast; William C. Fownes Jr., son of the Oakmont founder; and John Jr. and Archie Reid, sons of St. Andrew's (Yonkers) founder John Reid.

The finals gave Travis the chance to gain a measure of revenge on young Eben Byers, who had sent Travis packing in the third round the previous year. The match started in dull, threatening, humid weather, with just a small gallery attending. Byers jumped out to a two-up lead after eight holes, but made numerous mistakes thereafter. Travis took advantage on each of the next five holes to assume a three-up advantage.

Byers wasn't quite finished, holing a miraculous 50-yard pitch from left of the

OPPOSITE PAGE: WALTER TRAVIS DRIVES
FROM THE FIRST TEE AT THE 1903 U.S.
AMATEUR. *(Golf)*

ABOVE RIGHT: THE FINALS OF THE 1903 U.S.
AMATEUR AT THE 18TH GREEN. *(Golf)*

BOTTOM RIGHT: BYERS AT THE FIRST TEE
DURING AN EARLY-ROUND MATCH. *(Golf)*

FOLLOWING PAGE: THE 15TH HOLE AT
NASSAU COUNTRY CLUB DEPICTING THE
CLASSIC BUNKERING OF DEVEREUX EMMET.
(L.C. Lambrecht)

14th green that so shook Travis that he double-bogeyed the 15th hole. Back within one, Byers returned to his sloppy play, losing the final three holes of the morning round to finish with a four-hole deficit.

In the afternoon round Byers played Travis on fairly even terms, although squandering numerous opportunities to narrow the gap. The end—and drenching rains—came on the 14th hole, Travis winning the title, 5&4.

Golf was introduced to Long Island's North Shore when the region was still part of New York City. Originally the Queens County Golf Club, the name was changed to Nassau on January 1, 1899, coinciding with the formation of Nassau County out of what previously had been the eastern part of Queens County, in conjunction with the creation of "Greater New York City."

The club's patriarch was Charles Pratt, whose oil business became part of John D. Rockefeller's Standard Oil empire. The founder of Pratt Institute in Brooklyn, Charles Pratt died in 1891, but not before acquiring in excess of 800 acres in Glen Cove, on which he, his six sons, and one of his two daughters built their estates.

Among the founding fathers of the Queens County Golf Club were two of Pratt's sons, Charles M. Pratt and Frederick Pratt; Percy Chubb, who built the insurance company bearing his name; and the Maxwells, Howard and J. Rogers. They would soon be joined by the Whitneys, Howard and Henry; G.P. Tiffany; and financier John Pierpont Morgan, all representing prominent "gold coast" families.

The club was organized in 1895 with a six-hole course on the Pratt estate. Remnants of the old course can be seen today on the grounds of the Pratt Maritime Institute, on a promontory between Red Spring Beach and Crescent Beach on the western side of the Glen Cove peninsula.

The original location, two miles from the present site, was considered inconvenient in the preautomotive era, so in 1898 the club purchased 107 acres adjacent to the Glen Cove railroad station. The members were then able to commute to the club by train, a one-hour ride from Manhattan. The present clubhouse, the club's second, is a massive Georgian structure opened in 1913.

Two holes on the original course bore colorful names, and so merit description. According to a 1900 article in *Golf*, the fourth hole, called "Mounds," was an uphill 318-yard par 4, and its green was "of a saucer pattern, and is protected by a semi-circular row of conical grassy mounds. Between the mounds are small sand-pits, and occasionally balls do run through them."

The 161-yard par-3 seventh hole was called "Circus." According to *Golf*,

"This is as picturesque and sporty a hole as one may see anywhere. The green is a punch bowl of from sixty to seventy yards in diameter, and is protected by a cop bunker and sandpit that completely invests its upper rim. It calls for a carry of 120 yards from the tee, and looks a great deal easier than it is."

Nassau enjoyed the national spotlight once again in September 1914, when the U.S. Women's Amateur visited. A record 91 entrants played in the qualifying round, including 26 from Long Island. Defending champion Gladys Ravenscroft (also the 1912 British Amateur winner) was not on hand due to the war in Europe. Georgiana Bishop, the 1904 champ, won the medal with an 85, overcoming a slow (7-6) start. Long Islanders Lillian Hyde (South Shore Field Club) and Marion Hollins (Westbrook Golf Club) finished among the first 10 qualifiers (both represented clubs that were located on Suffolk County's south shore, east of Islip). Hyde defeated Hollins in the first round, then won again before losing in the quarterfinals. Many had considered Hollins the tournament favorite.

Nassau played at 6,037 yards for the ladies, just as it had for the men in 1903, suggesting (perhaps incorrectly) that the ladies played from the men's tees. The

course had undergone considerable change in the intervening years. The weather for the week was sunny and hot, the continuation of conditions that had burned out the fairways and made the ground rock hard. The longer-hitting ladies, Hyde included, were driving the ball 250 yards, but the bounces were erratic and unpredictable.

Mrs. H. Arnold Jackson won the championship for the second time—she was the 1908 winner under her maiden name, Kate Harley—defeating Elaine Rosenthal 1-up. Alexa Stirling made her national debut (at age 16), losing in the first round. Both were teenagers destined to tour with Bobby Jones, playing for the benefit of the Red Cross, during World War I.

Elaine Rosenthal was involved in two separate situations that are worth recalling. In her semifinal match with Jean Barlow, the two ladies found their balls equidistant (three feet) from the pin on the eighth green, as measured by U.S.G.A. president Robert Watson, who then tossed a $10 gold piece to determine who would play first. Rosenthal won the toss, played first and missed. Barlow then holed her putt to win the hole, which proved quite significant when the match reached the 18th hole all-square. Sometimes, though, the breaks even out. Barlow missed an easy three-foot putt for a half on the last green, and Rosenthal advanced to the final.

There the same goddess of fate made a second appearance. Both Rosenthal and Jackson played the seventh hole poorly. Both reached the green in four, with Jackson away. She left her putt on the lip of the hole, laying Rosenthal a dead stymie. Rather than risk knocking her opponent's ball into the hole for a winning 5, Rosenthal elected to play to the side of the cup for a half.

The American Golfer described the final match in detail. The first passage describes Rosenthal's situation on the 11th hole (she was already 2-down in the match):

> *"...being completely demoralized in playing the eleventh. Her third shot found a bunker, from which she failed to get out on her fourth. The next ran clear across the green into another bunker. Her first attempt to get out was ineffectual, but on her second essay she got out so well that her ball careened across the green to a third trap in a far corner, after all of which mishaps she picked up and was three holes to the bad."*

Showing the composure of a veteran player, Rosenthal recovered from that embarrassment and cut her deficit to one hole going to the last. *The American Golfer* continued:

(61

Opposite page, top: The "Mounds" at the fourth green. *(Golf)*

Opposite page, bottom: Kate Jackson, winner of the 1914 US Women's Amateur. *(Golf Illustrated)*

"Both played their seconds short, but both got bunkered, Mrs. Jackson in a pot bunker to the left and Miss Rosenthal in a deep pit to the right. Mrs. Jackson's third was well out but a little strong, overrunning into the road just on the edge of the green. Playing the odd, she made a beautiful stroke, her ball being practically dead. Miss Rosenthal, meanwhile, in essaying a thirty foot putt for a win, overrunning some eight feet. This she ran down in splendid style, but Mrs. Jackson got hers down also and won her second championship."

There were several "side events" held during the week of the championship, including a bogey competition, mixed foursome's competition, a four-ball competition, an approaching and putting competition, and a long-driving competition. Marion Hollins won the latter with drives of 228, 218, and 218 yards.

Long Island's First U.S. Open Champion

When he won the 1906 U.S. Open in Chicago, Alex Smith became the first of just two (Gene Sarazen was the other, in 1932) professionals representing a Long Island club to win the national Open championship. Smith was Nassau's first professional, and quite an accomplished player. Known as "Miss 'Em Quick" Smith for the speed with which he lined up and played his putts, Smith came to Nassau in 1901, and remained on the scene for eight years.

At first, Smith seemed destined to play in the shadow of Willie Anderson, four times the U.S. Open champion during the years 1901–1905, with Smith the immediate victim on two occasions. The tide turned when Smith beat Anderson in a play-off for the inaugural Met Open in 1905. The following summer Smith ended Anderson's reign in the national championship, and in the process became the first player to break 300 in the U.S. Open, shooting 73, 74, 73, 75=295.

Smith also won the 1910 U.S. Open and added three more Met Open titles, giving him a total of four, still the record for the championship.

OPPOSITE PAGE: LILLIAN HYDE AT THE PAR-3 10TH IN 1914. *(American Golfer)*

ABOVE: ALEC SMITH. *(American Golfer)*

RIGHT: THE SMITHS OF CARNOUSTIE; WILLIE AND ALEC (BOTH U.S. OPEN CHAMPIONS) AT TOP, MAC SEATED IN FATHER'S LAP. *(American Golfer)*

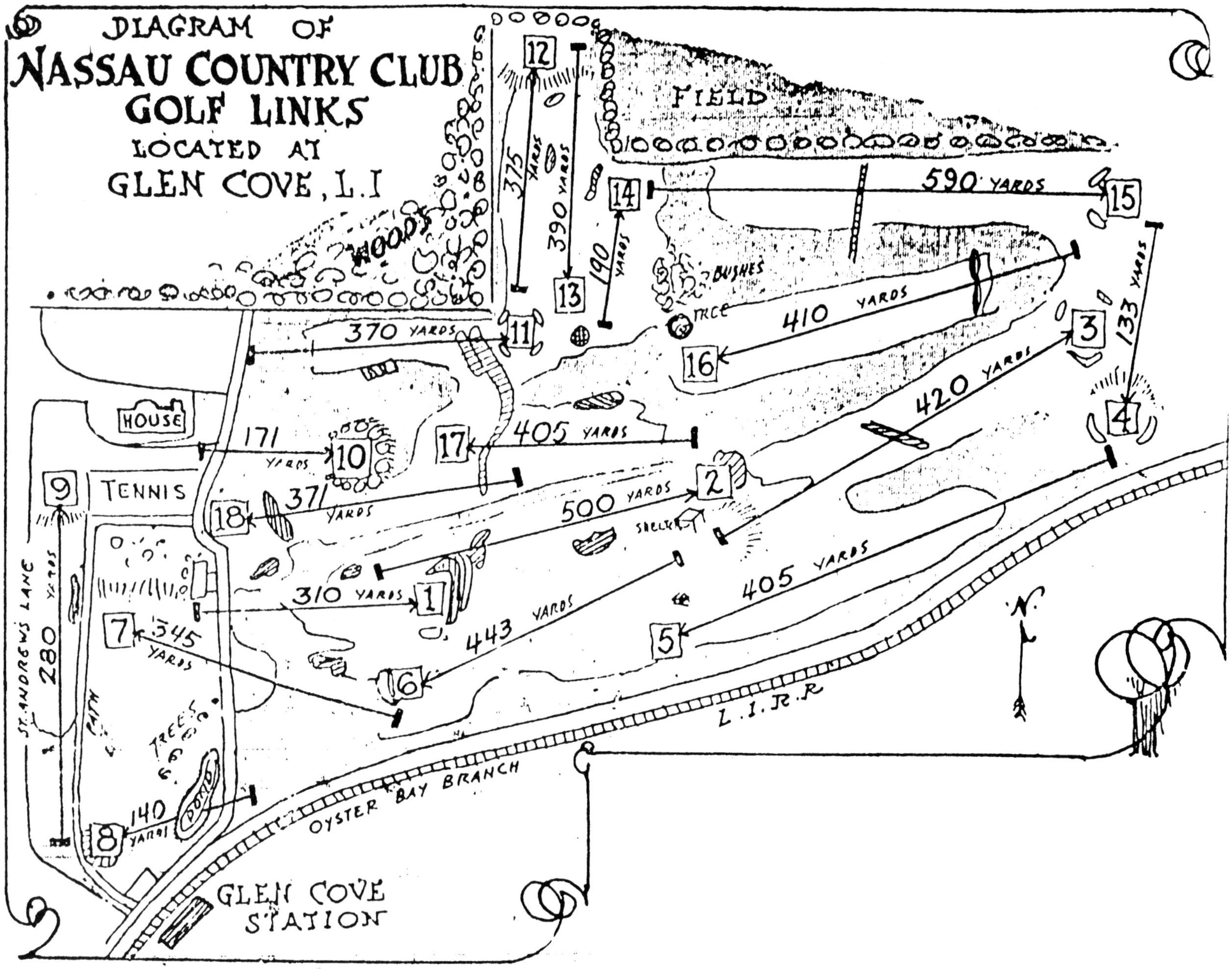

DIAGRAM OF
NASSAU COUNTRY CLUB
GOLF LINKS
LOCATED AT
GLEN COVE, L.I
WOODS
FIELD
BUSHES
TREE
HOUSE
TENNIS
SHELTER
375 YARDS
390 YARDS
190 YARDS
590 YARDS
410 YARDS
133 YARDS
370 YARDS
420 YARDS
405 YARDS
171 YARDS
371 YARDS
500 YARDS
310 YARDS
443 YARDS
405 YARDS
345 YARDS
280 YARDS
140 YARDS
ST. ANDREWS LANE
PATH
TREES
POND
L.I.R.R
OYSTER BAY BRANCH
GLEN COVE STATION
N.

The "Nassau"

In an article appearing in the *New York Times* in 1957 under Lincoln Werden's byline, Nassau member and former U.S.G.A. and M.G.A. president Findlay Douglas, twice the national Amateur champion, explained the origins of the "Nassau" bet as follows:

> "At the turn of the century, interclub matches were very much in vogue, with the results reported to the local newspapers. Many a prominent socialite and/or businessman would be embarrassed when a defeat by a score such as 7&6 became public knowledge. To avoid such embarrassment, J.B. Coles Tappan, a Nassau member, proposed the three-point match, with the front and back nines worth one point each, and the full 18 holes the other. With this format, the worst possible thrashing would be recorded painlessly as a 3-0 loss, and a player off his game one nine might be able to save one point with a better performance on the other side. So originally the Nassau bet was a scoring system named for the club of its origin. Later it would become a very popular betting system as well."

OPPOSITE PAGE: DIAGRAM OF THE NASSAU CLUB IN 1915. *(New York Telegram)*

BELOW: THE APPROACH TO TODAY'S EIGHTH GREEN, THEN A PAR 3. *(American Golfer)*

7

A Great Rivalry: Travis vs. Travers

Golf's greatest rivalry during the sport's first quarter century in America was between two men—Walter Travis and Jerry Travers—one considerably older than the other, whose golfing roots trace to Long Island.

Walter Travis was Australian-born, but came to this country as a boy. Disinterested in golf at first, he played his first rounds at the Country Club in Flushing at age 35. He joined the Oakland Golf Club in 1896, then became a charter member of the newly formed Garden City Golf Club in 1899, quickly becoming that club's most respected and influential member.

Travis himself was a notoriously short hitter, a fact generally attributed to his frail physique and the age at which he took up the game. To compensate, he was extremely accurate and consistent, and developed an excellent short game. Many golf historians regard him as the greatest putter the game has ever known.

Travis, or "the Old Man" as he was affectionately called (even at the beginning of his career), was a stickler for the rules of the game, and usually had little to say to his opponent during a match, preferring instead to concentrate his attention on the game at hand ... and the long black cigar that became his trademark.

When the U.S. Amateur came to Garden City in 1900, Travis was ready to assert himself. He successfully defended his title the next year at Atlantic City, then won the championship for a third time in 1903 at Nassau.

In 1904, Travis put America on the golf map with a stunning upset in the British

A RELATIVELY YOUNG WALTER TRAVIS. *(Golf)*

Amateur at age 42. His victory at Sandwich that year was the first ever by a foreigner, and was accomplished with the aid of a center-shafted Schenectady putter given to him on the eve of the tournament by his friend Edward Phillips. The putter had been produced in Schenectady, New York, and hence its name. The Royal & Ancient eventually banned the Schenectady putter from British tournaments. Ironically, Travis never putted well with the Schenectady after that tournament.

Jerome "Jerry" Travers first played golf at age nine on the front lawn of his family's estate in Oyster Bay. In 1900, at age 13, he began playing regularly at the Oyster Bay Golf Club, a relatively short-lived club that was among the first 20 established in this country. Its nine-hole course, situated on the Berry Hills about a mile and a half from the Oyster Bay railroad station, was built in 1894. The club's membership roster included many names from New York's upper social strata (including Teddy Roosevelt), being near their summer homes in the exclusive Oyster Bay colony.

After the Travers family joined Nassau in 1902, young Jerry soon caught the eye of Alex Smith. He approached Travers one afternoon after watching the teenager hit some balls, and challenged him to appear at the practice tee the following morning if he wished to make something of himself as a golfer. Travers accepted the challenge, and Smith gave him his first lesson that day.

The following season, Travers made his first appearance in the U.S. Amateur, held that year at Nassau, but bowed out in the second round. In 1904 he won the Interscholastic Championship, but the best was yet to come. For Travers was eagerly anticipating his first meeting in competition with Walter Travis.

That meeting came on October 8 in the finals of Nassau's Invitational tournament. Travis won the qualifying medal with rounds of 77-82=159, followed by Findlay Douglas, a former national champion and also a Nassau member (165), and Travers (168). According to the magazine *Golf*:

> *"The sensation of the event was the play on the last day, when Travers beat Douglas in the morning and Travis in the afternoon. This is an unexpected feat for a boy of seventeen. He played golf of the highest quality throughout ... and he won strictly on his merit."*

After defeating Douglas 2&1 in the semifinals, Travers felt that his putting was not up to par, and switched from putting with a cleek to a Schenectady for the finals. Travis was taken aback when he saw the Schenectady in Travers hand, and actually looked into his own bag to see if the youngster was pulling a prank. The match turned into a battle of the Schenectadies, with both players wielding hot putters. Travers never tasted the lead, and found himself 2-down with five holes to play. Undaunted, the youngster got back to even on the 17th hole, then won the match with a 12-foot putt for a birdie 2 on the third extra hole. Travis carded 76 for his round, Travers 77.

The following month, *Golf* reflected:

> *"At no period in the history of the game in this country has so young a player occupied so high a position. Travers has physique, a graceful and effective style, which should be lasting, and he seems to possess the proper golfing temperament. Travis later looked back at the match and commented: "There is no bitterness in such a defeat. It is a match I shall always recall with pleasure."*

This was the first of many matches between the two, the start of an at times unpleasant rivalry that would be the talk of golfdom for the next several years. Perhaps the best of their head-to-head confrontations came in the semifinals of the U.S. Amateur at Garden City Golf in 1908, a match won by Travers on the final hole. It was a classic confrontation that overshadowed the finals that year, in which Travers whipped Max Behr 8&7. Travis had won the qualifying medal at 153, nine strokes better than Travers.

The *New York Times* reported on the significance of the match:

> *"More than fifteen hundred persons witnessed the play ... more than a score of automobiles followed the players from green to green, watching the play from the sandy roadway and they were rewarded by golf of marked brilliancy, rare steadiness, with a succession of exciting features that will make the game go down in history as one of the greatest contests ever seen in this country."*

and then, taking the match from the 12th hole home:

> *"The short twelfth was one of the critical holes of the match. Travers was on the green from the tee, but his putt was obstructed by the edge of the mound on the green. Travis also had a hogback formation to putt over. Travers over putted ten feet, while Travis ran up within three feet. Amid breathless silence the champion putted, and*

Jerry Travers as a boy. *(American Golfer)*

when the ball ran down the enthusiasm was expressed by loud clapping. Travis was evidently disconcerted at this, for he missed, and losing the hole left honors even again. Travers made an unusually short drive to the next, and then fell into the sand pit near the green, the veteran winning handily in 5, and the latter won the next, Travers driving into a sand bunker and, striking at his ball irritably, missed getting out and had to take another.

"There were only four more holes to go and things looked dubious for the champion, as he was two down. Few persons in the crowd would have believed that he could win the next four holes, but he did it in fine style. He had good luck on the fifteenth, for from a long approach his ball grazed a man's shoulder near the green and bounded off to the far edge. Sand bunkers troubled Travis at the next. Both made beautiful drives at the seventeenth, Travis, from a long putt, just missed going down by an inch and Travers won 4 to 5, being one up with one more to go."

Garden City's 18th is unusual for a finishing hole, being a relatively short par 3 over a pond to a devilishly- bunkered green. At first glance it does not appear that difficult. But it had already earned a reputation as a giant killer, a hole where any score was possible, often at the most inopportune time.

Travis was about to rediscover that firsthand, his tee shot finding the deep bunker to the left of the green—the "Travis bunker," as it was called, because it was Travis himself who installed it in 1906, then adamantly refused to remove it even though the majority of the Garden City membership thought it unnecessarily harsh. Travis's ball never got out of his bunker that day—two attempts to move it elsewhere proved futile. Travis then emerged from the bunker, ball in hand, to congratulate his rival, whose tee shot had landed safely on the green, 15 feet from the hole. Travers went on to defeat Max Behr in the finals, while Travis no doubt remained on the scene to accept the condolences of his fellow members. "Well, that's one time the Old Man dug his own grave," one of them is reputed to have said.

A year later, *The American Golfer* looked back at Garden City's deep bunkers:

"Last year we ventured to say that some of the hazards on the last green were too deep. We were thereupon derided by the gentleman responsible for these excavations, and were told by this self-constituted oracle that the hazards were not too deep because they were exact duplicates of pot bunkers at St. Andrews. Unfortunately, there was a mistake ... and the bunkers at Garden City were made about twice as deep as the famous Strath and Shelly."

OPPOSITE PAGE, TOP: JERRY TRAVERS AT AGE 17 IN 1907. *(American Golfer)*

OPPOSITE PAGE, BOTTOM: WALTER TRAVIS. *(American Golfer)*

Head-to-Head Matches

Travis and Travers met in major amateur competition (U.S. Amateur or Met Amateur) a total of seven times, but only the 1908 U.S. Amateur was played on Long Island. A summary follows:

1905 Met Amateur (second round) at Fox Hills on Staten Island; Travers won 7&6

1906 U.S. Amateur (quarterfinals) at Englewood (NJ); Travis won, 3&2

1908 U.S. Amateur (semifinals) at Garden City; Travers won, 2-up

1911 U.S. Amateur (first round) at Apawamis (Westchester); Travers won, 3&2

1912 U.S. Amateur (second round) at Chicago Golf Club; Travers won, 2&1

1914 U.S. Amateur (semifinals) at Ekwanok (Vermont); Travers won, 5&3

1915 Met Amateur (second round) at Apawamis; Travis won, 1-up (at age 53)

To stay alive in that tournament, Travis had to stage what was called at the time "one of the grandest uphill fights ever seen" in his second-round match. Travis found himself 6-down at the 24th hole to young Henry H. Wilder, captain of the Harvard golf team and the Intercollegiate champion of the year. The *New York Times* described Travis's reaction to his desperate situation as follows:

> *"Not a muscle of Travis' face, not the slightest movement in his methodical, easy gait betrayed the fact that Wilder's big lead was of the least consequence to him."*

The match turned momentarily when Wilder was overcome by a temporary illness which cost him four consecutive holes. But Wilder settled suddenly, and was 4-up at the 15th tee. He then found bunkers at #15 and #16, could not match Travis's birdie at #17, then three-putted the final green to allow Travis to even the match. Travis won on the 41st hole when he hit his approach shot next to the hole.

In that same round, Eben Byers, the 1906 winner, parred the 40th hole to defeat John Montgomery Ward, who had won three of the last four holes, the 18th with a birdie (nearly a hole-in-one) to force extra holes.

All told, Travers was a four-time U.S. Amateur champion (1907, 1908, 1912, and 1913) and won the 1915 U.S. Open at Baltusrol as an amateur. Although Travers's national titles came while a member either at Montclair or Upper Montclair in New Jersey, he did achieve his first successes in golf while a junior member at Nassau. In addition to his national titles, Travers took home the Met Amateur trophy on five occasions—1906, 1907 at Nassau, 1911 at Garden City, 1912, and 1913.

Travis numbered among his personal achievements four Metropolitan Amateur titles (1900 at Nassau, 1902, 1909 and 1915) in addition to his three national Amateur championships. Travis's last major victory came in the final tournament of his career, the 1915 Met Amateur at Apawamis, appropriately via a 30-foot putt on the last green. He was 53 years old at the time, and beat the younger Travers in the second round in the last head-to-head confrontation of their rivalry.

During his later years, Travis devoted considerable energy to his role as editor of *The American Golfer*, a magazine he founded. He also proved to be a noted golf course architect, designing, among others, the two courses at the Westchester Country Club. The "Grand Old Man" passed away in 1927.

8

The Epic 1913 U.S. Amateur

72) The 1913 U.S. Amateur Championship at Garden City was newsworthy for two reasons. One was the roller-coaster ride that carried Jerry Travers to his fourth national championship—and almost out of the championship at times. The tournament also served to introduce Francis Ouimet to the golfing world, just two weeks before his landmark victory over Harry Vardon and Ted Ray in the U.S. Open at The Country Club outside Boston. At the time, the 20-year-old Ouimet was virtually unknown outside Massachusetts.

The course played at 6,411 yards for the championship, which was held during the first six days of September. The weather improved from hot and humid early in the week to almost ideal conditions later, helping the course stand up to the rigors of tournament play. According to *The American Golfer*:

> *"Never has there been such interruptedly good weather at Garden City. Ordinarily it blows there more or less—usually more. The championship week was marked by absolute freedom from wind, and rain too."*

Ouimet led the field of 145 through the first day of qualifying with a 75, followed closely by Travis and Eben Byers at 76 and Travers at 79—a back nine 35 bailed out a disastrous front nine 44. Of special interest was the fact that 17 golfers tied for the final nine places (of 64), and had to play-off for the right to continue.

The famous British journalist Bernard Darwin was on hand to cover the happenings for the American magazine, *Golf*, and he filed the following report on the playoff:

"At the end of the day it was discovered that seventeen players had tied for the last nine places in the 64, but the shades of night had fallen too far and too fast for the ties to be played off that night. At half-past eight the next morning, I was up and toiling across the course, which was still wet with dew, toward the fourteenth tee to behold a spectacle, to British eyes quite unique. The roll call was solemnly called, and sixteen heroes responded, one sluggard apparently preferring his bed. The players were then dispatched in parties of four, to play the fourteenth hole. Of the first four, two drove from the tee with wooden and two with iron clubs, and I rejoice to say that it was the two brave men who got the 4's. In the second batch there were two 4's, in the third only one, and in the fourth three. Three gallant 4's they were, too, for no single man was actually on the green in his second shot, and there was some courageous pitching and putting. Of the sixteen, eight were now safe, and two who had taken six or more were irretrievably dead. Six remained to play off for one place, and the fifteenth hole against the wind, with dewy grass, made a searching test. Four died the death, but Mr. Bowers and Mr. Marston both got fine 4's, Mr. Marston holing a nasty, curly downhill putt amid much applause. The struggle ended at the sixteenth, though in an unexpected way. After three shots, Mr. Marston lay apparently dead, Mr. Bowers eight or nine feet away; Mr. Bowers holed out, Mr. Marston missed, and the tale of nine was complete."

THE 12TH HOLE AS IT LOOKED IN 1913.
(AMERICAN GOLFER)

(73

The second qualifying round rivaled the first for its bizarre finish. On the one hand, Chick Evans rallied with six 3s on the back nine, including four consecutive birdies (on holes 13, 14, 15, and 16), and two holed-out chip shots, for a round of 39-32=71 to win the medal at 148, and lead the select 32 into match play. Travers, on the other hand, had his problems, rallying from another bad front nine (he took a 7 on the first hole, including three shots from the bunker that, he said, "took 10 years off my young life," only to stumble with a 7 on the 18th hole to fall into a 11-way tie at 165 for the final 10 places. According to Darwin:

> *"Meanwhile, Mr. Travers was keeping his supporters on tenter-hooks by taking an unconscionable number for the first nine holes; then he pulled himself together and played so heroically that he arrived on the last tee with a three for 82, which would have made him as safe as a church. He had to wait some while watching Mr. Byers performing prodigies of ineffectual valor with his niblick in the bunker to the left of the green, and this sight must have had some hideous mesmeric influence, for when his turn came to play, the ball flew straight into the heart of the very same bunker. This is really a desperate bunker, with precipitous sides and plenty of cheerful heel marks at the bottom of it, and it came near to giving America a new champion. Mr. Travers only got out at the third attempt; three putts swelled the total to seven, and he was in the direst jeopardy."*

Of the play-off that ensued, Darwin wrote:

> *"These eleven poor wretches came out to play off the tie for ten places. They played the first hole together, and but for its tragic ending, this hole was the joke of the world. After the tee shots, the course looked as if there had been a small local snowstorm, for nine balls out of the eleven lay on the fair green. Of the other two, Mr. Perrin got his ball out of the rough in two, and pitched onto the green in three, trusting very wisely to the subsequent indiscretions of others. Mr. Ulmer tried too much, and planted his ball in the bunker, where Mr. Kerr soon joined him. After this came a sequence of successful pitches broken only by the unfortunate Mr. Schmidt, who in this championship certainly did not live up to the reputation he won so worthily at St. Andrews. Some demon entering into him untimely caused him to lay aside his mashie and take a much-lofted niblick. With this club he tried, quite unnecessarily, to get right under the ball, but got under a vast divot instead, and the ball went with the "sickening thud" of the halfpenny novelette into the bunker. The contest now became one between Mr. Schmidt and Mr. Ulmer. Mr. Schmidt's first effort out of the bunker sent the ball hurling against the timber, whence it rebounded playfully some sixty yards backwards over his head; the next put it gently into the bunker again, the next being the fifth in all landed it on the green. Mr. Ulmer now becomes temporarily the hero of the story; his first niblick shot left the ball where it was*

before, and his second sent it scuttling over the green into the high grass beyond. Mr. Schmidt holed out in two putts, making seven shots in all, so that Mr. Ulmer had two strokes to beat him. The first was lamentably short and a prolongation of the agony seemed likely, but he holed out with rare nerve and so secured the vacant place. It was hard luck for Mr. Schmidt, but assuredly that second shot of his deserved what it got."

The first, and only, 18-hole round of match play took place that afternoon, with Travers once again in the spotlight. His opponent, U.S.G.A. president Robert C. Watson, birdied the first three holes to assume a quick 3-up lead. According to Travers:

"Watson was much surprised to learn that I could play a mashie shot off the shank of the club and send the ball away to the right. He told me he thought he had a patent on that particular shot. He had made it so often at Westbrook, he explained, that his club mates called it "the Watson." However, there was nothing the matter with his mashie when he played me, for he took the first three holes straight in 3, 2, 3, one under par for each hole, and nearly gave me heart disease. As the round was an 18-hole affair, 3up was a big lead. Fortunately for me, our popular president failed to keep up this phenomenal exhibition of golf under par, and I finally won the match."

(75

HEINRICH SCHMIDT'S FIFTH SHOT TO THE
FIRST GREEN IN THE PLAYOFF FOR A MATCH
PLAY SLOT. *(Golf)*

"WHO'S AWAY?" ON THE 11TH HOLE.
(Golf Illustrated)

Travers rallied to win the seventh through 12th holes, and eventually beat Watson 4&3.

Two matches highlighted second-round play. In one, Eben Byers holed several long putts to come from 6-down against Chick Evans and force extra holes, only to lose at the 39th. In the other, Travers and Ouimet matched 74s in the morning, with the turning point coming at the eighth hole in the afternoon, just after Ouimet had assumed a one-hole lead at #7. We again turn to Darwin for his account, as well as some overall comments on the match:

"Now came the turning point of the match. After two good tee shots, Mr. Ouimet played a great iron shot to within some three yards of the hole; it was a cru-

cial occasion for Mr. Travers, and he rose to it, as he always seems to do. With the joy of battle in his eye, he played a still finer shot—one of those long, firmly-hit iron shots at which he excels— and was nearer the hole than Mr. Ouimet. Mr. Ouimet nearly holed out; Mr. Travers did hole out for a three, and that three settled the match. It was not that Mr. Ouimet "cracked" in any sense of the word, but just a little of the steam had been knocked out of him by that desperate blow. Slowly, but surely, Mr. Travers surged ahead, taking no rest and giving nothing away, and on the sixteenth green he won a really great game by 3 and 2."

The third round was rather uneventful, the only match of interest being the one between Travis and Evans. Travis felt the effect of the heat, and fought an inaccurate long game all day. Evans, on the other hand, continued to battle his putter, and found better results using his cleek on the greens, winning the match 5&4.

In the semifinals, John G. Anderson upset Evans 2&1, rallying from 2-down at lunch, when he decided to go with his driver for the afternoon round. Anderson had used his driving iron in the morning, sacrificing considerable yardage in the process. In the other semifinal, Travers dumped Fred Herreshoff despite shanking two balls into the pond on the 18th hole at the conclusion of the morning round.

Anderson continued his excellent play in the finals, firing a 77 in the morning round to stay on even terms with Travers, who scored a couple of strokes higher. But after winning the first hole following lunch with a 5, Travers proceeded to match or beat par on every hole thereafter, winning the match, and the championship, 5&4, before a gallery of between 4,000 and 6,000 spectators.

OPPOSITE PAGE: FRANCIS OUIMET DRIVING AT THE 14TH HOLE. (Golf)

RIGHT: JOHN G. ANDERSON (LEFT) AND JERRY TRAVERS BEFORE THEIR CHAMPIONSHIP MATCH. (Golf)

(77

9

The National Golf Links of America

At the turn of the twentieth century, Charles Blair Macdonald looked upon the American golfscape as a vast wasteland. Most of the American golf courses to that time had been built by "golfing illiterates," and could hardly be compared to the great championship tests in the British Isles, he thought. Knowing Macdonald's personality, it would be easy to dismiss his opinion to arrogance, or to his fierce loyalty to golf in the Scottish tradition. Macdonald, however, set out to do something about improving the overall quality of American courses.

Charlie Macdonald looked upon himself as "Mr. American Golf," the man chosen by divine edict to supervise and govern the growth of the game in the United States. Macdonald was a big man, stubborn and humorless, with an ego of unmatched proportions. On the other hand, he was an intelligent, articulate man, and a stickler for the Rules of golf. Above all else, he was devoted to St. Andrews and everything the Royal & Ancient represented in golf.

Macdonald was born in Niagara Falls, Canada, but moved to Chicago as a youth. His father was a wealthy man of Scottish descent, and when the time came, sent his son to Scotland to be educated at St. Andrews University. Although at first not impressed with golf, Charlie soon became addicted, and developed into a fine player during his college years, one capable of playing on nearly equal terms with the leading players of the day, the likes of Young Tom Morris, David Strath, and Tom Kidd. Upon graduation, he returned to a golfless United States. During the

CHARLES BLAIR MACDONALD. *(Golf Illustrated)*

years 1875–1892, Macdonald played infrequently, and then only when business travel took him abroad.

In 1892 the World's Fair came to Chicago, and with it British visitors wishing to play some golf. Macdonald laid out a makeshift course for them. Soon a local club took an interest, and Macdonald built a nine-hole course for the fledgling Chicago Golf Club. That course was expanded to 18 holes in 1893, becoming the first regulation length course in this country.

Quite naturally, Macdonald was regarded as the father figure of Midwestern golf, and being a man highly influential in financial circles, was invited along with some Chicago friends to participate in major events held on the East Coast. Indeed, it was Macdonald's refusal to accept as "official" the results of tournaments held in 1894 at Newport and St. Andrew's (Yonkers) to crown a national champion that led to the formation of the United States Golf Association. Macdonald would emerge an easy victor at Newport in 1895 of the first official U.S.G.A.-sponsored Amateur Championship. That was the culmination of his career as a golfer.

Macdonald often thought of building a "classical" course in this country, and Long Island, he always felt, was the ideal location for such a course. In 1900, his business interests moved to Wall Street, and the Macdonalds took up residence in Garden City. The die was cast.

In 1901 Macdonald was further inspired by a series of articles entitled "Best Hole Discussions" appearing in London's *Golf Illustrated*. The magazine had invited the leading professional and amateur players to nominate the best one-, two-, and three-shot holes in Great Britain. Macdonald then conceived the idea of "transatlantic translation," whereby he would build a course in this country including holes that, if not direct copies, at least embodied the principles of the great holes abroad.

Macdonald wanted to show Americans what a first-rate British course was like. He wanted to "build a classical golf course in America, one which would eventually compare favorably with the championship links abroad, and serve as an incentive to the elevation of the game in America." He was to succeed admirably, creating what golf historian Herbert Warren Wind would later call "America's first great golf course."

After traveling abroad in 1902, then again in 1904, soliciting reaction and suggestions from leading figures in the game, Macdonald returned with a plan firmly in mind. Later in 1904, an agreement was drawn up incorporating the National Golf Links of America. Seventy subscribers from many sections of the country (hence the club's name) contributed $1,000 apiece for a share in the club. Among them were W.K. Vanderbilt, J. Borden and Herbert M. Harriman, H.P. Whitney,

Devereux Emmet, Findlay Douglas, J. Horace Harding, Clarence Mackay, and Robert T. Lincoln, son of the martyred president.

Macdonald, his son-in-law James Whigham, and noted amateur champion Walter Travis, and eventually architect Devereux Emmet, were charged with creating the golf course. Macdonald traveled to Great Britain again in 1906, and after a four-month stay, returned with surveyor's maps and sketches of the great holes, or interesting features he found on other holes.

Macdonald traveled the East Coast from Cape Cod to Cape May searching for the ideal terrain. In the spring of 1907, he found his land on Long Island, a 205-acre site on Sebonac Neck, including a quarter-mile frontage on Peconic Bay and a full mile along Bull's Head Bay, on the south fork of Long Island, about 100 miles from New York City. "A God-endowed stretch of blessed seclusion," Macdonald called it.

The land was of great scenic beauty and Scottish flavor, and adjoined the Shinnecock Hills course. Under the direction of engineer Seth Raynor, many truckloads of topsoil were hauled in to create the "natural" settings Macdonald wished for his holes. Raynor, incidentally, was a native of Southampton, and later an outstanding architect in his own right, always adhering to the Macdonald style.

Macdonald and Raynor had the course ready for its official opening in September of 1911, which featured an invitational competition won by Harold Hilton, who was fresh from his victory in that year's U.S. Amateur. More than 500 sand bunkers dotted the landscape, a few of them exceeding 200 yards in length.

Macdonald's creation was an immediate sensation on both sides of the Atlantic. Horace Hutchinson, the noted British player and writer, called the National "far and away the best in the United States. It has no weak point." Bernard Darwin was lavish in his praise of the course, commenting in 1922 that "those who think it is the greatest golf course in the world may be right or wrong, but are certainly not to be accused of any intemperateness of judgment."

The course did have its detractors, those who found it too exacting, without a single "let-up" shot. Some called it a "test of superman golf." To quote Darwin once again, this time from a 1913 article in the *Times of London*:

(81

OPPOSITE PAGE: THE "PUNCHBOWL" AS IT APPEARS TODAY, STILL ONE OF THE MOST INTRIGUING GREEN DESIGNS SEEN. *(L.C. Lambrecht)*

ABOVE: THE CLUBHOUSE *(Golf Illustrated)*

"If there is one feature of the course that strikes one more than another, it is the constant strain to which the player is subjected; he is perpetually on the rack. He is mercilessly harried all the way round from the first tee to the 18th hole. The National is truly a great course."

Those same critics soon changed their tune about the National when the Lido and Pine Valley courses were unveiled! But during the 1920s, those three courses—Lido, Pine Valley, and The National—were universally regarded as America's finest—and two of them were on Long Island.

Macdonald's course had an enormous influence on American golf architecture. It was not an uncommon sight to see delegates from other clubs studying the National, taking voluminous notes.

The National was the first strategic course built in this country. While rewarding a bold drive over severe rough, bunkers, or water with a simplified

82)

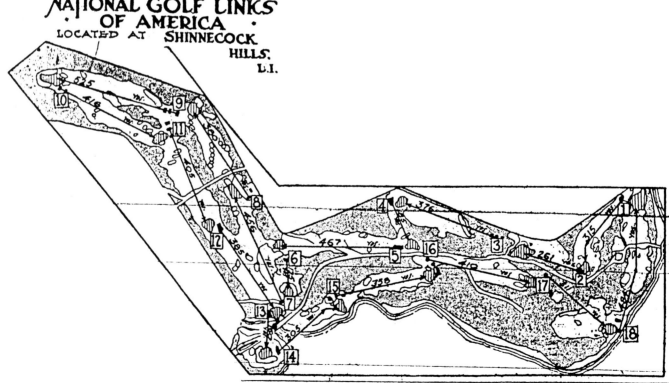

approach shot, each hole also offered an alternate route to the green to suit the games of average players, even good players under adverse weather conditions.

Although Macdonald regarded trees as a serious defect on a true links-style course, and the original landscape was relatively devoid of them, the numerous trees now present and the rolling hills Macdonald found or built combine to give today's National more the look of Gleneagles or Sunningdale, rather than St. Andrews.

Charles Blair Macdonald died in 1939, and was buried in Southampton. He spent most of his last 30 years at the National—his home was on the hillside across Bull's Head Bay—tinkering with the course, trying to make it perfect. Late in life, he admitted that, even then, he was not sure the course was "beyond criticism."

Charles Macdonald would have liked nothing better in his lifetime than to have been recognized as the "father of American golf." His personality no doubt prevented this from happening. He was the type whose friends would wire in Europe, "We hope you are enjoying your holiday. We are." Looking objectively at his life and accomplishments, though, one must admit that no one else came close to matching his contributions to the sport in its early years in this country.

(83

OPPOSITE PAGE: THE PLASTER PORTRAIT OF CHARLES BLAIR MACDONALD THAT STANDS IN THE CLUB LIBRARY. *(Golf Illustrated)*

OPPOSITE PAGE, BOTTOM: MACDONALD'S ORIGINAL COURSE DIAGRAM. *(New York Telegram)*

BELOW: SETH RAYNOR. *(Golf Illustrated)*

The National, Hole-by-Hole

Since the National is such an architectural landmark, it must be looked at in detail:

"Valley" (#1) 327 yards, par 4 sweeps down from an elevated tee next to the golf shop into a tumbling fairway that curves gently to the left, then back up to a humpbacked green. The key to this hole is the series of eight bunkers in the left rough through the drive zone. The ideal tee shot is over these bunkers, thereby opening up the green for a short pitch shot. A drive to the safer right side forces the player to contend with a huge bunker at the right front of the green, actually set several yards ahead of the green to make judgment of distance a bit tricky. The green can be driven, indeed has been driven. One evening, after playing the course for the first time, Macdonald's nephew, Peter Grace, indicated that he was not overly impressed with the layout, and singled out the short first hole for special criticism, claiming that the green could be reached from the tee. Macdonald disagreed, protesting that such a feat was impossible. They proceeded to the first tee, and Grace promptly drove the green. Macdonald stormed off the course, and quickly retreated to his home nearby. He called his lawyer the next morning, and had Grace removed from his will!

"Sahara" (#2) 330 yards, par 4 is modeled after what once was the third hole at Sandwich (Royal St. Georges) in England. In its native habitat, the "Sahara" was (it was revised in 1975) a long par 3 over sand hills to a green hidden in a blind hollow. Macdonald's "Sahara" is a short par 4 with the tee shot aimed at a lone pine on a hill behind a 3/4-acre sand bunker, requiring a carry of more than 200 yards into the prevailing wind. The alternate route to the right will leave the drive in a blind hollow, and demand a short pitch to a wide, elevated green that falls off sharply behind and to the right.

LEFT: THE "SAHARA" HOLE (#2). *(Golf Illustrated)*

OPPOSITE PAGE: LOOKING AT AND FROM BEHIND THE "ALPS" (#3) GREEN. *(Golf Illustrated)*

"Alps" (#3) 426 yards, par 4 is Macdonald's version of the famous 17th at Prestwick in Scotland, and is almost certainly the toughest hole on the course, a consequence not simply of its length but also because of the prevailing breeze against the player. The drive is played across a large "echelon" bunker that runs diagonally from left to right preceding the fairway, challenging the player to cut off as much as he dares. A strong, safe drive to the left will easily carry the bunker but may run through the fairway into knee-deep weeds or one of two bunkers set behind the fairway. The blind second shot must carry a huge rough-covered "saddle-back" hill (the "Alps," after which the hole is named) to a wide, rolling green (18,000 feet) that is set 20 yards beyond a long frontal bunker, with a few others to the right. Macdonald offers the average player the alternative of playing the hole as a par 5, following the fairway to the right around the hill after a conservative drive. Still, the third shot will be a testing one, over rough to the elevated, well-protected green. Until one learns exactly where the green is, and how far away it is, this hole will remain a difficult challenge. A bell behind the green is rung after a group putts out to notify players back in the fairway that the green is clear.

"Redan" (#4) 195 yards, par 3 is Macdonald's version of the famous 15th hole at North Berwick in Scotland. It is one of the great water-free par 3s in America, a hole that many feel is better than the original. The shot is played with a long iron to a green that is set diagonally to the slightly elevated tee, sloping away from the golfer from right front to left rear, behind a gaping bunker at least 20 feet below green level. The player willing to gamble by shooting at the pin over the bunker will be rewarded with a reasonable birdie putt, but punished severely if he misses his target. The player choosing to play safe to the right front of the green will face a long downhill putt to get close enough for a par, and must be careful not to overclub, because an equally ferocious bunker lies in wait at the right rear of the green. Quite challenging in concept and design, Macdonald is said to have included at least one such hole on each course he built. Unlike Macdonald's later adaptations, though, the

original hole at North Berwick played from a ground-level tee, leaving a rather blind shot to the sharply elevated green. The name "Redan," incidentally, comes from a type of fortification at Sevastopol that was stormed by the British in 1855 during the Crimean War. Long Island has a number of Redan holes, including the third at Piping Rock, the seventh at Shinnecock Hills, the eighth at Westhampton, and left-to-right versions at The Creek (#8) and two new courses in Suffolk County, TallGrass (#8) and Stonebridge (#4).

Left: The "Redan" hole (#4)
(Golf Illustrated)

Below: The tee shot on the fifth hole.
(Golf)

Opposite page: The "Short" hole (#6)
(Golf Illustrated)

"Hog's Back" (#5) 478 yards, par 5 is a moderate par 5 where the ideal drive will carry a series of bunkers to a ridge running across the fairway. A more conservative play to the right will force the second shot to carry over another series of bunkers cutting diagonally into the right side of the fairway. From there, the fairway rolls downhill to a green that is lightly bunkered, at least by National standards.

Like the "Redan," the **"Short" (#6) 141 yards, par 3** became a standard on Macdonald courses. It is a short par 3 to a green totally surrounded by bunkers, with a large horseshoe-shaped ridge (called the "donut") in the center of the green. To quote Darwin once again, "a most terrifying little hole, the green fiercely guarded by a timbered bunker and the hole cut in a hollow shaped like a horseshoe — a little paradise to which the roads from all other parts of the green are beset with shocks and switchbacks worthy of Coney Island." The third at Cold Spring, the 14th at TallGrass, and the 17th at both Piping Rock and The Creek are outstanding replicas of the original "Short," as is the 15th at Stonebridge.

"St. Andrews" (#7) 478 yards, par 5 is Macdonald's adaptation of the famous "Road Hole" (#17) at St. Andrews in Scotland. Although Macdonald didn't have railroad sheds or a hotel at his disposal

to protect the corner of his dogleg, he did fill that area with a large expanse of scrub-filled bunkers, and added a surprise bunker in the left-center of the fairway to catch the unwary player who decides to play it safe. But the real feature of this hole is the green area, and the two bunkers there that so dramatically affect the play of the second and third shots on this par 5. To the left front of the green sits a 10-foot deep pot bunker that may be more severe than its counterpart on the Old Course. The shallow green is set diagonally to the fairway, and is guarded behind along its full length by a huge bunker, Macdonald's "road." The ideal approach is a "bump and run" shot played into the opening of the green from the right side of the fairway. Any approach carrying to the green must be perfectly hit with backspin, or face the very real possibility of running through the green into the rear bunker. The ninth hole at Cold Spring is a marvelous rendition of this hole.

Bottle (#8) 424 yards, par 4 is the unsung hole at the National, although one of the most memorable on a course replete with outstanding holes. Modeled after the "bottle" hole (#3) at Sunningdale outside London, its character is defined by a series of bunkers that run diagonally into the fairway from the left rough. The golfer is given an option off the tee. He may attempt to carry the bunkers to the upper (left) half of the fairway, cutting off as much of the bunkers as he dares, to get a better look at the tightly trapped elevated green. More likely, though, he will choose to fade his drive to the lower (right) part of the fairway. From there, another series of fairway bunkers must be traversed. These serve to tighten up the fairway, and confuse one's judgment of the distance remaining to the green.

"Long" (#9) 540 yards, par 5 is just that, but really doesn't capture the playing qualities of its namesake (#14) at St. Andrews, if ever it was intended to do so. The tee shot must carry a huge bunker across the fairway, and a pond to the right front of the tee, which really doesn't come into play unless the player muffs his shot. The second shot must carry another huge bunker extending across the full width of the fairway, possibly Macdonald's rendition of the Hell Bunker on St. Andrew's "Long" hole. The green itself is virtually unprotected.

"Shinnecock" (#10) 450 yards, par 4 is a stiff par 4 running parallel to the third hole on the Shinnecock Hills course on the other side of the trees. The drive must carry an expanse of sand and a cross bunker to reach the fairway, and an approach from the left side of the fairway must carry at least 150 yards of bunkers and rough that separate the landing area from the green area. This hole, and the 11th to follow, are considered the most difficult on the back nine.

"Plateau" (#11) 432 yards, par 4 plays uphill from the tee to the top of a hill, then rolls back downhill across a road to an "L"-shaped three-tiered green set some 30 yards behind an unusual pot-style bunker known as the "Parson's Nose." Both the left front and the rear portions of the green are raised, with the "lip" at the left front dictating that the approach shot be played in "bump and run"

style. The "Parson's Nose" once had railroad ties shoring up its sides, but these were removed after a member was knocked unconscious when a rebound from a skulled explosion struck him in the head.

"Sebonac" (#12) 435 yards, par 4 bends to the left, with a series of deep bunkers set on a diagonal at the corner, challenging the player to carry as much as he dares. From there the hole runs downhill through a series of swales to an elevated, humpbacked green bunkered down below the left side and rear.

"Eden" (#13) 174 yards, par 3 is Macdonald's close reproduction of the famous par 3 (#11) at St. Andrews. Play revolves around a pair of greenside bunkers. "Strath," at the right front is a severe pot bunker, although nowhere as dangerous as the one at the seventh green. "Hill" is the larger bunker at the left side of the green. The normal reaction on the tee is to avoid "Strath," often causing a pulled shot that finds "Hill." Since the green slopes sharply from back to front, anything less than a feathery explosion from "Hill" may run off the green into "Strath," and therein lies the greatness of the design. Macdonald added one touch to his "Eden" —a pond in front of the tee, designed to prevent a topped shot from running onto the green, an often-heard criticism of the original "Eden." Walter Travis's 18th hole at Garden City Golf Club is possibly the greatest American "Eden," and predated (and likely influenced) Macdonald's hole at the National.

"Cape" (#14) 365 yards, par 4 is the best known of Macdonald's original creations at the National. It requires a moderate carry over a pond to a tumbling fairway that bends slightly to the right en route to a green that is almost totally surrounded by sand. Unlike later adaptations of this concept, the

Opposite page: A plaster mold of the original "Cape" hole (#14). *(Golf Illustrated)*

Below, right: The "Cape" tee. *(Golf Illustrated)*

National's "Cape" offers little incentive to gamble from the tee and cut the corner of the dogleg. A second pond near the right front of the green serves more as a deterrent to this strategy than as a hazard on the approach shot. Originally, the green on the "Cape" extended out into the sea, surrounded on three sides by water.

"Narrows" (#15) 397 yards, par 4 plays across a pair of ponds fronting the tee, then a large bunker, to a rising fairway protected along both sides from the drive zone to its sharply sloping green by an endless series of bunkers. A really pretty hole, and like the eighth, quite unsung.

"Punchbowl" (#16) 404 yards, par 4 also plays over a pond in front of the tee. The ideal line is over a big bunker on the right side of the fairway, but this requires a good poke. The more conservative drive to the left, if struck perfectly, may well roll into a deep "punchbowl," or even worse, finish on the side of the bowl, from which a full shot is virtually impossible. The big hitter playing over the bunker will find a similar effect to the right should he push or slice his drive. The green is set 20 yards behind a huge cross bunker, in a smaller punchbowl, and cannot be seen from the fairway. Back in 1919, a member thought that a windmill would look rather nice sitting on the hillside overlooking the left side of this green. Macdonald had one built, a 50-footer, and left the bill in the member's locker! The green at the Creek's signature sixth hole traces its heritage to the 16th at the National.

Golf magazine rated **"Peconic" (#17) 375 yards, par 4** as the tenth best hole in the country in 1986, quite an accolade for a relatively short par 4. From the elevated tee, the golfer looks out upon a beautiful vista of Peconic Bay. When he focuses his attention on the task at hand, he will notice that once again he is offered a choice. The ideal drive, one that opens up the green to the approach, must be on the left side of the fairway, but to get there it must carry a morass of rough and bunkers requiring

OPPOSITE PAGE: APPROACH TO THE "CAPE" GREEN. *(American Golfer)*

THE GREEN ON THE "NARROWS" HOLE (#15). *(Golf Illustrated)*

(91

a solid stroke of at least 200 yards. A more conservative drive to the right must avoid a couple of fairway bunkers, and the approach will have to carry a large inverted bunker that hides the putting surface from sight.

"Home" (#18) 502 yards, par 5 plays slightly uphill and passes the clubhouse on the left, with Peconic Bay at the foot of the hill along the right side of the fairway. A pair of large bunkers in the left rough force most drives to the right, away from the clubhouse. The second shot must carry a cross bunker and thread its way through a series of bunkers. Should either the second or third shot be pushed, or the final approach played too firmly, the ball will face a "sheer drop into unspeakable perdition," to quote the noted British golf writer, Bernard Darwin, who praised the hole in 1913 as the finest finishing hole in the world. Arnold Palmer once tempted "perdition," trying to draw his second shot around the flagpole that stands at the edge of the cliff in front of the clubhouse. Arnie's ball was never seen again. Nor was the search party!

Above, left: The 16th tee. *(Golf Illustrated)*

Below left: The home hole. *(Golf)*

Above: The 17th hole. *(Golf Illustrated)*

Opposite page: The 17th hole at National is still one of the most beautiful views in all of golf, with Peconic Bay in the background. *(L.C. Lambrecht)*

10

Lido: An Engineering Marvel

Back in the "Roaring Twenties," the crown jewel of New York area golf was the links course at Lido Beach, an engineering marvel built by Charles B. Macdonald on land reclaimed from the sea. It was possibly the most daring experiment in golf course architecture ever conceived. The group behind the Lido Golf Club included, among others, Otto Kahn, Cornelius Vanderbilt, and Henry Rogers Winthrop. It was the latter who suggested to Macdonald the idea of building a golf course on marshland and swamps. At first Macdonald thought the idea utter folly. But when Winthrop added that Macdonald would have complete freedom to create whichever holes he wished, he struck a sensitive nerve. Winthrop knew that Macdonald still had in mind holes he had seen in the British Isles for which he had never found a suitable setting in this country. "To me, it seemed a dream. It really made me feel like a creator," Macdonald would recall.

The group originally purchased a 200-acre "rectangle" extending from the Atlantic to Reynolds Channel, of which 115 acres of tidal marsh on the east, including a 10 to-15-acre lake, were ticketed for the golf course. The desolate terrain, filled with sand, reeds, and briny water, was more suitable to frogs and wild birds than golfers. But that would soon change.

Macdonald did indeed incorporate several ideas from abroad in his design, as well as versions of originals first seen at the National. To gain some variety, though, he enlisted the aid of British journalist Bernard Darwin, who sponsored a contest

BELOW: THE TERRAIN THAT BECAME THE FAMOUS FOURTH HOLE. *(Golf Illustrated)*

OPPOSITE PAGE: A DIAGRAM OF THE GOLF COURSE WITH THE CHANNEL HOLE ON THE LEFT BORDER. *(Golf Illustrated)*

in *Country Life* magazine, asking his readers to design a classic par 4-hole of 360 to 460 yards. Alister MacKenzie's design was declared the winner from among 81 entries. Macdonald adapted MacKenzie's plan, with slight alterations, as Lido's 18th hole, thereby giving great impetus to MacKenzie's budding career as an architect. MacKenzie's hole was the ultimate in strategic design, including three separate "tongues of fairway" to aim at from the tee, each requiring a carry over some very rough country, with the more daring drive rewarded with a simplified approach to a green protected by bunkers and grassy hollows. When he saw the hole in person, Darwin said that he was more convinced than ever that the committee had chosen the proper design as the prizewinner.

Seth Raynor, Macdonald's engineer, built Lido. He is said to have pumped 2,000,000 cubic yards of sand from the channel floor to shape the various contours Macdonald wished to create. A lagoon was built to form the island fairway for Lido's famous fourth hole, the "Channel Hole," one that Macdonald considered the best two-shot hole in the world.

(95

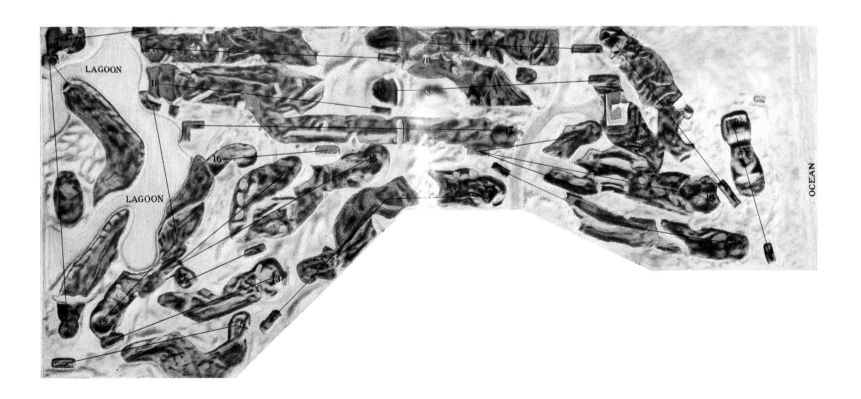

Work began at Lido in 1914, one week before World War I broke out, but the course wasn't playable until 1917, at about the time the United States entered the war, and wasn't opened officially until after the war. The total cost was nearly $800,000, a staggering sum in those days. The course received high praise, with many experts rating it among the five best in the country.

During the late 1920s, the magazine *Metropolitan Golfer* conducted a survey of 50 prominent professionals, asking each to list what he considered the leading courses in the country. The consensus opinion was that Pine Valley ranked first— some things never change— with Lido second, ahead of such highly regarded Long Island courses as the National, Garden City Golf, and Inwood.

Lido was recognized as the nearest thing to a British seaside links in this country. When asked in 1922 by *The American Golfer* to compare Lido, Pine Valley, and the National, Bernard Darwin had this to say:

> *"I should say that Lido was the finest course in the world, Pine Valley the hardest course in the world, and that I would rather play on the National than either of them."*

At 6,604 yards from the championship tees, Lido was considered three to five shots harder than the greatest British links. No less than seven holes demanded sufficient length off the tee to carry a huge bunker or series of bunkers guarding the "entrance" to the fairway—a feature reminiscent of the National. The sand-based bentgrass rough was so thick that it usually was difficult to find one's ball, and even then impossible to do anything with it but play a niblick recovery back to the safety of the fairway.

The Channel Hole's C-shaped fairway was bordered along the left by the lagoon, which had to be carried from the tee and again on the approach, with a huge cross bunker 80 yards short of the green. The tee shot offered the intriguing alternative of a long and risky carry of 210 yards over water, rushes, and sand to a separate fairway, a small target 100 yards long and 30 yards wide. If the shot was carried off successfully, the player was left with a grand second over the lagoon; if short or off-line, the player was left with a dif-

BELOW LEFT: THE PAR-3 THIRD HOLE, LIDO'S "EDEN." REYNOLDS CHANNEL REPLACED THE EDEN ESTUARY AS A DANGEROUS BACKDROP. *(Golf Illustrated)*

BELOW: LOOKING ACROSS THE THIRD GREEN TOWARD THE CHANNEL HOLE (#4). THE CONSERVATIVE ROUTE IS OVER THE BRIDGE; THE DARING ROUTE PLAYS TO THE RIGHT OF THE BRIDGE. *(Golf Illustrated)*

OPPOSITE PAGE, TOP: SKETCH OF THE CHANNEL HOLE. *(Golf Illustrated)*

OPPOSITE PAGE, MIDDLE: THE LAGOON HOLE (#11), WITH THE 17TH TO ITS LEFT AND MOUNDS BACKING UP TO THE 10TH GREEN (RIGHT). ALL OF THIS WAS MANUFACTURED, INCLUDING THE HAND-PLANTED REEDS. *(Golf Illustrated)*

OPPOSITE PAGE, BOTTOM: THE PAR-3 OCEAN HOLE (#8), CIRCA 1925; ALREADY SHORTENED TO 160 YARDS, BUT STILL QUITE A CHALLENGE FOR THE GOLFER. *(Golf Illustrated)*

OPPOSITE PAGE, RIGHT: THE RIGHT-DOGLEG SIXTH HOLE. *(Golf Illustrated)*

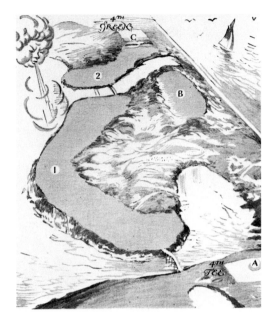

ficult recovery from knee-deep "eel grass." In fact, Lido's hole offered two entirely distinct routes, one playing as a par 4 of 466 yards, the other as a par 5 of about 510 yards "around the horn." Darwin called Lido's fourth "the most majestic two-shot hole I have ever seen, truly awe-inspiring."

Immediately to the left of the "Channel Hole," on the other side of the lagoon, was the 12th, a long dogleg par 4 that played around the lagoon to a punchbowl green. The eighth hole also was a new Macdonald concept. Called the "Ocean Hole," it was a 160-yard par 3 to a raised green, with the beach along the right, somewhat similar in concept to the famous 15th at Portmarnock in Ireland. When the prevailing southwesterly breeze blew, the tee shot had to be played out over the beach. Another hole that attracted considerable comment was the sixth, a 90-degree dogleg to the right that called for a long, blind second shot over sand hills and a forest of giant sea rushes.

In 1928, Lido unveiled its new Spanish Mission-style clubhouse just to the east of the seventh green, overlooking the ocean. It was as large and as lavishly appointed as the most palatial American hotel of the time, and included 400 guest rooms. The 1,500 members enjoyed outdoor dancing to live orchestras on the

(97

building's broad verandas, an umbrella-studded promenade along the ocean's edge, and a casino with adjoining grandstand overlooking the club's tennis courts.

The glory that was Lido's was short-lived, however. During World War II, the United States Navy took over much of Long Beach Island, including the Lido property. The club ceased operations after the 1942 season, only to reopen in 1949 with a new Robert Trent Jones course located entirely on the Channel side of Lido Boulevard. The private club lasted until 1977 when it fell victim to financial difficulties. Since 1978, Lido has been operated as a public facility, and only recently has undergone a successful rejuvenation.

Space considerations no doubt mitigated against preserving the old Channel hole, although the present 16th hole is similar in concept. The Channel hole likely

OPPOSITE PAGE: PRESENT DAY 13TH HOLE OF LIDO BEACH GOLF COURSE, PART OF WHICH WAS LIKELY THE ORIGINAL CHANNEL HOLE. (*L.C. Lambrecht*)

THE LIDO HOTEL/CLUBHOUSE ON THE BEACH. (*Golf Illustrated*)

played from a tee alongside the present 12th green in the opposite direction up the 14th fairway, then across the Lagoon to the second part of today's 16th fairway. The separate alternate fairway was located somewhere on the present 13th hole, not far from the green.

During its heyday, Lido was a force in Metropolitan golf, hosting major regional events on a regular basis, more frequently than any other club in the region. Included were two Met Amateurs, the inaugural Long Island Amateur, and three Met Opens.

The scores in the 1922 Met Open attested to the difficulty of Macdonald's original design. Marty O'Loughlin won that year with a four-round total of 309 under very windy conditions. Johnny Farrell was second at 312, and Jim Barnes came in at 315. Gene Sarazen's score was 320, including two 84s, 32 strokes higher than his winning score that year in the U.S. Open. Pat Doyle's third round 73 established a new course record. According to the *New York Times*, it was a day when:

> *"... most of the leaders were struggling, striving to keep their scores down in the low 80s."*

O'Loughlin led most of the way, leading by two after 36 holes and by four after 54. Willie Ogg was his closest pursuer, with Farrell and Barnes seven and ten strokes back, respectively. We let the *New York Times* take us through the front nine of the final round:

> *"As a result of the closeness of the competition—for seven or eight shots mean nothing at Lido—there was considerable excitement when the final dash was started in the afternoon. Attracted by the deeds of O'Loughlin, the New Jersey champion started out with a big following at his heels, but Marty, unable to put forth his best efforts with so many eyes focused upon him, gave early evidence of a collapse. Starting off with a pair of 6s, followed two holes later by a 7 and three fives, O'Loughlin was soon deserted, and everyone flocked to see what Barnes and Farrell were doing, it then appearing that it lay between them, especially after the news got around that Ogg had killed his chances by taking a 9 on the seventh hole."*

Ogg was three strokes ahead at the time and playing well, when suddenly, according to the *New York Times*:

> *"Left with but a short pitch to the green on his third, he found his ball lodged*

into the fork of a piece of wood just off the fairway. Instead of taking his penalty, he elected to play the shot, and the ball flew out at right angles into the bushes, and when it was all over he had used up nine shots."

Despite an outgoing 45, O'Loughlin found himself tied for the lead with Johnny Farrell, who immediately compromised his own chances by deciding to "play it safe" on the back nine, a strategy that quickly resulted in a crucial pair of three-putt greens. O'Loughlin steadied himself at the turn, and carded a back nine 38 that won him his second title of the year, and the $500 first prize.

For all its regional activity, however, Lido never hosted a major national event. The closest it came was in 1925 when sectional qualifying for the U.S. Open was held at the club. Playing what he called "some of his greatest golf," Bobby Jones qualified with rounds of 72-71, the first round played in a downpour from start to finish. Mac Smith's duplicate 35-35=70s led the qualifying, and were considered at the time one of the greatest displays of shot making ever seen.

(101

O'LOUGHLIN'S WINNING PUTT ON #18 IN 1922, "WHILE DELUDED GALLERY FOLLOWS FARRELL." *(Golf Illustrated)*

11

Engineers: An Instant Sensation

The "yellow dog" brooded over dinner. Earlier in the day he had thrown away a golden opportunity to win that first national championship he so coveted. The pressure and the frustration were beginning to get to him. His only consolation came in the fact that he would have the chance to redeem himself the following day in a play-off.

The setting for the foregoing was the dining room at the Engineers Country Club in Roslyn Harbor. The "yellow dog," to use his own words, was none other than Bobby Jones. The occasion was the 1923 U.S. Open, held cross-island at the Inwood Country Club. That Jones would venture to the North Shore that evening might seem unusual, even though the Inwood clubhouse had suffered a major fire just before the tournament. But Engineers was a club that Jones knew well, a friendly atmosphere in which he felt comfortable.

Although still a young club at that time, Engineers had already witnessed two national championships over its links, the 1919 PGA and the 1920 U.S. Amateur. No other club of comparable age had ever been so honored. Jones, of course, had been on hand in 1920 as a carefree 18-year-old who feasted on pie a la mode at lunch between rounds. According to Jones, it was after the Amateur at Engineers (his third) that he began to take matters more seriously, and worry if he would ever break through to win a major tournament.

Due to the large number of entrants, qualifying for the 1920 Amateur was held at two clubs, Engineers and nearby North Shore, on September 6. Jones emerged comedalist at 154 with another 18-year-old, Fred Wright, and took the medal home when he defeated Wright in their third-round match. Both Jones and Wright shot 79 at Engineers, then 75 at North Shore, to lead all qualifiers. The cut came at 165.

Four top British amateurs, Cyril Tolley, Tommy Armour, Roger Wethered, and Lord Charles Hope, came over for the event, but only Armour was able to qualify, and he was eliminated in an early round. Meeting with a similar fate was a group of 12 leading Canadian players, who had come to Engineers the week before the Amateur to compete against a team of American amateurs, including Jones. The unusual number of upsets in the qualifying and early rounds of the tournament was attributed to a period of dry, hot weather that left the greens "iron-hard." The Engineers course played to a par 70 at 6,362 yards for the championship.

In the finals, which brought together the two leading players in the country, Chick Evans played some superb golf to defeat Francis Ouimet 7&6. During one 19-hole stretch starting at the 10th hole, Evans played just 71 strokes. A gallery estimated at

Opposite page: The original Engineers clubhouse. *(Golf Illustrated)*

Davy Herron driving from the 15th tee in 1920. *(American Golfer)*

13,000 witnessed the victory, which most observers attributed to brilliant iron play.

Two matches earlier in that championship have received more attention, in retrospect, than did the finals. In the second round, Evans was fortunate to get by Reggie Lewis of Greenwich. One down going to the 18th, Evans pulled his drive into a bunker, then left his recovery in the rough 100 yards short of the green. Lewis, meanwhile, was just over the green in two, seemingly in position to close out the match. Evans pitched to 14 feet, then Lewis, with just a fair chip, put his ball inside Evans. To prolong the match, Evans had to sink his putt, and Lewis miss his—which is exactly what happened with Evans holing a difficult sidehill putt. Evans eventually won on the 41st hole, one of the longest matches in U.S. Amateur history.

Jones, meantime, advanced to the semifinals, where Ouimet eliminated him, 6 and 5. He later considered that match, which was played before the largest gallery he had seen to that point in his career, as his "last trouncing as a kid." An incident on the seventh green during the afternoon round supposedly ended his childhood. As he was about to putt, a bee landed on his ball. Jones chased it away, but it returned. He chased it again, and this time it came to rest on the green nearby. A gallery official placed his megaphone over the bee, which promptly escaped through the mouthpiece, and flew back to Jones. Bobby then proceeded to chase the bee around the

104)

green, and finally persuaded it to leave. He then returned to his ball, only to 3-putt, falling another hole behind at a crucial juncture in the match. Charles Blair Macdonald happened to be in Jones's gallery at the time, and commented to his companion, "Mark my words, he will not win. He lacks concentration." Apparently, Jones got the message.

The United States vs. Canada competition had some historic importance in its own right. Those matches, which were held twice, in Canada in 1919 and at Engineers in 1920 one week before the Amateur, were the forerunner of the Walker Cup, being a first attempt at international competition. The United States was the victor on both occasions.

Engineers' first national championship, the second edition of the PGA Championship, took place in September of 1919. The inaugural had been played at Siwanoy in 1916, after which World War I intervened for two seasons. Jim Barnes won the 1919 PGA at Engineers—he had also won at Siwanoy—defeating Fred McLeod 6&5 in the finals. *The American Golfer* recounted the turning point in the match:

(105

"As in 1916, there was an Englishman and a Scot in the finals. Barnes was as cool as the proverbial cucumber, sizing up every shot very much after the fashion of James Braid, particularly when on the putting green. It was six feet three versus five feet three on the Saturday, but one would never have guessed this when drives were compared, for McLeod was well up with his bigger opponent..The theory that the nearer you are to the ground, the better putter you are was rudely smashed in this final go. McLeod, after a brilliant day of green work on Friday, started off on the first ten holes as if he were the David of the links, confident in his ability to smite the Goliath of golfdom. Out in a splendid 36, which included a 6, he found himself 2-up and going strong. At the eleventh hole, McLeod's approach was a bit too strong and he lost, just at a time when it appeared another hole would be added to his string. He was admittedly still thinking of this error when he putted on the next green, and the result was a miss by several inches of a foot and a half putt. This disturbed the equilibrium of the Scot so much that he proceeded to lose five of the next six holes, making a clean sweep for Barnes and a comfortable lead of five at the lunchtime hour."

Barnes reached the finals by eliminating Bob MacDonald 5&4, despite being outdriven consistently by 20 to 70 yards. McLeod parlayed five consecutive one-putt greens to defeat George McLean of Great Neck and gain his berth in the finals.

REGGIE LEWIS AND CHICK EVANS.
(American Golfer)

The average score for the tournament was 78. The professionals and the tournament officials were lavish in their praise of the course and club facilities, and so Engineers was offered the following year's Amateur.

Members of the Engineers Club of Manhattan, a swank social group comprised of wealthy, blue-blooded engineers from across the country, established the Engineers Country Club on January 21, 1917. The Engineers purchased the 210-acre W.R. Willett Manor House and estate in Roslyn Harbor in March of 1917. The property included several small ponds, and featured a boathouse and jetty on Hempstead Bay. The club's original intent was to build two 18-hole golf courses, but that plan was soon amended. In the end, 150 acres were dedicated to their 18-hole golf course, and the other 60 acres to homes for members. The rambling brick and frame Manor House, on an eminence overlooking the water, was converted into a clubhouse, but was destroyed by fire on November 2, 1917, just after the inaugural ball. Rather than rebuild, the extensive stable facility on the grounds was converted at very little expense into an unusual, though thoroughly modern, clubhouse for what at the time was a men-only club. Its facilities were considered among the most luxurious in the country.

To design their golf course, the engineers engaged Herbert Strong, who also served as the club's first golf professional. Their mandate to Strong was simple—build 18 distinct golf holes unlike any others in the country. Soon, the course was recognized as one of the sportiest and toughest in the country, the "last word in golf

OPPOSITE PAGE, TOP: PUTTING AT THE 17TH GREEN DURING THE 1919 PGA. (*American Golfer*)

OPPOSITE PAGE, FAR LEFT: PLAYING FROM A GREENSIDE BUNKER AT THE 14TH HOLE. (*Golf Illustrated*)

BELOW: THE TREACHEROUS APPROACH TO THE 16TH GREEN. (*American Golfer*)

RIGHT: APPROACHING THE 18TH GREEN. (*American Golfer*)

construction, or even a couple beyond that," to quote one golf journalist of the era. Some thought Engineers to be the finest course in the country, others felt it was no more than a "bag of tricks."

But the glory days ended with the Depression, and Engineers was fortunate to survive the next two decades, operating primarily as a public course, also using such names as Roslyn Harbor Country Club and Rolling Hills Country Club. In 1951, a group from the Oceanside Golf & Country Club joined with other individuals from the north shore to purchase Engineers and form the present club.

The Engineers course is an old-fashioned one, replete with several blind shots, that has undergone little revision over the years. The old "2 or 20" 14th hole—the most infamous at Engineers—was a 90-yard par 3 that played directly over a frontal bunker to a tiny plateau green perched precariously atop a knoll. Two bunkers protect the right side, one to the left, and another pair at the rear of the green—actually, most of these bunkers prevent an errant shot from rolling 80 to 90 feet down the hillside into extremely formidable rough. It was once written about Engineers' 14th that "more malediction, praise, and lamentation has been bestowed upon this particular creation than any other short hole in existence." Two golfing immortals, Bobby Jones and Gene Sarazen, went for "double figures" on this hole.

Equally challenging—and scary—is the relatively short par-4 16th hole, where the fairway falls off a cliff into a morass of bunkers, mounds, and rough, with the green perched precariously above a brook closely bordering its right side.

(107

12

Birth of the Long Island Golf Association

The Long Island Golf Association was organized in late March of 1922. A statement issued by the association read as follows:

> *"The Long Island Golf Association was organized for the purpose of promoting the game of golf and forming a closer relationship between the clubs and players on Long Island.*
>
> *"All members of clubs belonging to the association shall be eligible to play in tournaments.*
>
> *"The championship tournaments of the association shall be amateur, open, junior, and golf team. The golf team championship shall be decided by the lowest aggregate scores of any five members of the same club playing in the qualifying round of the amateur championship of the association."*

John M. Ward of Garden City Golf Club was elected the association's first president. The first championship conducted was the Amateur, and the site chosen, the formidable Lido Club, added to the luster of the event. The field included the Metropolitan Amateur titleholder, Gardiner White of Nassau, and Grant Peacock of Cherry Valley, who was runner-up to White in 1921. The first Long Island Amateur champion, however, was Howard Maxwell of Nassau, who defeated Donald McKellar of North Hempstead in the finals. Cherry Valley was selected to

John Montgomery Ward

John Montgomery "Monty" Ward is a member of baseball's Hall of Fame. He played for the New York Giants as well as the Providence and Brooklyn teams in the National League, and the Brooklyn team in the Players League, during the years 1878–1894. He hit .371 in two different seasons, led the Players League with 207 hits in 1890, led the National League in stolen bases three times, and was an outstanding fielder at shortstop and second base. Like Babe Ruth, he started as a pitcher, winning 158 games during that phase of his career, including 44 in 1879 and 40 in 1880. He pitched a perfect game, an 18-inning shutout, and won two complete games in one day. Also an excellent golfer, Ward won the 1905 New Jersey Amateur.

host the inaugural Long Island Open in 1922, a tournament won by Willie Klein, then a young assistant at the Garden City Country Club. Klein repeated in 1923, and won again in 1933.

The Long Island Amateur has had some memorable renewals over the years, starting with the 1923 edition. Eddie Driggs of Cherry Valley, a former fullback at Princeton, led most of the way, only to be collared by John Stearns of Nassau on the 17th hole. With the match even on the home green, Stearns's birdie putt stymied Driggs's short putt for par, and when Driggs attempted to jump Stearns's ball, he accidentally hit his opponent's ball into the hole for a match- and championship-winning birdie! Driggs rebounded, winning the tournament three times, in 1925, 1929, and 1930.

Others to win the Long Island Amateur include 1933 U.S. Amateur champion George Dunlap of Garden City Country Club (in 1932) and 1937 British Amateur winner Robert Sweeny of Meadow Brook (in 1955). Frank Strafaci, a member at Pomonok and later at Garden City Country Club, won five Long Island Amateur

ABOVE: WILLIE KLEIN, WINNER OF THE FIRST TWO LONG ISLAND OPENS. (*Golf Illustrated*)

RIGHT: THE FOUNDERS OF THE LIGA (L TO R): GARDINER WHITE, A.S. BOURNE, JOHN M. WARD, A.T. HAIGHT, GRANT PEACOCK. (*Golf Illustrated*)

BELOW: EDDIE DRIGGS. (*Golf Illustrated*)

titles (1938, 1941, 1947, 1949, 1951), and his brother Tom added two more (1944, 1945) to the family account while Frank was in the service at the end of World War II. John Humm, a 25-time club champion at Rockville Links (at one time a national record), won the Long Island Amateur three times over a remarkable 31-year span (1948, 1952, 1979), defeating Frank Strafaci in the finals in 1952. Future Tour winner George Burns won in 1972 while a member at Wheatley Hills—just a footnote, actually, when compared to his Wheatley Hills club mate Gene Francis, who won the title seven times (1963, 1969, 1973, 1976-1978, 1988), the last at age 50.

The Long Island Open was contested at 72 holes through 1948, and thereafter scheduled at 54 holes. Al Brosch set the 72-hole record with a 276 at Wheatley Hills in 1939, while the 54-hole record is 200, done twice by Bruce Zabriski at Bethpage Red (1991 and 1993). Al Brosch, at different times professional at Bethpage, Cherry Valley, Woodmere, and Sands Point, won a record 10 Long Island Open titles (1939, 1946-1951, 1953, 1956, 1959). Brosch played on the Tour at times, and, in fact, was the first player ever to shoot 60 in a Tour event. The immortal Gene Sarazen was an early winner of the Long Island Open, taking the 1927 renewal at Salisbury (#4 course). Macdonald Smith of Lakeville dominated that era by winning four times

ABOVE: THE 17TH AT POMONOK PRIOR TO RENOVATION, WITH THE 18TH HOLE AND CLUBHOUSE LOOMING IN THE BACKGROUND. *(Golf Illustrated)*

Opposite page, left: 1933 U.S. Amateur champion George Dunlap. *(Golf Illustrated)*

Opposite page, middle: British Amateur champion Robert Sweeny. *(American Golfer)*

Opposite page, right: Frank Strafaci, winner of a record seven Met Amateurs and five Long Island Amateur championships. *(Metropolitan Golf Association)*

Below: "Long Jim" Barnes, winner of the U.S. Open, British Open, and PGA Championship during his illustrious career, professional at Plandome and Huntington Crescent during the 1930s. *(Golf Illustrated)*

Right: George Voigt. *(American Golfer)*

(1925, 1929, 1930, 1931). Joe Turnesa was the only member of the illustrious Westchester clan to win the Long Island Open, doing so three times (1934, 1938, 1940) while professional at Belleclaire in Queens.

"Long Jim" Barnes, winner of the first two editions of the PGA Championship, a U.S. Open and a British Open, won the Long Island Open late in his career (1937) while professional at Huntington Crescent.

A number of outstanding Tour players captured the Long Island Open during the third quarter of the century while serving at Long Island clubs. The list includes Jay Hebert of Woodmere (1954), Tom Nieporte of Piping Rock (1962, 1964, 1965, 1973, 1975), Jerry Pittman of The Creek (1968), and Jimmy Wright of Inwood (1969, 1970, 1972, 1974). Wright finished fourth in the 1969 PGA Championship, a record for a modern-day club pro. Of more recent vintage is Jim Albus of Piping Rock, winner of the Long Island Open twice (1987, 1988), who left club life to go on to outstanding success on the PGA Senior Tour. Among his accomplishments was a victory in the Tournament Players Championship over the likes of Nicklaus, Player, and Trevino.

George Voigt of North Hills remains the only amateur to win the Long Island Open, and in fact, the only player to win both LIGA titles in the same season (1928). Voigt gained a measure of international fame in 1930 when he led Bobby Jones late in an early round match in the British Amateur at St. Andrews, narrowly missing putting a stop to Jones's Grand Slam in its first leg.

The only father-son duos to capture major LIGA titles are the Gallettas. Mal Galletta Sr. won the Long Island Amateur in 1946, not to mention numerous club championships at North Hills, Wheatley Hills, and Brookville. Mal Galletta Jr. won the Long Island Open three times (1977, 1979, 1981), and grandson Mal Galletta III won the Long Island Amateur in 1992.

Since 1948 the Long Island Golf Association has conducted a third

(111

"major," the Richardson Memorial at Seawane. The tournament honors William Duncan Richardson, who was a reporter for the *New York Times* for nearly four decades (1921-1957), and also a regular contributor to *Golf Illustrated*. Richardson's sporting interests transcended golf — he was equally fluent in baseball, football, track, rowing, and horse racing. The taciturn, witty Richardson was, above all else, a gentleman. He routinely attended sporting events dressed in a jacket and tie. On the beat, he came to be known as "the Gentleman from the Times."

The Richardson is played in May at the beginning of the local season. The roster of winners over the years is impressive—names such as Humm, Galletta, Strafaci, Siderowf, Courville, Francis, Burns, Zahringer, and Baldwin adorn the trophy. Charles "Chick" Evans, who won both the U.S. Open and U.S. Amateur in 1916, made the trip from Chicago for the first Richardson. Although his partner, bandleader Fred Waring, was unable to play, the 58-year-old Evans went out in the driving rain and played six holes, "just as a tribute to Bill."

The Richardson is played at the Seawane Golf & Country Club in Hewlett Harbor, which was founded in 1927 and named after the Indian term "sewan," meaning copper beads. Helen Hicks, perhaps the greatest woman golfer ever developed on Long Island, and the first woman to turn professional, practiced regularly at Seawane—her brother, Jarvis, was a member. Hicks felt that if she could master Seawane, she was ready for major competition. The most notable feature of the Devereux Emmet-designed course are the two deepwater canals that come into play on several holes.

Although not conducted by the Long Island Golf Association, the Havemeyer Memorial at Southward Ho! Country Club in Bay Shore has also become a fixture on the local golf calendar. Scheduled the week after the Richardson, the Havemeyer honors the central role in club history played by Horace Havemeyer, the club's financial "angel." The Havemeyer was first played in 1951.

For several generations, before and after the turn of the century, the Havemeyer family was identified with the sugar industry in America. Several members of the family were, in turn, known as "The Sugar King." Among them were William F. Havemeyer, who served three separate terms as mayor of New York City, and Theodore Havemeyer, one of the organizers and first president of the United States Golf Association.

Southward Ho was organized in 1923, and turned to A.W. Tillinghast to design their golf course. The greens resemble those at Tillinghast's Winged Foot—pear-shaped, pitched back-to-front, with bunkers pinching in at the front corners.

OPPOSITE PAGE, TOP: AMERICA'S FIRST FEMALE GOLF PROFESSIONAL, HELEN HICKS. *(American Golfer)*

OPPOSITE PAGE, BOTTOM: THE 18TH GREEN AND CLUBHOUSE AT SEAWANE IN 1934. *(Golf Illustrated)*

OPPOSITE PAGE, FAR RIGHT: HORACE HAVEMEYER. *(Golf Illustrated)*

13

The Walker Cup: Born on Long Island

The National Golf Links was the venue for the first Walker Cup matches, which were held in 1922. According to C.B. Macdonald, the original idea of an international team competition between the United States and Great Britain was his, with the matches to alternate between his own National Golf Links and his beloved St. Andrews in Scotland. However, the National's membership treasured their privacy and preferred to keep their course out of the spotlight that accompanies tournament golf, so the Walker Cup has since moved around to different courses in the United States and Great Britain.

George Herbert Walker, donor of the Walker Cup, was a member at the National, and the maternal grandfather of former United States president George H.W. Bush, himself the father of current president, George W. Bush.

The idea of an international golf competition arose in the aftermath of World War I, "expanding" a concept born in 1919 when an American team, captained by W.C. Fownes Jr. of Oakmont defeated a Canadian team at the Hamilton Golf Club in Ontario. The Americans won a return match in 1920 at Engineers. Simultaneously, British and American golfers were seriously seeking each other's championships.

At a meeting of the USGA Executive Committee in December, 1920, Walker, who was President of the USGA at the time, proposed the idea of an international golf championship, and offered to donate an International Challenge trophy which

the press, to his embarrassment, dubbed the "Walker Cup."

Early the next year, the USGA invited a number of countries to send teams to compete for the trophy, but no country was able to compete that year. Not to be discouraged, Fownes put together an American team that defeated a British team in an informal match at Hoylake just prior to the British Amateur in 1921, thereby laying down a challenge to the British. Early in 1922, the Royal & Ancient Golf Club in St. Andrews announced that it would send a team to compete for the Walker Cup later that year.

The matches were played on August 28-29 at National, four 36-hole foursomes matches the first day, then eight 36-hole singles matches the second day. The date was selected to allow the British players to play in the U.S. Amateur, which was held a couple of weeks later at The Country Club near Boston. The American team won that first Walker Cup by a score of 8-4. All eight team members—Bobby Jones, Francis Ouimet, Jess Sweetser, Chick Evans, Robert Gardner, Jesse Guilford, Max Marston, and W.C. Fownes—were, or would become, U.S. Amateur champions. Guilford was the defending (1921) champion, and Sweetser would win two weeks later. The British team was led by Cyril Tolley and Roger Wethered; the 1922 British Amateur champion Ernest Holderness was unable to come due to business considerations. When the British captain, Robert Harris, became ill at the last moment, journalist Bernard Darwin, who was covering the event for the *Times of London*, joined the team and won his singles match over Fownes. Darwin was no slouch on the links, having reached the semifinals of the 1921 British Amateur.

Golf Illustrated also covered the Walker Cup, and had the following to say about the #1 and #2 singles matches:

OPPOSITE PAGE: GEORGE HERBERT WALKER. *(United States Golf Association)*

A CASUAL GROUP SHOT OF THE 1922 TEAMS. *(Golf Illustrated)*

Top: The gallery along the 16th fairway. *(Golf Illustrated)*

Bottom: The gallery approaching the 17th green. *(Golf Illustrated)*

"A year before at Hoylake, Tolley defeated Guilford by two and one, and this time it was only by remarkable putting that Guilford was able to be only two down when the first round was finished. In the afternoon it was Tolley's putting that failed while Guilford went on to heights unknown in putting excellence and eventually won by two and one. It was a terrific battle between two giants who made things look so ridiculously easy by their long slugging and masterful iron shots to the green. Roger Wethered's was similarly affected. After taking the lead in the morning, his putter forsook him and away went his margin, and only by winning the last hole was he able to get within reaching distance of Bobby Jones, who was thus able to start the afternoon round one up. It was a great battle in the afternoon. They see-

sawed all the way out and although Wethered placed every iron shot from the seventh to the thirteenth inside Jones, it did him no good for he lost three of these holes by poor putting. Bobby did not falter for a moment, and went on to score a victory by three and two."

Jess Sweetser earned the dubious distinction of losing the only overtime match in Walker Cup history. *Golf Illustrated* reported:

"The only match that came to the home green saw C.V.L. Hooman stage a great comeback during the last five holes and square the match at the seventeenth and halve the eighteenth. For some unknown reason, President Byers ordered the match to be played off, contrary to general principal [sic], and Sweetser put himself out of the running hooking badly to the left and never had a chance to get near the green in less than five."

After the first year, it was decided that no man should be expected to play more than 36 holes a day for his country, and thereafter ties became a part of Walker Cup scoring.

(117

In September of 1924 the Walker Cup matches were contested at the Garden City Golf Club, the second time these international matches were held in this country, indeed the second time on Long Island. The Americans had won at St. Andrews in 1923 by the narrow margin of 6 1/2 to 5 1/2.

The American team at Garden City included Jones, Ouimet, Evans, Sweetser, and team captain Robert Gardner. Much of the prematch publicity centered on the absence, for business reasons, of five key players from the British team. Among the missing were Roger Wethered, generally regarded as Britain's leading player of the time, and Ernest Holderness, the 1924 British Amateur champion. The only member of the 10-man British team ever to have won the British Amateur, indeed to possess an international reputation, was Cyril Tolley, the team captain.

The Americans defeated their British rivals 9-3, although the contest was much closer than the final tally suggests. The only foursomes match that was even close—the Americans were handy winners of the other three—involved Michael Scott (45 years of age and the oldest player in the competition) and Robert Scott Jr. (no relation), who came from 3-down after 18 holes to beat the team of Bobby Jones and W.C. Fownes Jr. on the final green. This was the only loss Jones ever suffered in international team competition. The *New York Times* detailed the match:

Opposite page, top: The winning 1924 American team with the Walker Cup. (L to R: Bobby Jones, Chick Evans, Jess Sweetser, Francis Ouimet, Robert Gardner, William Fownes, Max Marston, Jess Guilford, Oscar Willing, and Harrison Johnston. *(Golf Illustrated)*

Opposite page, bottom: The British team at Garden City (L to R): Eustace Storey, William Hogue, Dennis Kyle, Major Charles Healot, Cyril Tolley, Tony Terrance, A.C. Brislowe, William Murray, Michael Scott, Robert Scott. Seated is Henry Cullen, secretary of the Royal & Ancient Golf Club. *(Golf Illustrated)*

"This was the only one of the four matches that supplied any thrills whatsoever, the outcome of the other three being never in doubt after the first few holes had been played in the afternoon round. Ouimet and Guilford played the best golf to finish one-up on Tolley and Hezlet in the morning. They had a round of 74, in spite of two 6s at long holes. It was the two Scots who put up the most magnificent battle of them all, a battle that might not have gone as well for them had not Fownes thrown a monkey wrench into the machinery at two of the last three holes when he once putted weirdly and then missed a tee shot on a hole of such dimension that a long drive is essential in order to reach the green with the second. Going to the ninth hole, Michael Scott topped his drive and it took the British pair three to reach the green. On top of that, Jones missing a twelve-footer on the green left the Honorable Michael with a stymie, the nearest ball being not more than a foot away from the cup and the two balls not more than seven inches apart. Unfazed by the unpleasant situation, Michael took out his trusty niblick and jumped his ball into the cup for a half. It was at the sixteenth that Fownes offset a great deed performed by the great Bobby. Both balls were trapped on the way to the green, Fownes putting his approach into a deep bunker at the left of the green and Michael reached a pit on his recovery out of the rough, where Robert had put him with a bad tee shot, Robert Scott brought forth applause when he pitched out within holing distance, but Jones outstripped him with a superb recovery to within two feet. His work went for naught, however, for Fownes missed and gave the Britons a chance to halve the hole. Fownes then proceeded to miss his drive, going to the seventeenth, and it was through the great run-up shot by Bobby that the hole was saved and the match carried on to the home green. Coming up to the home green, the match was all even. Robert Scott's iron landed close to the hole, while Jones fell far short. Fownes then gave his ball a chance to look into the hole, but it went two yards beyond. It looked as if a halved match might result, for Jones had a two-yarder to hole for a par 3, while Robert Scott was within three feet of the hole. Bobby's putt, however, was of the downhill variety and his ball, after starting for the cup, turned aside. The Glasgow golfer then confidently tapped his ball into the hole for the solitary British victory."

The eight singles matches the next day included several pivotal moments that turned the competition in the Americans' favor. Two matches in particular grabbed the headlines. In one, Francis Ouimet defeated Eustace Storey, a Cambridge University student, 1-up with an eight-foot birdie putt on the final green—after

Storey had missed from 10 feet. In the other, Tolley defeated the 1923 U.S. Amateur champion, Max Marston, 1-up with a birdie at the 17th hole. Tolley had built a four-hole lead in the first six holes after lunch, but Marston came back to even the match—despite fighting a persistent slice.

The Walker Cup has since returned to Long Island just once, in 1977 at Shinnecock Hills, and the American team once again was the winner, by the score of 16-8. The team included future U.S. Open champion Scott Simpson, budding Amateur star and future Senior Tour player Jay Sigel, and reigning Amateur champion John Fought, but only Dick Siderowf, the 1973 and 1976 British Amateur titleholder, had previous Walker Cup experience. Sandy Lyle, destined to become a British Open and Masters winner, was a member of the British team. In truth, in an era when the career amateur had become nearly extinct, there were no household names competing, as had been the case in 1922 and 1924.

The format for the matches had been changed in 1963, and now each day's play consisted of four foursomes matches in the morning, then eight singles matches in the afternoon. The matches were held on Friday-Saturday, August 26-27.

Herbert Warren Wind, writing in *Golf Journal*, reported on the key stroke in Friday's foursomes, which happened on the 18th hole in the final group, with the Americans ahead 2-1 in matches:

120)

"...on the home hole, Michael Brannan , a muscular fellow from Brigham Young University, locked up the match when he hit a magnificent 2-iron approach a yard from the pin on that elusive green. If you're an invading team, with understandable hopes of going to lunch 2-2, it's quite a jolt to find yourself down 3-1 instead."

After the Americans won six of the eight singles matches that afternoon, there was talk that the Americans' success could be attributed in part to the fact that the Shinnecock fairways had not been cut down low, and consequently the smaller British ball sat down in the grass. Whatever the reason, it was noted that the eight British players were 41 over par that afternoon! The British attempted to rally on Saturday morning, leading all four matches after nine holes. Eventually they won two, with Scott Simpson holing a 53-foot putt on the 17th hole to win a key point. The Americans then clinched the Cup by winning the first two singles matches in the afternoon, one coming as the result of Lindy Miller's curling, downhill 50-foot putt on the 18th green.

And so the Walker Cup has been played on Long Island three times, once at each of the Island's three highest-ranked courses, each of them with a distinctive British flavor, and the American team has won on all three occasions.

(121

OPPOSITE PAGE: USGA PRESIDENT WYNANT D. VANDERPOOL PRESENTING THE WALKER CUP TO UNITED STATES TEAM CAPTAIN ROBERT GARDNER, WITH BRITISH CAPTAIN CYRIL TOLLEY LOOKING ON. *(Golf Illustrated)*

RIGHT: THE 1977 U.S. WALKER CUP TEAM (L TO R): FRED RIDLEY, VANCE HEAFNER, LINDY MILLER, SCOTT SIMPSON, JOHN FOUGHT, BILL SANDER, CAPTAIN DICK SIDEROWF, JAY SIGEL, MIKE BRANNAN AND GARY HALLBERG. *(United States Golf Association)*

14

Golf's First World Series

The Sound View Golf Club in Great Neck was Long Island's most colorful club during the Roaring Twenties, a reflection of the membership, which came in good numbers from the theatrical and literary set of Manhattan. They were great fans of the game, and in 1921 attempted to write their own place in golf history.

Their ploy was the staging of the first "World Series of Golf," matching the year's American and British Open champions, Jim Barnes and Jock Hutchison, respectively, for the "unofficial" world's championship. The *New York Times* summarized the match as follows:

> *"The long angular figure of Jim Barnes cast a diminishing shadow over the illustrious record of Jock Hutchison on the links of the Sound View Golf Club here today, and at the conclusion of 32 holes of the scheduled 36-hole match for the unofficial supremacy of the golf world, the man who defeated the elect of American and British golf artists a few weeks ago was announced the winner by 5&4. In addition to the title and prestige at stake, the American champion's victory was worth $1,000 and the Sound View silver cup, while the holder of the British Open championship received $500, the solace of the vanquished."*

Barnes won the first hole with a 25-foot birdie putt, and never looked back. According to the *New York Times*, Hutchison was

SOUND VIEW PRESIDENT FONTAINE FOX PRESENTING THE TROPHY TO JIM BARNES, WITH JOCK HUTCHISON LOOKING ON. *(Golf Illustrated)*

"...never in the hunt, always down, fighting bravely to overcome the fast-moving American, but never quite equal to the task."

Barnes led by three holes after the first nine, then by four after 18 and 27 holes. He carded a 74 in the morning round to his rival's 78, then outscored him once again in the first nine holes after lunch, 38 to 39. Hutchison's one rally came immediately after lunch. After narrowly missing from 25 feet on the first green, he won the next two holes to cut his deficit in half. Barnes responded to the challenge, however, winning the next three holes to put the match out of reach. Barnes closed it out by matching his rival's par 4 on the 14th hole.

Neither Barnes nor Hutchison played well, and it was Barnes's steadiness on the greens that carried the day. According to the *New York Times*:

(123

> *"So far as brilliancy went, the match was a disappointment; for neither Barnes nor Hutchison ever succeeded in pulling himself up to the expected heights. In only one department did Hutchison approach anything like his latent ability, that being off the tee where he more than held his own with his rival – in fact, outdriving Barnes in the majority of cases. But his trusty mashie – an implement in the use of which he takes rank second to none – failed him miserably and cruelly, while his putter – what a temperamental thing a putter can be! Jock's actions on the greens were similar to those of Eliza on the ice. He was very unsteady."*

The idea of a world's championship proved popular, the series being continued for the next several years, although at different clubs, and with different formats, and never again on Long Island.

Sound View was located in the southwestern corner

LEFT: DIAGRAM OF THE GREAT NECK
COURSE IN 1915. (*New York Telegram*)

OPPOSITE PAGE: SCENES AT THE ANNUAL
SHAMROCKS VS THISTLES DAY AT SOUND
VIEW IN 1922. (*Golf Illustrated*)

of the Great Neck peninsula, in what is now Great Neck Estates, overlooking Little Neck Bay and the Long Island Railroad. Among the club's members were Ring Lardner, Gene Buck, Ed Wynn, H.B. Warner, Oscar Shaw, and Grantland Rice.

During its heyday, Sound View staged an annual "Shamrock" vs. "Thistle" match, pitting the club's Irish and Scottish members in mortal combat, clad in the traditional garb of their homeland. Sound View was, indeed, a fun place in those days—from the parrot behind the ninth green, who loved to yell "fore," to the group of members who tried to organize a national "club throwers" association in the mid 1920s.

With the Depression, Sound View fell upon hard times. The end came after the 1947 season, when the property was sold to real estate developers. A number of former members then moved on to help found the Glen Head Country Club, which began operating in 1948.

15

The Gold Coast Era

In his classic novel *The Great Gatsby*, F. Scott Fitzgerald immortalized the "Long Island Set," the fabulously wealthy denizens of Long Island's North Shore, which was known as the "Gold Coast" while it glittered. Theirs was a time of elegance and splendor, private yachts, formal gardens, and castles surrounded by polo fields. A typical summer's day on the Gold Coast started with a morning round of golf, then lunch on the terrace at the Piping Rock Club. In the afternoon, it was off to a game of polo at Meadow Brook, then to a dinner party that more often than not would last into the wee hours of the morning.

Perhaps the most famous Gold Coast party took place on September 6, 1924, in honor of the Prince of Wales. The future short-reigned King Edward VIII of England, considered the world's most eligible bachelor at the time, was visiting Long Island for the Westchester Cup polo matches between the United States and Great Britain at Meadow Brook.

The party took place at Harbor Hill, a 52-room French chateau on the 600-acre Roslyn estate of Clarence Mackay, and was attended by 1,200 guests. Trees bordering the mile-long entrance drive sparkled with thousands of blue lights, and the numerous fountains on the grounds were aglow with still more lights.

Clarence Mackay was among the founders of two of the Gold Coast's most exclusive clubs, Piping Rock and The Creek. Piping Rock, the older of the two, was organized in 1909 to "supplement" Meadow Brook. The membership rosters at the two clubs overlapped considerably, each club serving a different purpose. Meadow Brook was primarily a gentleman's polo and hunt club; Piping Rock was more of a family-oriented country club offering a wide array of social and sporting activities—including polo. There were three polo fields on the grounds at Piping Rock.

Piping Rock, which opened in 1912, took its name from the "piping rock," which is located on a hill on the north side of Piping Rock Road, although no longer visible from the road. The rock, which is hundreds, perhaps even thousands, of years old, was situated on what once was the main trail between Oyster Bay and Glen Cove, and was used by the Matinecock Indians and later the Hessian soldiers (during the Revolutionary War) as a resting place. Tribal leaders would meet there as well, to smoke the peace pipe.

Charles Blair Macdonald designed the Piping Rock course, and it would not prove to be his favorite project. His fierce dedication and loyalty to golf clashed with the club's primary role as a polo club. Horses often thundered across his fairways and, according to Macdonald, his front nine was "sacrificed to the polo fields"

DIAGRAM OF THE PIPING ROCK COURSE IN 1915. *(New York Telegram)*

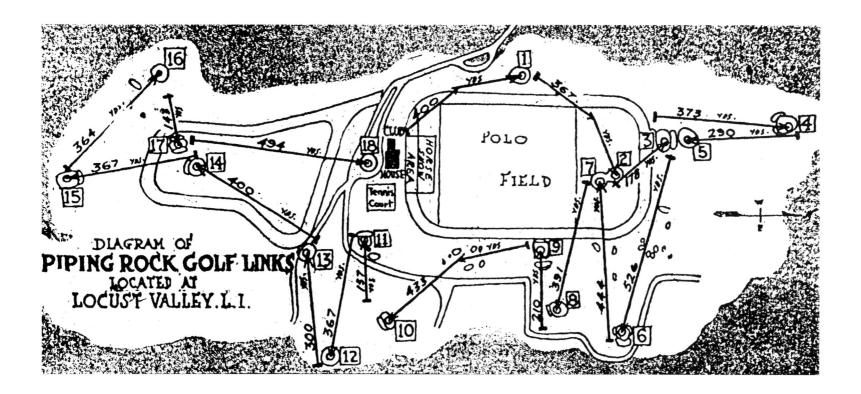

128) in the sense that the holes had to be routed clockwise around the fields, inhibiting his use of the terrain.

An early generation of Piping Rock members participated in an annual cross-country match against Nassau, over the two-plus miles of countryside between the two clubs. In 1917, for instance, Nassau professional Jim Maiden took top honors, playing the "course" in just 22 strokes; Marion Hollins won the ladies' competition with a score of 30.

As the 1920s dawned, Piping Rock became the "place to be," and in fact became overly crowded. And so a group of 11 of Long Island's most prominent and wealthy sportsmen, Piping Rock members all, decided that a more private retreat was needed. The group included Vincent Astor, George F. Baker Jr., Marshall Field, Clarence H. Mackay, J.P. Morgan, Herbert L. Pratt, Harry Payne Whitney, John R. Ryan, Harvey Gibson, Frank Crocker, and Charles B. Macdonald.

Together they financed a new golf club, which they named The Creek after Frost Creek, an inlet of Long Island Sound that was to play a significant role in the character of the first five holes on the back nine. The land purchased by the club was just a small part of the 600-acre estate of Paul Cravath, a prominent New York lawyer, and a Piping Rock founder.

The Creek was one of the few clubs in the United States to have a beach club and yachting facilities on its property. Members were able to land their yachts at

ABOVE LEFT: THE 18TH HOLE AT PIPING ROCK. (*Golf Illustrated*)

ABOVE: TWO SCENES FROM THE ANNUAL CROSS COUNTRY MATCH FROM PIPING ROCK TO NASSAU. (*Golf Illustrated*)

OPPOSITE PAGE: THE BEAUTIFUL 14TH AT PIPING ROCK STILL PRESENTS THE GOLFER WITH NUMEROUS OBSTACLES AS WELL AS A STUNNING VISTA. (*L.C. Lambrecht*)

the Beach Club, and commence their round of golf at the 10th tee.

Seth Raynor built Macdonald's course at The Creek. It offers golfers the "best of both worlds," possessing a mix of parkland holes and seaside links. From the sixth tee the golfer can enjoy one of the most breathtaking views in Long Island golf, with both Greenwich and Stamford in sight across the Sound—not to mention one of Long Island's great par 4s. Its fairway tumbles down the hillside from an elevated tee, finishing at a punch-bowl green that is angled behind a huge bunker across its right front.

The Creek and Piping Rock, recall, both are rated among the top 100 courses in America in the 2001 *Golf* Magazine survey.

The Women's National Golf & Tennis Club was exclusively for women, a reaction in part to overcrowded conditions at Piping Rock and The Creek that prevented the women from playing on weekends. Women's National opened on Memorial Day of 1924, fulfilling the dream of Marion Hollins, quite possibly the most influential woman of golf's first half-century in America. The idea of an exclusive women's club was in the back of her mind for several years, and after winning

Opposite page, left: The "view" at The Creek. Included are the 6th (far left of photo), the 7th (top center), the 16th (middle) and 17th (bottom right). *(The Creek)*

Opposite page, below: Marion Hollins with the Long Island Ladies Medal Play trophy. *(Golf Illustrated)*

Right: Alexa Stirling. *(Golf Illustrated)*

Below: Marion Hollins was a great all-around athlete. *(American Golfer)*

the U.S. Women's Amateur in 1921, she channeled her energies toward making it a reality.

Devereux Emmet was asked to design a course that wouldn't defeat the better women players with excessive length, yet continually challenge them with the clever placement of its hazards. At most tees the player faced a challenging carry, although an alternate route was always provided, typically at the loss of one stroke, for those unwilling or unable to challenge the hazard. The placement of these hazards was keyed to the average carry of one of Alexa Stirling's drives, which was estimated to be 175 yards. Stirling, winner of three consecutive U.S. Women's Amateurs (1916, 1919, and 1920, a streak interrupted by World War I) was a member at nearby North Hempstead Country Club during the few years she worked in Manhattan.

Ernest Jones, recognized as one of the great golf teachers in the world, held sway as professional at the Women's National. Despite the handicap of having lost a leg while in the British army during World War I, he developed an excellent reputation as a teacher of ladies.

Because of their overlapping memberships, The Creek and Women's National merged in 1941 to economize the operations of both facilities. That spelled the end for Women's National. Ultimately the newly-formed Glen Head Country Club purchased the property in 1947.

Also catering to the polo set was the Sands Point Golf Club. All-time polo greats such as Tommy Hitchcock, J. Cheever Cowdin, Devereux Milburn, Winston Guest, Pete Bostwick, Ogden Phipps, and future New York governor Averill Harriman all played at Sands Point.

Sands Point has always been rich—in soil and natural resources—long before establishing its reputation as a focal point of Long Island's "Gold Coast" society. Indeed, it is rumored that part of Captain Kidd's famed treasure is buried on the

Sands Point peninsula. Sands Point's sand and gravel was used to build the streets and skyscrapers of Manhattan. Sands Point owes its growth to the extension of the Long Island Railroad in 1898. With a direct ride to Manhattan as a drawing card, prominent New Yorkers began visiting Sands Point for summer vacations. During the 1910s, Sands Point competed with Newport as America's summer social capital. Eventually, the summer guests remained year-round, building "Gold Coast" mansions.

Perhaps the most unusual hole on Sands Point's A.W. Tillinghast golf course was the 10th, a 100-yard par 3 (which no longer exists) that played to a small green (surrounded by three "ice cream cone" bunkers. There was a runway up the middle, which some members utilized to reach the green with a putter!

Many of the Tillinghast features of that course were covered over during a Robert Trent Jones renovation of the course. These were restored during the 1990s; many Tillinghast bunkers were "located" via old aerial maps, then excavated.

LEFT: WOMEN'S NATIONAL'S PICTURESQUE PAR-3 16TH HOLE. *(Golf Illustrated)*

ABOVE: A SMALL GALLERY AT A CLUB TOURNAMENT AT WOMEN'S. *(Golf Illustrated)*

RIGHT: ERNEST JONES, A CASUALTY DURING WORLD WAR I, BUT A GREAT TEACHING PROFESSIONAL THEREAFTER. *(Golf Illustrated)*

BELOW: THE CLUBHOUSE AT WOMEN'S NATIONAL. *(Golf Illustrated)*

16

A South Shore Jewel

Long Island's storied wealth was not concentrated solely on the Gold Coast. There was an isolated colony of millionaires on the South Shore in Suffolk County. Their Timber Point Club was considered among the most exclusive on Long Island, their golf course for many years ranking as one of the Island's most challenging.

The seed that eventually flowered as the Timber Point Club was planted in the early 1900s when a group of millionaires, led by Horace Havemeyer, the "Sultan of Sugar," built their mansions on a series of promontories below East Islip, and lived there in private splendor equal to that of the North Shore. When one of their number died in 1922, a group including Havemeyer, his brother-in-law Kingsland Macy, and Wall Street trader Buell Hollister bought the 231-acre estate and converted it into a private club with membership restricted to a select 100, all members of the Suffolk County Republican Club.

After organizing Timber Point in July of 1923, the club's founders hired the internationally-famous architectural firm of Colt & Alison to design and build an 18-hole golf course. It was nearly two years before the project was completed. Reportedly, it took a full year for the dredges to haul up enough sand to fill in the marshland, and reclaim 100 acres from the Great South Bay, allowing Alison to build 18 holes where only nine seemed possible. What resulted was a magnificent par-71 test of 6,825 yards among the sand dunes that quickly took its place among the country's finest courses, although it received only a smattering of play on any given day. Only one U.S. Open course to that date had played longer.

Perhaps the quality of Timber Point—its facilities and golf course—was defined in 1932 when the club hosted the annual Lesley Cup matches, an interdistrict competition among the Metropolitan, Massachusetts, Golf Association of Philadelphia, and Quebec Golf Associations that, at the time, attracted the leading amateurs in the Northeast. The Lesley Cup simply didn't go just anywhere—Timber Point joined Garden City Golf, Shinnecock Hills, and National as the fourth Long Island club to host the matches (Maidstone and Atlantic later were added to the list).

Privacy was an obsession with the Timber Point members, as two events of 1923 clearly demonstrate. When the Suffolk County Mosquito Commission asked for contributions to aid their work in controlling what had become a severe problem, the Timber Point members refused, preferring to contend with the insects rather than the masses who would find the area far more attractive should the mosquitoes vanish. They didn't, and Timber Point members played at times with mosquitoes all over their faces.

When a 1,500-acre estate adjacent to their golf course came on the market, they quickly raised $250,000 to purchase it, then converted it into a private hunting preserve which they seldom used. When New York's Parks Commissioner Robert Moses wished to purchase the property and convert it into a public park, Havemeyer, Macy, and Hollister acted swiftly and purchased the property themselves, hoping to subdivide it into 30 building lots and sell them to "the right kind of people," who would be invited to join the Timber Point Club. Not to be denied, Moses seized the land, and the rest—Heckscher State Park—is history.

The first nine at Timber Point played through forests of pines, with several holes possessing features mindful of Pine Valley. With the 10th hole, however, the course "emerged to the glistening sands and the water, with its inevitable tang of the sea," to quote from a February 1925 article in *Golf Illustrated*.

The feature holes on the course were on the back nine. The 11th, which was a 460-yard par 4 known as the "three-island" hole, was similar in concept to the 18th at Lido, offering the player a choice of three fairways from the tee, with the ideal line demanding a carry of 200 yards over sand and rough. The less daring could negotiate a shorter carry to the left or right, but would thereby surrender any chance of reaching the green in two strokes. The 12th ("Harbor") was a 140-yard par 3 with a magnificent view of the bay. Played over water from an elevated tee to an elevated green, it demanded deadly accuracy. The waters of the club's yacht basin extended

Left, top: A view from behind the 11th green at Timber Point. The par-5 eighth is in the background. *(Golf Illustrated)*

Left: The "Harbor" hole, only 140 yards, presented quite a challenge for even the best of players. A carry over part of the yacht basin to an elevated green surrounded by sand were just some of the penal aspects of this hole. *(Golf Illustrated)*

Opposite page: The 200-yard, par-3 15th. This was and still is one of the great par 3 tests on Long Island. Players tee off into the teeth of the wind, with water behind, and menacing sand everywhere else. If you can just hit the green. *(Golf Illustrated)*

from tee to green on the left, while a vast wasteland of sand engulfed the green. (137

The most memorable and unusual hole on the course may well have been the 15th, which was known as "Gibraltar." It was a long, uphill par 3 of 200 yards, with the green perched atop a bluff overlooking the Great South Bay. Vast expanses of sand on either side caught the offline shots of players straining to reach the green into the teeth of the prevailing southwesterly wind. Behind the green—memories of the 17th at Pebble Beach!

Both the 16th and 17th holes played along the bay, whose waters paralleled the left side of the two fairways. When the wind blew, the drive had to be played out over the water if the player hoped to avoid the rough on the right!

The original owners eventually sold out in the 1940s, and it was not until 1971 that Suffolk County purchased the property and began operating it as a public facility. In 1972 architect William Mitchell was engaged to build a third nine. To make room, it was necessary to destroy six holes from the original layout. The original third through eighth holes now play as the second through seventh on the Red nine, while the old 12th through 17th remain as the second through seventh on the Blue course. Unfortunately, the "three-island" hole no longer exists, although its green is used for the first hole on the Blue nine.

17

Bobby Jones's First Major

As he prepared to hit his approach shot to the 18th green at the Inwood Country Club during the 1923 U.S. Open Championship, Bobby Jones must have seen his career flash before his eyes. Just 21 years of age, he had been playing in major championships for seven years (this was his fourth U.S. Open) , albeit without a title to show for his considerable efforts. By his own reckoning, he had "failed" already on 11 occasions—success to Jones meant nothing short of first place!

And if a feeling of "deja vu" came over him, there was good reason. Jones had been in exactly the same position the day before, and muffed the chance. The date was July 15, 1923. It was a gray, overcast Sunday afternoon.

Jones's practice rounds at Inwood had been uninspiring. He was constantly in trouble, and found it difficult to break 80. Once the tournament started, though, Jones's swing returned. After the first two rounds on Friday, his 71-73=144 trailed Jock Hutchison (70-72) by two shots. Bobby Cruickshank (73-72), one shot behind Jones, was the only other player in close contention. Francis Gallett of Port Washington was next at 148.

With a 76, Jones widened his lead on Cruickshank (78) to three shots after three rounds, while Hutchison fell four strokes behind after an 82 on Saturday morning.

Jones continued to play well in Saturday's second round, and had the tournament well within his grasp when he set up to play his approach to the 16th green. We let the *New York Times* bring him home that afternoon:

BOBBY JONES, WINNER OF THE 1923 U.S. OPEN AT INWOOD. *(Golf Illustrated)*

"That left him with only pars for a 33 for the incoming nine, which would have put him so far in advance of the others that nothing could have prevented his winning. But at the sixteenth he put his second shot out of bounds into the automobile parking area, and only saved himself by means of a superb iron which dropped stone dead ten feet from the pin. By holing the putt he had done the hole in three strokes although credited with a 5.

"A 5 at the seventeenth followed, but his downfall came at the home hole. Once again he hooked his iron, this time with costly results. His ball landed among the spectators, and stopped near a post. Ordinarily he would have made the green easily, but as he was making the shot his head came up and he pitched squarely into a trap. His recovery was far past the cup and he finished with a 6. That proved to be the most disastrous 6 he ever took in his life."

Jones walked off the course a dejected young man, filled with self-doubt, and no longer the tournament leader.

Bobby Cruickshank, a Scot from Edinburgh whose gallantry during World War I left no doubt about his courage, was at the sixth tee when Jones finished, both players standing at +8. He knew exactly what he needed to win—1-under-par golf over Inwood's final 13 holes. Cruickshank responded to the challenge by playing holes 6 through 12 in 22 strokes (2-3-3-4-3-4-3), 3 under par. He needed only to par in from 13 to win by three shots. But he too met his match down the stretch at Inwood. Bogeys at 13 and 15 whittled his lead down to one stroke, Again, we let the *New York Times* bring him home:

"Playing the sixteenth, it appeared as if Cruickshank had lost his chances. After slicing his iron second to the rough at the right of the green, he played a poor chip and then took three putts. He now needed one under par for the next two holes to tie, and Jones was again able to breathe a sigh of relief."

After a par 4 on the 17th , Cruickshank reached the home hole:

"Headed for home, Cruickshank, grim and dour, laced into a tee shot that whistled its way down the fairway—straight down the middle, but not very far down. He had not quite got hold of it, and the wind which had freshened while he was playing the final nine holes, was directly in his face. A 3 looked impossible from where he was, but taking a number 1 iron, he sent the ball on the most direct path

toward its destination that any ball ever took. On it came, over the water guarding the green, stopping less than two yards from the hole. Cruickshank, habitually a fast player, took plenty of time studying his line. There was a tense hush as he took his stance, drew back his putter, and firmly tapped the mallet. It traveled straight for the rim of the cup and dropped in for the 3 he needed so badly. Cruickshank was on it like a flash, and had it clutched mightily in his hand almost as soon as it hit the bottom of the cup."

Cruickshank and Jones had tied after 72 holes with identical scores of 296. Nearly 10,000 fans attended the play-off the next day, for which Cruickshank was established the 10-7 favorite, a reflection as much on his strong finish the day before as on Jones's futility in the clutch to that point in his career. Indeed, Jones welcomed the play-off, not wanting to back into a major title after the kind of finish he had mustered the previous day. The play-off was a back-and-forth affair from the start, with the two players standing even as they went to the 18th tee after halving just three of the first 17 holes. Cruickshank had managed to stay close with some remarkable scrambling.

It was the melodramatic happenings on the 18th hole that day that earned Inwood its indelible place in golf history. The hole played at 425 yards over a yawning water hazard, a lagoon that crossed the fairway just in front of the green. Cruickshank drove first, and we pick up the *New York Times* report:

"Something happened to Cruickshank, for he almost missed his drive to the eighteenth hole completely, topping the ball and sending it into a patch of rough at the left of the fairway. Jones, thinking thoughts of his debacle of the day before, pushed his own drive well to the right, among the spectators that lined the course, ready for the mad rush to witness the finish, but Jones' drive, although in the rough, was perched up and within striking distance of the green, while Cruickshank had no possible chance of getting home, since his drive measured not more than 150 yards, and the distance between the tee and the green is nearly three times that. There as nothing left for him now but to play the ball out through the trees and down the fairway in order to get a chance to play his third for the pin. Not knowing what Jones was about to bring off, Cruickshank put everything he had into the stroke and got a good shot under the circumstances."

As Jones prepared to play to the green, he was in the driver's seat—as he had

OPPOSITE PAGE: THE CURRENT DAY 14TH HOLE AT INWOOD, SITE OF BOBBY JONES'S FIRST MAJOR CHAMPIONSHIP. *(L.C. Lambrecht)*

BOBBY CRUICKSHANK, RUNNERUP. *(Golf Illustrated)*

been the day before. But his shot would not be an easy one. He faced a 190-yard shot into the wind and over the hazard. If he chose to play it safe and lay up short of the lagoon, he would be on even terms with Cruickshank, and matching his own weakness against his rival's strength. On the other hand, if he gambled and lost, a mishit shot likely would bury his hopes in a watery grave. Jones did not hesitate, and the *New York Times* continues with the outcome:

> *"It was then that Jones played the shot that sent his fame around the world wherever golf is played. Without a moment's hesitation, Jones drew a No. 1 iron out of his bag, took a momentary look at the lie, glanced at the flag and swung. It was a superb shot made by a superb golfer in a superb manner. The ball flew off the face of his club, rose in the air and carried squarely on the green, 190 yards away. A tremendous shout went up when the ball struck on the green, bit its way into the turf, and brought up its journey about two club lengths away from the hole for a possible birdie three.*
>
> *Cruickshank, fighter that he proved himself throughout the entire tourney, doubtless felt his heart rattling around in the bottom of his boots when he saw his opponent's ball perched up close to the hole, but he didn't show it. He walked one hundred yards down the fairway, measured the distance and then made his last dying effort. Had he been able to get the ball dead to the hole, he could still save his championship for another day. It was a 100 to 1 shot, but he played it for all it was worth. He pulled it off to the left and saw it drop into a trap just at the left of the green."*

Cruickshank finished with a double-bogey 6. Jones won the title with a two-putt par, recording a 76 to his rival's 78. And, according to the *New York Times*:

> *"Then one of the greatest scenes of all was enacted. The crowd, perhaps biased in Jones's favor, since he has always been a favorite, rushed out on the green. Two of Bobby's fellow townsmen, who had made the journey all the way from Atlanta to see him win his first title, hoisted him on their shoulders and he was borne triumphantly toward the clubhouse. A kiltie, blowing away on the bagpipes, furnished the music. His youthful face wreathed in smiles, Jones was kept busy several minutes accepting the congratulations and plaudits of the golf-mad spectators who had witnessed one of the greatest of all playoffs."*

The significance of that stroke, as it affected one of golf's great careers, cannot

BOBBY JONES PUTTING ON THE THIRD GREEN. (*American Golfer*)

be underestimated. Had his shot fallen short into the lagoon, Jones's career may have "ended" before it really began. That one shot opened the floodgates that eventually resulted in 13 major championships. The shot also propelled golf, for the first time, onto the first page of the *New York Times*, which ran the headline

"Jones, An Amateur, Beats Cruickshank, Pro, For Golf Title"

That Inwood would someday play such a significant role in the history of golf certainly was not evident from its rather pedestrian beginnings. The club started life in 1901 as an engagement gift from Jacob Wertheim to Emma Stern. The fact that the original course resembled a potato farm did not bother the membership.

JONES AND CRUICKSHANK ON THE FINAL GREEN. *(American Golfer)*

OPPOSITE PAGE: THE FRONT-PAGE HEADLINE IN THE *New York Times* THE DAY AFTER THE PLAY-OFF. *(New York Times)*

"All the News That's
Fit to Print."

The New York Times

VOL. LXXII....No. 23,914.   •••   NEW YORK, MONDAY, JULY 16, 1923.

FRANCE WILL REFUSE ANY CONCESSIONS, ASSERTS POINCARE

Speech at Senlis Is Interpreted by Paris and London as Blow to Baldwin Plan.

WANTS NO EXPERT BOARD

And Blames England's Aloofness for German Resistance and Chaos.

DENIES GERMANY IS RUINED

And Insists That the Guarantees Promised to France Shall Be Carried Out.

By EDWIN L. JAMES.

Copyright, 1923, by The New York Times Company
Special Cable to The New York Times.

PARIS, July 15.—Premier Poincaré in his speech at Senlis today answered Prime Minister Baldwin's reparations declaration Thursday by affirming France's intention to carry out her policy toward Germany.

In that he did not refer to Mr. Baldwin by name nor mention the project of a reply to Germany, M. Poincaré evidently sought not to be discourteous to the British proposal, which is expected to arrive in Paris on Thursday. But in declaring that the Entente should leave each nation's conscience free, and in declaring against an international commission "to coalesce against us those whose interests are opposed to ours," M. Poincaré seems to indicate that if the British draft note to Germany does not begin by stating that passive resistance in the Ruhr must end before the negotiations, and if it proposes an international commission, Paris will not accept it.

One Steamer Sinks Another; Is Then Itself Hit and Sunk

LONDON, July 15 (Associated Press).—Three steamers were in collision in the fog in the North Sea today. Two of them were sunk, but their crews were rescued, and the third proceeded on her voyage in a damaged condition.

Owing to the heavy fog the Swedish steamer Eldorado hove to, and the Spanish steamer Begona No. 5, crashed into her. While the two vessels were locked amidship, and as the latter began to fill her boats were lowered and her own crew and that of the Eldorado, totaling forty-three men, reached the Sheridan. The captain of the Britisher sent a radio message to Yarmouth from which port tugs were dispatched and took off the survivors.

Later the British steamer Sheridan coming through the fog hit the Begona amidship, and as the latter began to fill her boats were lowered and her own crew and that of the Eldorado went to the bottom.

MINNESOTA DECIDES SENATORSHIP TODAY

Will Choose Low-Tariff Republican or Radical Farmer-Laborite to Succeed Nelson.

JOHNSON MEN CONFIDENT

Small Total Vote Is Expected After One of the Oddest Campaigns in State's History.

Special to The New York Times.

MINNEAPOLIS, Minn., July 15.—With the eyes of the whole nation focused on her, Minnesota will decide tomorrow, whether a conservative low tariff Republican or a radical Farmer-Laborite shall be sent to Washington as the successor of the late Senator.

JONES, AN AMATEUR, BEATS CRUICKSHANK, PRO, FOR GOLF TITLE

21-Year-Old Georgian Downs Scottish Star at 18th Hole, 76 to 78.

EACH HAS 72 AT THE 17TH

Brilliant Shot Going to Last Green Settles Issue in National Open Play-Off.

10,000 AT INWOOD COURSE

Victor Captures Championship After Three Previous Attempts—Fourth Amateur to Win Honor.

STROKE STANDING AT EACH HOLE.

	1	2	3	4	5	6	7	8	9
Jones	4	8	13	17	22	26	29	33	37
Cruickshank	5	8	12	17	21	24	28	32	37

	10	11	12	13	14	15	16	17	18
Jones	42	47	49	53	56	63	67	72	76
Cruickshank	43	48	51	55	59	63	68	72	78

Special to The New York Times.

INWOOD, L. I., July 15.—Robert Tyre Jones Jr. of Atlanta, Ga., 21 years old on March 17 last, is tonight America's national open golf champion for 1923.

In the playoff for the title, necessitated by the fact that Jones was tied yesterday by Robert A. Cruickshank, former Scottish amateur star who came to America and turned pro three years ago, with a score of 296 at the conclusion of the regulation 72-hole test at the Inwood Country Club, Jones was the winner today by two strokes, and it was not until the last hole was played that the question of who was to wear this

---

Girl Baby Abandoned in Hotel Wins Friends; Employes Name Her Mary Marlborough

A girl baby, a few weeks old, that was abandoned in a room of the Hotel Marlborough, Broadway and Thirty-sixth Street, may never again see or hear of her parents, but she has acquired a host of friends on Broadway and among the employes of the hotel where she received more attention than the best paying guest. The only clue to the child's identity is a line in the hotel register, which reads: "Mr. and Mrs. H. Williams, Baltimore." The police are searching the hospitals to learn if the child had received medical treatment, as the supposed mother had reported to the hotel clerk, Harry Levenson.

"The man and woman with the baby came here on Friday afternoon, in a private car, which the man drove away after he had registered," said Levenson. "Williams paid for the room in advance, displaying a large roll of money. I made some remark about the baby, and the woman replied that the child looked well, but they had brought her to New York for examination at a hospital."

The clerk recalled that the guests had a marked Southern accent. They were well dressed and their faces were tanned as if they had been traveling in an auto. Their baggage consisted of one bag, which they left behind. It contained clothing for the baby, on which there was no identifying marks.

Mr. and Mrs. Williams were seen about the hotel up to noon on Saturday. In the afternoon Mary Corrigan, a maid, heard an infant's cries in room 349 on the third floor. There was no response to her tap on the door. She entered and found the baby on the bed.

The maid held the baby for an hour, expecting its parents to return. Then other girls in the hotel took turns in caring for the castaway. On Saturday night Miss Mary Hicks, chief telephone operator, and her assistants took charge of the baby. Under the direction of Dr. C. Brandenberg, house physician, they prepared food for the baby, bathed and dressed her and otherwise were kept busy telling about the infant's plight to the guests.

Late yesterday Manager Franklin notified the police of the West Thirtieth Street Station. They ordered the baby sent to Bellevue and Miss Hicks and several maids and operators took her there. They named their charge "Mary Marlborough."

GOMPERS DEMANDS TRUTH ON SOVIET

Asks Senators King and Ladd Pertinent Questions on Conditions in Russia.

AS THEY GO ON INQUIRY

Sees Red Interference Here and Demands Guarantees Against This.

Special to The New York Times.

WASHINGTON, July 15.—In a letter written to Senators King and Ladd, who recently started for Russia on a tour

---

RODE WITH CONVICTS IN DASH TO LIBERTY

Motorist Kidnapped With Car in Philadelphia Escape Tells of Mad Drive Into Night.

SPEED DEMON AT WHEEL

Old Auto Thief Steers Across Three States—All Trace of Six Fugitives Now Lost.

PHILADELPHIA, July 15.—While the police continued their search throughout this and neighboring States for the six convicts who made a daring escape yes-

---

HARDING IN GAY MOOD AS HE SPEEDS NORTH UNDER MIDNIGHT SUN

He Runs the Locomotive for 26 Miles and Helps Paint a Building.

DRIVES A SPIKE OF GOLD

This Symbolizes the Connection of the Pacific and Arctic Oceans by Rail.

PEOPLE ARE MOST CORDIAL

They Wish to Show Their Appreciation of His Long Trip to Study Their Problems.

Harding Goes Farther North Than Any Other President

FAIRBANKS, Alaska, July 15 (Associated Press).—President Harding has reached a point further north than any other American President and with his arrival in Fairbanks tonight he was within 150 miles of the Arctic Circle.

His arrival here marked the end of a two and one-half days ride over the Government railroad from Seward. Tomorrow he begins the trip south over the Richardson trail.

Special Cable to The New York Times.

McKINLEY PARK, Alaska, July 15.—After spending the night at Broad Pass, near the top of the Alaskan range, where his special train was sidetracked on its arrival just before midnight, President

(145

Most of them knew little or nothing about golf.

The next spring the club contacted the Spalding Company for assistance in finding a new pro; the previous year's pro left to pursue a more lucrative career as a hack driver. The man Spalding had ticketed for the Inwood job turned up hopelessly drunk the morning of the interview. Spalding quickly substituted a sore-armed former baseball player by the name of Edward Eriksen, who knew absolutely nothing about golf. With little choice, Inwood hired Eriksen, and things worked out far better than anyone had a right to imagine.

Eriksen remained at Inwood for nine years, and developed into a highly-respected golf instructor. He also designed a more respectable nine-hole course than the one already in play— seven of its holes remain with modifications as part of today's course, including the original ninth, today's 18th.

In 1921, the PGA Championship was contested at Inwood, with Walter Hagen winning the 36-hole final over "Long Jim" Barnes, the first of five PGA titles Hagen would capture during his illustrious career. Hagen also became the first American-born professional to win that title. His march to the championship at Inwood was virtually unchallenged, although his pre-tournament status was uncertain, Some felt Hagen was "beginning to slip" following a poor year in 1920. Rumors circulated that he was considering retirement.

The tournament "favorites" were Barnes, the 1921 U.S. Open champion who had won the first two PGA Championships in 1916 and 1919, and Jock Hutchison, the defending champion who won the British Open earlier in the season. Barnes got through to the finals, while Hutchison was detoured in an early-round match.

Both players performed superbly in the finals. *Golf Illustrated* chronicled the match:

"This year's final, however, produced one of the most brilliant duels ever seen on a golf course. Barnes, playing as fine a brand of golf as anyone could wish to see, was unable to hold the sensational Hagen. Barnes had a 71 for his morning round, a figure that represented golf just a trifle better than perfect, but he found himself unable to match the game that Hagen unreeled on the front. The home-bred turned in a 69 and carried a margin of one-up into the afternoon round.

"In the afternoon Hagen played the first nine in 33, four shots under par, and driving for the fourteenth was no less than four under fours. Barnes made the mistake of letting his opponent get a flying start by taking the first two holes in fours, and this put him battling with his back against the wall. From that stage on, Hagen

146)

Calamity Jane

When Bobby Jones arrived on Long Island for the 1923 U.S. Open, he visited the Nassau Country Club. Nassau's professional was Jim Maiden, who along with brother Stewart, were Jones's mentors when he was a youngster at East Lake Golf Club in Georgia.

Jones was off his game prior to the tournament, with his putting stroke especially troubled. After Jones and Maiden finished a practice round, Jones waited on the final green while Maiden retrieved a putter from his shop. On his first stroke with "Calamity Jane," Jones dropped a 40-footer. After finding that he could hole six-footers with ease, Jones asked to borrow the putter. He never gave it back. Jones won the Open the following week with the original club, then made a copy the following year, and used "Calamity Jane II" successfully right through his Grand Slam in 1930.

Maiden himself shafted the original "Calamity Jane." It was misplaced while Maiden was playing a round upstate, and damaged when shipped back to Long Island. Maiden turned it over to his assistant, Joe Merkle, for repairs. Merkle saved the club, and eventually Maiden gave it to Jones.

WALTER HAGEN PUTTING AT INWOOD, 1921.
(*Golf Illustrated*)

ABOVE RIGHT: HAGEN DRIVING FROM THE
NINTH TEE IN THE 1921 FINALS. (*American
Golfer*)

never gave Barnes a winning chance. His drives were long and generally straight, and while his approaches were usually inside those of Barnes, Walter putted with unerring aim, while Jim, when he had a chance, did no more than hang them on the rim. As far as the fourteenth hole Hagen never made the semblance of a mistake, although with the playing of this hole Jim scored his first success. It was a little too late by then. A bunkered tee shot cost Hagen this hole, but this slight respite did not materially enhance Barnes's chances as he was three down with four to play, and two halves on the next two holes settled the issue."

The 1921 PGA is also remembered as the tournament in which Gene Sarazen first hit the headlines, pulling off what at the time was considered an astonishing 8&7 upset of Jock Hutchison. According to *Golf Illustrated*:

"Then Gene Sarazen, of Titusville, provided the great shock of the tournament when he defeated Jock Hutchison, the champion, in the second round by eight up and seven. Sarazen, a former Westchester County caddie, turned in a card of 69 against

Harry Hampton in the first round and duplicated this against Hutchison in their morning tilt, and then went out in thirty-six in the afternoon to make the affair sure. Hutchison was away off and Sarazen was well on.

"Sarazen, who is but twenty years of age, showed his lack of experience by letting the long waits between his opponent's shots get the better of his temper. Sarazen had been playing great golf up to his match with Walker and will go far, for it is his ambition to be a champion, and he should, someday, attain it. He needs seasoning. His match with Walker did him much good, for it taught him that in championship competition there is often more elements to combat than figures which appear on a scorecard."

There were several unusual incidents during the championship. Heavy rains interrupted the semifinals. Barnes and his rival agreed to resume play the following morning, but Hagen's opponent refused, and that match continued on to its conclusion. Hagen got wet, but presumably got his rest that night, while Barnes had to play 12 holes to conclude his match in the early morning before embarking on the 36-hole finals.

Perhaps the most unusual event of the week was the following, as reported in *Golf Illustrated*:

"...was the strange way in which a tree grew overnight between the eleventh and eighteenth fairways. Some of the players had been driving from the eleventh tee to the eighteenth fairway, thinking this method gave them as good a second shot and with less opportunity to fail to find a good lie as the eleventh fairway is narrow and calls for a very straight shot.

"When members of the club noted that Hagen, Barnes, and others were taking liberty with their course in such a manner, they engaged workmen and overnight a large tree was taken out by the roots and planted in such a position that in order to land on the eighteenth fairway from the eleventh tee it would be necessary to slice or hook around it."

Inwood also was the scene of a memorable edition of the Met Open in 1968. Jerry Pittman won, his 274 total eight strokes ahead of runner-up Jimmy Wright. Pittman set a new course record with a 65 in the third round. During an 11-hole span in the final round, he and fellow competitor Wright carded an amazing 14 birdies!

Located across an inlet of Jamaica Bay from Kennedy Airport, the course is

GENE SARAZEN, AN UNKNOWN AT THE 1921 PGA. *(Golf Illustrated)*

148)

exposed to the winds and is often played under difficult weather conditions. The foundation for a good score must be laid over the first five holes, all of which offer birdie opportunities to the better players. The course was redesigned for the two championships. The hole marked #14 became the first; the pair marked #6 and #7 were eliminated; additional holes were built at the upper right while the 10th became the 11th. The 17th and 18th remained the same, as shown here. The 16th, 1st and 2nd holes, as diagramed here, became the 3rd, 4th and 5th holes, all par 5s.

DIAGRAM OF THE INWOOD COURSE IN 1915.
(New York Telegram)

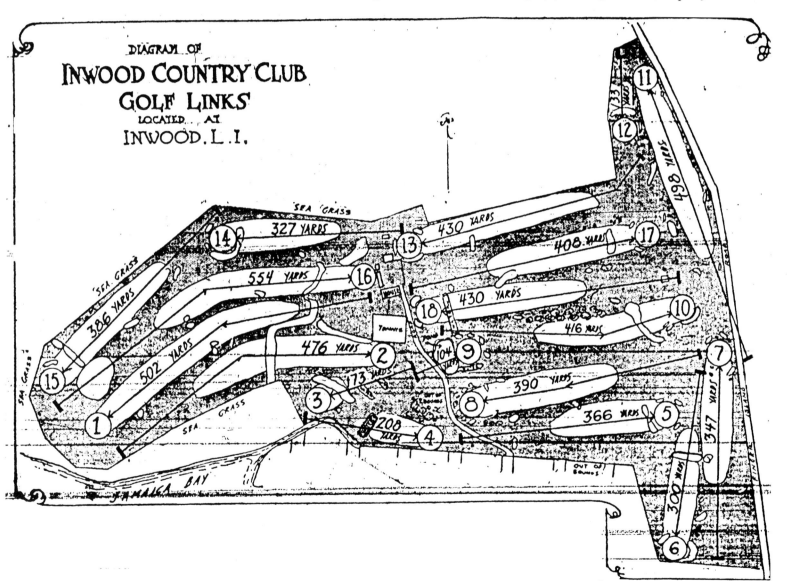

18

All My Children: The Salisbury Links

In 1899, the privatization of the Island Golf Links, creating the Garden City Golf Club, left a void for many Garden City residents and guests of the Garden City Hotel. The vacancy was filled by the creation of the Midland Golf Club that same year. The Midland golfers had a major impact on the mid-Nassau County golfscape, playing a key role in the formation of four major clubs, including two that would become sites for national championships.

At the start, Midland's members maintained their own nine-hole golf course and clubhouse, which lasted for less than a decade. The land, situated in the heart of the village, was given to the club rent-free by the Garden City Company, but taken back in 1907 when it was needed for real estate development. The Midland golfers remained together as a club, however, playing at a new public facility a few blocks to the west, also created under the banner of the Garden City Company.

The new course was called the Salisbury Links after a road that crossed the property, and was available to "all approved players, male and female." To quote course architect Walter Travis, the course offered a "good game for all classes of players, from the very top-notcher to the veriest duffer." The course was advertised as "playable the year round."

Salisbury Links proved very popular, with strong social overtones. Too popular, in fact. The course became crowded, and the Midland members contemplated leaving and forming their own club. Although the idea was vetoed, a splinter group

OPPOSITE PAGE: A 1908 AD FOR THE SALISBURY LINKS. (*American Golfer*)

The SALISBURY LINKS at GARDEN CITY

is a public subscription course, OPEN TO ALL GOLFERS.

Unlike most courses, it is adapted for BOTH the BEGINNER and the EXPERT, *and it is playable all the year round.*

It is owned and maintained by the Garden City Company.

Its 18 holes—FULL OF VARIETY—are 5900 yds. in length.

It is ONLY 18 MILES FROM NEW YORK and within ten minutes walk of the Railway Station and Hotel.

Its commodious club house adjoins the first tee and provides ample locker rooms, baths, lounging room, bar and luncheon-room—with separate accommodations for ladies—all the facilities, in short, of a first class club.

The professional, R. Wakerly, is a first-class instructor and has a well-equipped shop for the repair and sale of clubs, balls, etc.

Annual Subscription for men, $35.00 ; for ladies, $25.00

Other charges to players are as follows:

One day	.$ 1.00
One week	5.00
One month	10.00
Six months	15.00
Annual charge for locker	5.00

FOR FURTHER INFORMATION APPLY TO THE

GARDEN CITY COMPANY, Garden City, N. Y.

proceeded to found the Wheatley Hills Golf Club in East Willaston, which opened its doors in 1913.

Devereux Emmet revised his original golf course after the 1931 season. The occasion for the change was the building of the Northern State Parkway—as far as nearby Jericho Turnpike at that time. The new roadway cut across the eastern end of club property, destroying a few holes in that area.

Through its early years, the club's property was bisected by the Long Island Motor Parkway, which divided the golf course into two nearly equal pieces, connected by a tunnel joining the ninth green and 10th tee. The club had its own private entrance from the Parkway,

The Salisbury Links continued on, still congested. In 1916, it was decided to reorganize as a private club, named Cherry Valley after the road, lined with wild cherry trees, that ran diagonally through the property, just west of the clubhouse.

Cherry Valley would, a decade later, host a national championship, the 1927 U.S. Women's Amateur. Miriam Burns Horn from Kansas City defeated local heroine Maureen Orcutt of White Beeches (NJ) 5&4 in the finals. Among the also-rans were Mrs. H. Arnold Jackson (the 1908 and 1914 champion now from the Nassau Country Club), Glenna Collett (six-time winner, 1922, 1925, 1928, 1929, 1930, and 1935), Virginia Van Wie (who would win three consecutive, 1932-1934), Alexa Stirling Fraser of the North Hempstead Country Club, a three-time champion (1916, 1919, 1920), Dorothy Campbell Hurd (winner in 1909, 1910, and 1924), Rosalie Knapp of

(151

Women's National, and Mrs. J.L. Anderson of Cherry Valley.

Mrs. Horn had the more difficult route to the finals, beating Mlle. De La Chaume, the British and French titleholder, in the quarterfinals and Alexa Stirling Fraser in the semifinals, while Miss Orcutt ousted the Canadian champion, Ada Mackenzie, in her semifinals match. The *New York Times* reported on the final hole of the Horn-Fraser match as follows:

"That left Mrs. Horn dormie, and hung the issue on the home hole. Mrs. Fraser drove and her ball stopped just off the green, but so close to the rough that she had an awkward approach to play and left herself fifteen feet from the pin.

"Mrs. Horn, meanwhile, had driven almost on the green and chipped four feet past. There was a tense moment or two then. With great deliberation, a characteristic of her play throughout the match, Mrs. Fraser considered the putt carefully and then holed it, putting the strain on her opponent, who had to hole a very missable putt to keep the match from going extra holes.

"It was a tight pinch to be in, but Mrs. Horn, a grim fighter with nerves of steel, never flinched and tapped the ball in the cup for the much needed half, which gave her the match and sent her into the final round."

(153

Opposite page: The Northern State Parkway extension sliced off a piece of the Wheatley Hills course (bottom). The road immediately above the Northern State is the old Motor Parkway. Hillside Avenue is on the left. *(Wheatley Hills)*

Above: Glenna Collett and Mlle. de la Chaume. *(American Golfer)*

Right: Marion Horn, winner of 1927 U.S. Women's Amateur at Cherry Valley. *(American Golfer)*

Neither Horn nor Orcutt had ever advanced beyond the third round in the championship, and their nerves were evident during the finals, especially so the younger Orcutt. Horn was 2-up after the first 18 holes despite shooting an 88 to Orcutt's 91—both players had carded 78s in the medal round, which had been in the rain. As evidence of this comedy of errors, we present the *New York Times's* account of the play of the first and 10th holes of the morning round:

"Miss Orcutt had two chances to win the first hole, but scorned both of them. The first came when Mrs. Horn, after driving to the left of the fairway, pitched into the big bunker between her and the green. Miss Orcutt, after a fine drive, had an open road to the green, but attempted to pitch and run and went into the same bunker.

"Mrs. Horn again left the door open by failing to get out on her first endeavor, but Miss Orcutt did likewise. She was then weak with her chip from the long grass, but so was Mrs. Horn, and the hole was halved in 6s."

"The tenth was a travesty. With two gorgeous wooden shots, Miss Orcutt was only seventy-five yards from the green, while her opponent, after driving into the gravel on the left, dubbing her second short of the road and still in the rough on her third, played five and was not on the green. Miss Orcutt apparently had the hole sewed up, but before she got through she managed to amass a large 7 and she had to hole a missable putt for that.

"She began by going into the rough on her third. Her next was just out, twenty feet short, and she took three to get down from there and gave Mrs. Horn a very generous half."

The first round was a case of mistakes and missed opportunities for both players. After lunch Miss Orcutt quickly closed the gap to one hole, but the turning point came at the seventh hole when she hit a bad drive and fell 2-down again. Mrs. Horn took control of the match at this point, and went on to become the first woman from west of the Mississippi to win the national championship.

The Cherry Valley course, as played for the Women's Amateur, evidenced a dramatic change from the original Salisbury Links, and at the same time was somewhat different from the present course. At various times, the course extended across Cambridge Avenue and First Street, and into what in 1929 would become the Adelphi University campus. Devereux Emmet was as much responsible for the 1927 course as was the original architect, Travis.

Perhaps the most prominent of Cherry Valley's golfers was Edmund H. Driggs Jr. (a former football star at Princeton and football coach at Adelphi), winner of the 1927 and 1944 Met Amateurs as well as the inaugural (1923) and 1933-1934 New York State Amateurs. Also a member there, was one of Long Island's most accomplished women golfers, Ruth Torgerson. She was the W.M.G.A. champion in 1941, 1949, and 1950, and also won three Long Island and four New York State championships. She reached the quarterfinals of the 1941 U.S. Women's Amateur, her best showing in the championship.

When Cherry Valley became private, a new publinx, opened in 1917, was built at the foot of Stewart Avenue, just to the east of Garden City. Those Midlanders unable to join Cherry Valley continued to play at the new Salisbury until 1920, when several of those surviving joined with a group of Hempstead businessmen to organize the Hempstead Golf & Country Club, whose golf course, in part, was designed by A.W. Tillinghast. The Hempstead clubhouse is an expansion of the former Parsons farmhouse, which dates back to 1756 and was occupied by Tories during the Revolution. The clubhouse also is historic in the sense that it was within

(155

OPPOSITE PAGE: MARION HORN DRIVING FROM THE NINTH TEE. *(American Golfer)*

CHERRY VALLEY'S (THEN) PAR-3 SEVENTH HOLE. *(American Golfer)*

its walls that Hofstra University was conceived in 1935, the university's founders all being club members. A depleted Midland Club ceased operations in 1924.

When Cherry Valley was made private, many residents of the western side of Garden City were left without a golfing home, and so formed the Garden City Country Club in 1916. The club leased the Gordon estate straddling the railroad tracks, and their Walter Travis-designed golf course opened in 1917.

Just two blocks to the north of the new clubhouse was the former site of the Nassau Boulevard Air Field where, in 1911, the first airmail flight in American history took off and flew all the way to Mineola! Pilot Earl Ovington carried a bag containing 640 letters and 1280 postcards. That flight was reenacted in 1936 when a plane landed on the 14th fairway, a substitute for the Nassau Boulevard Air Field that no longer existed, and took off with the mail for Roosevelt Field. Play was delayed while photographs were taken.

In 1918, J.J. Lannin, proprietor of the Garden City Hotel, entered the picture. He purchased the transplanted Salisbury Links, its clubhouse, and 326 acres with the intent of developing the land for golf. The first course (#1) was the highly-acclaimed site of the 1925 United States Publinx Championship, during which the club housed and fed all the contestants.

During the golf boom of the 1920s, #1 was followed in rapid succession by four more courses. Salisbury came to be known as the "Sports Center of America." Devereux Emmet designed all five Salisbury courses, and two of them—#3 and #4—were operated as a private club. Both were used for championship play, although the latter was generally regarded as the club's showcase. The #4 course was unique in that it included just two par 3s and two par 5s.

All five courses were located within the boundaries of today's Eisenhower Park with two clubhouses serving the public and private golfers separately, both located off Merrrick Avenue. Across the street at the time were the old Meadow Brook Club's links and polo fields.

The year 1926 was a banner one for Salisbury, with three major events contested there. In July, a memorable edition of the Met Open, played on the #3 course, resulted in a 54-hole play-off between Macdonald Smith and Gene Sarazen, after the pair tied at 286 over the 72-hole route, then again at the end of their first (70) and second (72) play-off rounds. Smith finally emerged the victor after a third extra round, shooting a 66 to his rival's 70. The 126 holes played were considered a world's record for a major championship. For his superlative effort, Smith earned the princely sum of $250!

The *New York Times* summarized the 36-hole conclusion of the tournament as follows:

> "Sarazen, starting the third round with a three-stroke deficit to Smith, shot a brilliant 68, within a stroke of the record for the No. 3 course. To all appearances, he had the tournament won then and there as he was leading Smith by three strokes going into the fourth and final round. But with the championship tucked away in his pocket right up to the last hole, Gene wavered long enough to permit Smith to tie.
>
> "He took three putts on the next to the last green, and then, after a good drive to the last hole and a second shot that rolled over the corner of the green and stopped hole high, he chipped back short and missed his twenty-foot putt for a 4.
>
> "Smith had picked up two strokes by the time he reached the seventeenth tee, but even after he holed the green in par figures to get back another one, no one dreamed that it would be possible for him to tie with a 4 on the last hole.
>
> "After Smith's tee shot his prospects seemed to be far more remote than ever, for his ball was sliced in among the trees that border the right-hand side of the fairway. His second shot still left him sixty yards short of the green. His third, a beautiful pitch, landed on the green, but four or five yards above the hole, a downhill putt staring him in the face.
>
> "Not one of the throng gathered around the putting green as much as breathed as Smith took his bead on the line, drew back his putter, paused, and then hit the ball. Straight on the line it went and when it tumbled for the much-needed four, gave Smith the chance to wage another war for the title. It was a great finish, and one that proved his mettle."

FINALLY! THE WINNING PUTT IN THE 1926 MET OPEN. *(Golf Illustrated)*

Sarazen played the final two rounds in 68-75, Smith in 74-72 to finish on even terms at 286. Sarazen made five birdies en route to a back-nine 31 in his morning round.

Sarazen and Smith returned the next day (Sunday) to settle the issue at 18 holes, but after both carded 70s, they played a second round, this time both shooting 72. The *New York Times* reported:

"Few matches with so much at stake have had so many dramatic moments as this one, and in few matches has the golf been so monotonously superb ... but at night-fall every one was as much in the dark as ever."

The two rounds were played in strong winds. In the morning, the match was close all the way, and Sarazen finally got the lead for the first time when he dropped an eight-yard putt for a birdie 2. The *New York Times* describes the final two holes of the morning round:

> *"One stroke to the good and two holes to play, Sarazen threw his advantage away by driving into the face of the trap at the seventeenth and then failed to put his recovery near the hole. Smith was on and down in two putts for a par 3.*
> *"At the last hole, Gene sliced his second and was short of the green on his third, but holed a good five-footer for his half. Smith was on the green in three, five yards above the hole, but was short on his down hill putt for a 4."*

Thus a sixth round was mandated, starting after a heavy shower during lunch. Smith played the better golf in the afternoon, but Sarazen parlayed a hot putter and courage in the face of several bad breaks to stay close. Smith opened a two-stroke lead and Sarazen caught him with a birdie 3 at the 14th hole, then took the lead at the 15th with a 25-foot birdie putt. A poor approach cost Sarazen the 16th hole, and the match was again even. Then, according to the *New York Times*:

> *"Fate, which had dealt Sarazen several jolts during the match, gave him two belts in succession at the last two holes. His putt for a 2 from ten feet hung on the lip of the seventeenth and another putt, this one a four-footer, did the same on the last hole. As a matter of fact, he should have won the hole any way, for Smith's second shot was badly sliced and the only thing that kept it from going out of bounds was that it hit an automobile and a tree and bounded back on the fairway."*

The *New York Times* reported that the seventh (and any subsequent) round would be played the following Saturday:

> *"Another attempt will be made to settle the vexatious problem on Saturday, and if the two principals continue to play as they have for the last four days, they will be lucky indeed if they get out of the trenches by Christmas. So far, as the records of golf*

MAC SMITH AND HIS DOG. *(American Golfer)*

show, there has never been such a long stretch of holes played in any major championship.”

Smith led by two strokes after a front-nine 35, then both players wielded hot putters over the back nine. Smith had six one-putt greens en route to a 31, and Sarazen was close behind with four one-putts and a closing 33. One final stroke of bad luck sealed Sarazen’s fate. It came at the 11th hole, as the *New York Times* reported:

> *“After the eleventh it was all over but the shouting, for here again Gene got a bad break. He hooked and Mac sliced. There was no earthly reason why Sarazen should have been any worse off than Smith, but he was, for his ball was up against the side of a mound where he couldn’t get at it, while Mac’s was in among some mounds on the other side, but not close enough for any interference.*
>
> *“Gene’s second shot, made difficult by the way the ball was lying, was hooked and it stopped close to a tree in the rough again, while Mac’s was up near the green. Sarazen then played a masterful shot to the green, but by now Smith’s putter was functioning and another stroke disappeared into his pocket.”*

The national PGA Championship came to Salisbury #4 in September, and the outcome of the final match between Walter Hagen and Leo Diegel was decided on the greens. According to the *New York Times*:

> *“It was a pitiful sight to see a great golfer putt so lamentably as Diegel did on Saturday, especially when his weakness in this all-important department of the game had to be contrasted with the beautiful putting of Hagen ... never in its charmed life did that putter perform more valiantly than it did today. Six one-putt greens in the morning round, and four one-putt greens in the afternoon tell the story better than words.*
>
> *“Diegel, always a bundle of unbridled nerves, was worse than ever this morning. Hagen, on the contrary, was the Hagen of always—the calm, undisturbed, unruffled golfer who takes things as they come in golf, with his every thought concentrated on the next shot, none on the one that has been played.”*

The tone of the match may have been set early. According to the *New York Times*:

> *“The second shot of the match was the one that foretold the outcome. Diegel was yards ahead with the green open to him, and Hagen’s second shot in the rough above*

the hole on the right. Here was Leo's chance to get the jump on his man. Instead he topped an iron and did well to get a half."

And then, on the fourth and fifth holes:

"It looked as if nothing but a miracle could prevent his squaring the match there, but Hagen, playing his ball off the slope of the green, got back on and holed in one putt, giving him a half when Diegel failed to hole his putt.

"Hagen's recovery on the short fifth was even more miraculous and more disturbing to his opponent. His pitch landed in a trap short, while Diegel's stopped in the short rough beyond the edge of the green from where he almost holed after Hagen had recovered weakly. There was no more than a sixteenth of an inch of daylight between Diegel's ball, lying two inches from the hole, and the line Hagen had to take, but away went the putt and down it dropped. Those two breaks seemed to nettle Diegel all the more."

160)

Diegel eventually evened the match after 11 holes, only to watch Hagen respond by almost holing out his approach on the 12th. Hagen led by two holes after the morning round, and never was threatened thereafter, eventually beating Diegel 4&3 to capture his third consecutive PGA title.

In the semifinals Hagen shot a course-record-equaling 68 in the morning round and defeated Johnny Farrell 6&5. Hagen was eight under par for the 31 holes, and Farrell two under. The match was won when Hagen won two of the last three holes before lunch and the first two after lunch. In the other semifinal match, Johnny Golden staged "one of the greatest uphill fights ever seen" against Diegel, coming from 5-down to extend the match to the 18th green, where he narrowly missed holing a chip shot for a birdie that would have prolonged the match.

Finally, in mid-October, the Metropolitan section of the PGA held its first-ever championship at Salisbury. J.J. Lannin provided a beautiful solid silver trophy for the winner, which to this day bears his name. Lannin also donated prize money for the inaugural tournament. Mike Brady won the qualifying medal with 71-73=144 in wind and rain, then eliminated Gene Sarazen and Jim Barnes in the first two rounds before losing to Joe Turnesa in the third round. Meanwhile Willie Klein put out Mac Smith and Johnny Farrell before suffering elimination in the third round at the hands of St. Albans' Joe Silvester. Turnesa and Silvester advanced to the finals, with Turnesa a decisive winner, playing the final 31 holes in just one over par.

OPPOSITE PAGE, TOP: THE FOUR SEMIFINALISTS IN THE 1926 PGA CHAMPIONSHIP (L TO R): WALTER HAGEN, LEO DIEGEL, JOHNNY FARRELL, AND JOHNNY GOLDEN. *(New York Times)*

OPPOSITE PAGE, BOTTOM: LEO DIEGEL DRIVING FROM THE FIRST TEE IN THE SEMIFINALS. *(New York Times)*

Unfortunately, the Salisbury Country Club did not survive the Depression. It was taken over by the county in 1940. The Nassau County Park was created December 4, 1944, at which time two courses (#1 and #4) remained in use, the others having been neglected. In 1950 and 1951, respectively, the new White and Blue courses were opened, and at the same time the #1 course was abandoned and its land developed for picnic grounds, athletic fields, and a man-made lake. The new courses were unusual in the sense that both were "twin short hole" courses, each including 22 holes, with duplicate versions of the par-3 holes side by side to allow faster players to play through slower groups. Robert Trent Jones Sr. designed both new courses.

At the same time, the old championship course (#4) was renamed the Red course and today remains a reasonable facsimile of the course that saw the club through its glory years. Only the first and 18th holes are entirely new, having been built in 1946 to accommodate the new clubhouse site. The new clubhouse and pro shop were opened in 1950.

The facility was renamed in honor of former president Eisenhower on September 7, 1969.

LEFT: ONE OF TWO SALISBURY CLUBHOUSES. *(Metropolitan Golfer)*

OPPOSITE PAGE: BROTHER JACK HAGEN, SALISBURY PRO, AND OWNER J.J. LANNIN ESCORT WALTER HAGEN TO WINNER'S CIRCLE AFTER 1926 PGA. *(Golf Illustrated)*

19

The Miami Beach of the North

If the vision of one man had not run headlong into the Depression, the character of the East End of Long Island might have been changed forever.

That man was Carl Graham Fisher, the batteries tycoon who had built Miami Beach from a tangle of mangrove swamps. Fisher liked what he saw when he first visited Montauk on his yacht, and soon thereafter, the "Miami Beach of the North" was on the planning board. Fisher and four associates purchased 9,000 acres of land at Montauk for $2.5 million, and plans were drawn up for a golf course, marina and yacht club, polo fields, tennis courts, and a luxurious 200-room hotel to be called the Montauk Manor. Fisher envisioned Montauk becoming a point of departure for Long Islanders traveling to Europe by boat, replacing the trip to Manhattan with a railroad ride to the end of the Island.

To make his dream a reality, Fisher employed 800 men daily; miles of new roads were built and water pipes laid. Tudor-style homes were built on the hillsides, and a channel was cut through Lake Montauk to give larger boats access to the yacht club. But when the stock market crashed in 1929, the effect on Carl Fisher and his dream was devastating. Although a great many of his projects were left unfinished, enough were completed to make Montauk a meeting place for presidents, foreign dignitaries, and the world's elite.

The Montauk Downs Golf Club opened for light play in 1927. The course was a natural links designed by Captain H.C. Tippett, likely with an assist from Charles

Opposite page: Carl Fisher as he appeared in an article on Long Island history. *(Montauk Library Collection)*

Above: The Montauk Manor House, with the course in the foreground. *(American Golfer)*

Blair Macdonald. Tippett, who was British, was a member and club champion at Lido, and runner-up in the 1923 Met Amateur.

The course rolled through a "cluster of rounded hills and valleys, with here and there a gash of a ravine cutting across the landscape," to quote from an article in the September, 1928, issue of *Metropolitan Golfer* magazine. There wasn't a level hole on the course, nor was there any trace of artificiality. The terrain was barren linksland, where trees abound today. Montauk Downs was said to be "as close an approach to the famous seaside links of the British Isles as may be had anywhere."

Montauk Downs received its acid test under fire in early August of 1928 when the club staged a 72-hole tournament that attracted many of the area's leading professionals. During the morning round on the first day, with the winds calm, several low scores were recorded, headed by Joe Turnesa's course record 67. When the winds kicked up in the afternoon, however, Turnesa soared to a 75. The following day, under even more turbulent conditions, only four in the field were able to better 75. The unanimous opinion was that Montauk Downs was a "stern, exacting test of golfing skill."

Despite the Depression, the damaging hurricane of 1938, and World War II, when Montauk temporarily became a military base, the golf club and hotel survived. Finally, an investment group took over in 1966. The hotel, which had closed its doors in 1964, was converted to condominiums in 1974.

TOP LEFT: MONTAUK DOWNS. *(Golf Illustrated)*

BOTTOM LEFT: SOME MEMBERS ARRIVED BY PRIVATE AIRPLANE DURING THE 1920S. *(Golf Illustrated)*

OPPOSITE PAGE: VIEW FROM THE 18TH FAIRWAY OF THE 430-YARD, PAR 4 DEMANDING HOME HOLE, WITH THE CLUBHOUSE IN BACK-GROUND. *(Golf Illustrated)*

By 1969 Montauk Downs possessed a brand new Robert Trent Jones golf course that was fine-tuned under the watchful eye of son Rees Jones.

The investors did not fare well, however, and the state took over the operation in 1978. Today, the state-operated facility at Montauk Downs handles nearly 50,000 rounds of golf each year, an amazing number considering its isolation, and yet is maintained in superb condition.

One's most enduring impression of the modern course is of the many long par 4s, most of which play uphill to elevated greens. Two of Montauk's par 5s challenge the longer hitters with the option of going for the green in two—over water. The seventh cascades out of the woods down to a lake, calling for a 150-yard carry into the green. The 13th features a lateral water hazard along the right side over the final 200 yards which eventually crosses in front of the elevated green.

20

Golf's First "Charge"

Arnold Palmer's popularity derived in part from his dramatic come-from-behind "charges" into the winner's circle at major championships. He was far from the first. Gene Sarazen staged a memorable late rush—the last 28 holes in 100 strokes—to win the 1932 U.S. Open on Long Island, at the old Fresh Meadow course in Queens.

Sarazen at one time had been Fresh Meadow's professional. "The Squire" came aboard in 1925, and brought with him Al Ciuci, his former mentor as a teenager, to teach and run the pro shop. Fresh Meadow's fully stocked golf shop quickly gained recognition as one of the first and finest operations of its scale in the country.

Fresh Meadow first gained national prominence as the site for a major event when the PGA Championship came to the Flushing club during September of 1930. In those days, only the final 32 contestants surviving qualifying competed at match play for the title. Among the 32 at Fresh Meadow that year were Sarazen, Tommy Armour, Horton Smith, Bobby Cruickshank, Johnny Farrell, Craig Wood, "Wild Bill" Mehlhorn, Billy Burke, and "Long Jim" Barnes. The course was in excellent shape, considering the long drought that had plagued the New York area, and the selective watering policy the club had been forced to adopt.

William D. Richardson, covering the tournament for the *New York Times*, described the conclusion of the final match between home pro Sarazen and Armour:

"After proving a bitter disappointment to him virtually throughout the match,

Tommy Armour's putter finally came to his aid on the eighteenth hole at the Fresh Meadow Country Club yesterday and gave him a victory over Gene Sarazen in the final round of the Professional Golfers Association championship tourney.

"Up to then there had been little to choose between Armour and Sarazen, who is terminating his career as pro at Fresh Meadow. On the whole, Armour had out-played Sarazen up to the greens, but Gene had more than held his own on them.

"They had battled for thirty-five holes and were just where they started. Armour had squared the match by a remarkable recovery from the rough on the short thirty-second. He had saved halves on the next three—two of them hard halves to get.

ARMOUR PUTTING ON THE NINTH GREEN WITH SARAZEN LOOKING ON. *(Golf Illustrated)*

(169

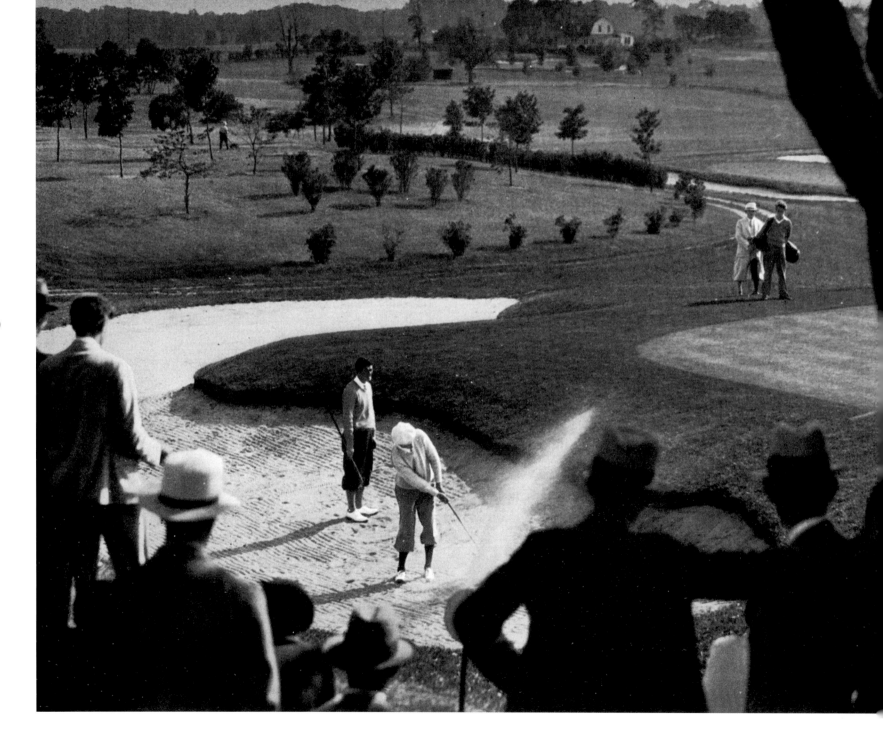

"It was his honor and he drove to the left, just off the fairway. Sarazen's drive wound up in a trap, and his recovery landed short of the trap in front of the green and popped in. A gasp went up when Armour followed suit, for it looked like a great opportunity wasted. Afterward it developed that Tommy, seeing Gene's ball where it was and his own lying not too well, had tried to play safe and lost in the gamble.

"Sarazen chipped out ten feet past the hole. Tommy, after much deliberation, came out twelve feet to the right and beyond the hole. As he was about to putt a camera enthusiast, standing directly back of him, disturbed him and he stopped. Finally he hit the ball. It rolled slowly toward the hole and had just enough momentum to topple in.

"Sarazen was unable to hole his, and the wooden-headed putter that Armour had thought of discarding earlier in the round had made him the PGA champion."

Richardson called the match "one of the finest finals ever played in the event." The two players were never more than two holes apart; Armour held a 1-up lead after the morning round. Ironically, after all the excellent shots, both players snap-hooked their drives on the final hole.

With the following year's U.S. Open scheduled to be contested at his home club, Sarazen resigned his position at Fresh Meadow early in 1931, and took a similar position at the nearby Lakeville Golf & Country Club. Sarazen sincerely believed that the "home pro jinx" had cost him the 1930 PGA, and was taking no chances of a repeat performance in the Open.

Nevertheless, Sarazen was accorded a hero's welcome at Fresh Meadow when he returned to this country a week before the Open, for he brought with him the British Open trophy, which he had won with an easy front-running romp at Sandwich, establishing a new record for that venerable classic in the process.

Sarazen and his fellow competitors were greeted by New York City's finest as they arrived at Fresh Meadow. According to an article in the *New York Times*:

"The golf course of the Fresh Meadow Country Club in Creedmor, Queens, where the National Open Championship is scheduled to start on Thursday, was being guarded by police yesterday and roads in the vicinity were being patrolled by radio cars as a result of an alleged plot to damage the greens. The plot is said to have grown out of the refusal of the championship committee to permit bookmakers to operate on the grounds during the play."

OPPOSITE PAGE: HORTON SMITH COMING OUT OF A BUNKER AT THE NINTH GREEN DURING THE PGA CHAMPIONSHIP. *(American Golfer)*

TOMMY ARMOUR. *(American Golfer)*

Olin Dutra, a descendant of the first Spanish settlers of the Monterey Peninsula, fired a brilliant 69 to take a four-stroke lead after the first round, which was played on a day, according to the *New York Times*:

> *"when the course was swept by a wind of half-gale proportions that wrecked scores and golfing reputations."*

Fresh Meadow's par-70, 6,829-yard course played difficult that day. Leo Diegel was second at 73, followed by Sarazen and Jose Jurado, the slender Argentinean who, the *New York Times* reported,

> *"Hits a tremendous drive for a player his size and his bold play has caught the fancy of the galleries. No shot is too dangerous for him to attempt. He was leaving himself considerable to do with some of his putts."*

BELOW: THE ARGENTINEAN SENSATION JOSE JURADO. *(Golf Illustrated)*

OPPOSITE PAGE: SARAZEN HITTING HIS TEE SHOT TO THE PAR 3 NINTH GREEN IN 1932. *(American Golfer)*

The winds continued to blow on the second day, and on all upwind holes the tees were moved forward, shortening the course by 100 yards. Phil Perkins, the British Amateur champion of 1928 who had turned professional in 1932, tamed the winds with a 69, and finished the day tied with Jurado. Dutra, Diegel, and Walter Hagen were third, fourth, and fifth, followed by Sarazen, who carded 36-40=76 for 150, five strokes in arrears.

Much has been made of Sarazen's "safety-first" tactics, as he looked to avoid the severe bunkers flanking the greens, preferring to take his chances instead with the relatively-flat putting surfaces. His strategy has been questioned primarily because it ran counter to his usual gambling style of play. It looked even more questionable in light of his recent mastery of his newly-devised sand iron. Sarazen was so effective with this new weapon that he considered himself even money to get up and down in two strokes from any greenside bunker. Perhaps too much has been made of Sarazen's strategy, and not enough of his lethargic play. Sarazen simply wasn't hitting his irons well, tired no doubt from his trip abroad.

By the time Sarazen reached the ninth tee Saturday morning, he was four over par for his round, and had lost another two strokes to the leaders. The ninth was a 143-yard par 3 completely surrounded by sand, and Sarazen's 7-iron rolled 15 feet past the pin near the back apron. The ninth green was next to the clubhouse, and Sarazen had used it often as a practice putting green. He knew its contours well, so it came as no surprise when he rolled that putt in for a birdie, a stroke that touched

off one of the great finishes in Open history. Throwing caution to the winds, and shooting for the flag on every hole, Sarazen played the back nine on Saturday morning in 32 strokes, moving to within one of leader Perkins. Bobby Cruickshank was one stroke behind Sarazen as the final round began.

William Richardson, writing in the *New York Times*, tells the story of the final round which Sarazen played with fellow Long Islander, Willie Klein:

"Never has there been such a last-round drive as took place over the Fresh Meadow course yesterday and at the finish there wasn't a person in the gallery who was not completely overcome by the excitement of it all.

"The afternoon was a series of thrills which began when Perkins, playing superbly, refused to crack under the terrific strain of a championship, and posted his brilliant 70 to give him a seventy-two-hole score of 289. At the time it looked as if that mark would make Perkins the champion and provide one of the greatest achievements in the history of the game. Knowing full well how much trouble the course had given so many of the stars, no one believed it would be possible for any one to equal his mark.

"But suddenly, out of nowhere, Cruickshank hopped into the picture with the score of 33 on the outgoing nine holes, a score that left him with par to tie Perkins for the lead. And then came word from the front that Sarazen was burning up the course. By the time he reached the turn in 32, giving him a 64 for the last nine holes in the morning and the first nine in the afternoon, Gene had topped Perkins' and Cruickshank's sixty-three hole totals.

"All he had to do then in order to win was to play the last nine holes in 36 strokes, and after watching his golf for a few holes, no one ever had

any doubt of his ability to do that.

"One look at Gene was all that was necessary to convince any one that there was a new Open champion, the man who would soon join hands with Bobby Jones as the only two men ever to win the two major titles in the same year.

"It was the Sarazen of old out there on the course. The same kind of bold, flashing player who as a boy had won the United States Open at Skokie ten years back. The only difference was that he was a far better shot-maker now than then.

"A tremendous gallery, perhaps 10,000 wild-eyed enthusiasts ... launched a wild dash with the centre of the putting green as their objective, and in spite of the efforts of the marshals, messengers, police, and volunteers, the crowd surged ahead until three-fourths of the putting green was occupied as Sarazen came up to play the final hole. It was so dense and so unruly that even the players had a hard time getting on to the green to finish.

"Gene's second shot, following a perfectly placed drive, went a bit too far to the right and dropped into a bunker, from where almost without waiting for quiet, he pitched out roughly eight feet wide of the pin.

"Even when something like quiet and order were restored, it was utterly impossible to get the crowd back to the limits of the putting green. Actually, Sarazen and Klein barely had room to swing their putters.

"Sarazen had that putt for a 66, something almost unheard of in a champi-

ABOVE: SARAZEN PLAYING FROM THE BUNKER AT THE 18TH GREEN DURING THE 1932 U.S. OPEN CHAMPIONSHIP. HE GOT UP AND DOWN FOR PAR AND WON HIS SECOND OPEN TITLE. *(Golf Illustrated)*

LEFT: SARAZEN'S PUTT ON THE FINAL GREEN. *(Golf Illustrated)*

OPPOSITE PAGE: USGA PRESIDENT HERBERT RAMSEY OF NATIONAL PRESENTS SARAZEN WITH THE HAVEMEYER TROPHY. *(Golf Illustrated)*

onship, and when the ball rolled straight and true right into the cup, he was engulfed in a throng that swept him away, paying not the slightest attention to the expensive green on which they were tramping.

"Sarazen was borne away to receive the historic cup, the $1,000 first-prize that goes to the winner, and fame and glory."

Sarazen played his final 28 holes in exactly 100 strokes, finishing the tournament with rounds of 70-66 to equal the Open record of 286. His last round, the lowest in Open history (to that date), gave Sarazen a three-stroke margin over Cruickshank, who himself finished with 68, and Perkins, who shot 70 in the last round. As so often happens with emotional players like Sarazen (and later, Arnold Palmer), one shot or one putt can ignite the flame that sparks the "charge."

Bobby Jones was on hand at Fresh Meadow and called Sarazen's last round "the finest competitive exhibition on record" while touting Sarazen as the "greatest living golfer."

Fresh Meadow was barely a decade old when it hosted its second national championship. The club was located just south of what is now the Long Island Expressway, near 183rd Street. The Fresh Meadow Cinema and adjoining shopping center and housing development now occupy the site.

From the very beginning the club decided to travel first class. They wanted their course to be one of the great examinations of golf in the country, and they wanted it to test the leading players of the day in major competition. To this end, they engaged noted architect A.W. Tillinghast to design their course, which opened in 1923. The following quote from the club's official history describes the kind of course it was, and the reception it received:

"News of the Tillinghast Course in Flushing, New York, had started to spread throughout the golfing world. When the course was officially opened large numbers of golf celebrities and experts came from far and near to test its rigors. What they found was a course in exquisite condition, as though it had been groomed for a decade, and of scenic delight. It contained holes of fascinating variety, some fairways finding their ways through groves of towering trees, others with water obstacles on the way to the greens; doglegs with treacherous sand traps as they curved around corners to the left and to the right; out of bounds galore to plague the "hooker" and "slicer" alike; the famous Tillinghast pear-shaped greens fiercely trapped. All these features created one of the finest tests of golf anywhere."

(175

21

From Brooklyn to Huntington

Among the earliest golf courses on Long Island were a threesome in Brooklyn—Dyker Meadow, Marine & Field, and Crescent Athletic—located in close proximity to one another, overlooking the Narrows and Staten Island. In fact, the first two were neighbors, situated within the confines of what is now Dyker Beach Park. The latter eventually moved to Huntington as the Huntington Crescent Club.

The earliest of the Brooklyn clubs was Dyker Meadow, which was organized in 1895 and located in Fort Hamilton, off 7th Avenue and 92nd Street, at the southwest corner of the park. Marine & Field, which was organized in 1895, was located at the northern boundary of the park, with its clubhouse at 13th Avenue and 86th Street.

Both clubs possessed nine-hole courses designed by Tom Bendelow. In 1909 they consolidated their golf courses, with Marine & Field playing as the front nine, Dyker Meadow as the back. By 1928 they had been superseded by the public Dyker Beach (at times called Shore View) course.

That course served as the training ground for the Strafaci brothers, Frank and Tom, both winners of the Met Amateur, and as home base for many years for one of Long Island's top playing professionals, Wiffy Cox. A member of the United States Ryder Cup team in 1931, Cox finished fourth in the 1931 U.S. Open, fifth in the 1932 Open at Fresh Meadow, and third in the 1934 Open.

The Crescent Athletic Club (established 1896) was the golf wing of the Crescent Athletic Association, which was incorporated in 1888. The latter was located adjacent to the yachting anchorage off Bay Ridge, on the east cliff of the Narrows overlooking New York Bay, between First Avenue and Colonial Road, 83rd and 85th Streets. The clubhouse was a fortress-like structure with several piazzas. Of the parent club's 1,500 members, only two hundred had an interest in golf. Lacrosse, baseball, and track were the primary interests of the "new moons" (as club members were often called).

The Crescent's first nine holes were increased to 18 holes by 1899, and measured just 4,548 yards, with the 346-yard first hole the longest. Even then, the club's property was the target of real estate developers, and the club began looking elsewhere for greener fairways. By 1908 nine holes had been surrendered, but the other nine remained intact through 1931, when the club moved to Huntington. In 1930, the Crescent Athletic Club joined forces with the Hamilton Club of Brooklyn to form a 3,000-member base which they called the Crescent Athletic-Hamilton Country Club, a name that would be changed in 1938 to the Huntington Crescent Club.

Led by Judge James C. Cropsey, president of the Crescent Club, the new organization purchased the estate of Roy Rainey, 300 acres of rolling woodland, formal gardens, and a swimming pool with a frontage on Huntington Bay. There they planned athletic facilities that were to include 24 tennis courts, fields for soccer, cricket, baseball, lacrosse, and polo, a toboggan slide, a yachting anchorage, and

(177

Wiffy Cox, Dyker Beach's long-time golf pro. *(American Golfer)*

Right: The Rainey mansion. *(Golf Illustrated)*

cabanas at the beach. The Depression intervened, however, and the plans did not fully materialize. In particular, the beach club and yacht anchorage were not built. The club engaged the architectural team of Emmet & Tull to design two 18-hole golf courses. The (shorter) East Course was seeded that fall and opened for play on July 4, 1931. The championship West Course opened the following spring. Huntington Crescent was Long Island's "mega club," the only one with two 18-hole golf courses.

Huntington Crescent's first golf professional (1931–1940) was "Long Jim" Barnes. The 6-foot, 4-inch Barnes was recognized as one of the very best players in this country. He won the first two PGA Championships (1916, 1919), a U.S. Open (1921) by nine strokes, and a British Open (1925). In 1940 he was among the original 12 men inducted into the PGA Hall of Fame.

In June of 1939, the club acquired the property of the Huntington Bay Club, which it used as a center for bathing and yachting. The Bay Club had been organized in 1920 with a very prestigious membership roster. Its facilities, spread over 130 acres, included an 18-hole golf course that straddled Huntington Bay Road. That course had turned to weeds by 1939 when the bank foreclosed on the property.

The colorful Bustanoby brothers, three Frenchmen who built "Beaux Arts," a $1 million gambling casino there, had purchased the property, which included a 44-room Victorian hotel called the Clark House, in 1906. Designed by Stanford White along the lines of the casino at Monte Carlo, it sat atop an underground series of tunnels built to help the clientele (many of whom arrived by steamer from Manhattan or Stamford) escape the police. The Bustanobys also renovated the hotel and renamed it "The Chateau." It was a total resort, supplemented with luxurious villas. Unfortunately, the brothers suffered a series of financial reversals, and were forced to sell "Beaux Arts" in 1913.

Huntington Crescent planned to restore the Casino to its former beauty, with a new pier, cabanas, and yacht basin. At the same time, the old hotel/clubhouse was razed. But the war years were difficult, and by 1956 the club decided that the "joint

BELOW: THE EIGHTEENTH GREEN AND CLUBHOUSE ON THE EAST COURSE AT THE CRESCENT-ATHLETIC HAMILTON CLUB. *(Golf Illustrated)*

OPPOSITE PAGE, TOP: THE SHORT 122-YARD, PAR-3 EIGHTH HOLE ON THE WEST COURSE AT CRESCENT-ATHLETIC HAMILTON CLUB. *(Golf Illustrated)*

OPPOSITE PAGE, BOTTOM: THE WELL-GUARDED FOURTH GREEN ON THE WEST COURSE. *(Golf Illustrated)*

178)

operation" was not working, and so a separate beach club, the Head of the Bay Club, was formed, and a good portion of the intervening land sold for real estate development. A full 18 holes were lost, effectively destroying the West Course. Only the front nine on the East Course remains relatively intact today.

The Huntington Bay Club's golf course was not the first in Huntington. That honor goes to the Huntington Country Club, which had been organized in 1910 by former members of the (by then defunct) Oyster Bay Golf Club, one of Long Island's first (1894).

Many of the original members made Huntington their summer residence; others lived on the numerous grand estates in the vicinity. Their number included club founder Walter Jennings, William K. Vanderbilt II, Marshall Field II, Frank Melville (and later his son, Ward Melville), and August Heckscher. The layout, designed by Devereux Emmet, opened in 1911.

Huntington is unique among Long Island's country clubs in that it has an ice skating rink on the grounds, and a separate winter club whose membership transcends the country club.

22

Depression Born: Bethpage State Park

The Depression and subsequent war years had a telling effect on American golf, strangling many clubs financially, and forcing a number of clubs, including some prominent ones, to close their doors forever. There was one positive, however: Long Island's Bethpage State Park complex, born as a Work Relief project during the Depression.

Bethpage's origins trace back to 1695, when an Englishman named Thomas Powell purchased a large tract of land on what is now the eastern border of Nassau County, some 35 miles from Manhattan. It was located on the road joining Jericho on the north with Jerusalem to the south. The biblical connection was obvious, and a passage from St. Matthew's gospel (21:1) provided the name:

> *"and as they departed from Jericho, a great multitude followed Him, and when they drew nigh unto Jerusalem and were come to Beth'phage, unto the Mount Of Olives..."*

Literally translated, Beth'phage meant "house of figs," but Powell gave it a looser interpretation as "land of fruit or plenty." For the publinx golfers of Long Island three centuries later, he could not have chosen a more appropriate name.

The seeds for golf at Bethpage were not planted until 1912 when Benjamin Yoakum, a wealthy Texas railroad magnate, purchased 1,368 acres of rolling woodland and farmland that was part of Powell's "Bethpage Purchase." In 1923, the

Lenox Hills Country Club came into existence on land leased from Yoakum. The club was ideally situated, with an entrance to the old Motor Parkway at its doors. Lenox Hills was meant to be an inexpensive club offering high-class golf to its members at a nominal seasonal fee. It featured an 18-hole Devereux Emmet course that eventually would evolve into Bethpage's Green Course. The first nine holes, a "lovely winding course between wooded hills," opened to rave reviews on Decoration Day 1923.

The clubhouse was located off the "Melville-Huntington Road" (now Bethpage Road) near the current seventh tee on the Green Course, on one of the highest hills around Farmingdale, and offered a panoramic view across Long Island, as far as the Fire Island Lightship in the Great South Bay. It was destroyed by fire in 1945. Yoakum's "summer home" was situated off Round Swamp Road in the area between what is now the second tee and 14th green on the Black Course.

Yoakum died in 1930, and the following year the Long Island State Park Commission attempted to purchase his estate for development as a state park. The

THE 18TH GREEN AND CLUBHOUSE AT LENOX HILLS. *(Metropolitan Golfer)*

funds needed to purchase the property were hard to find during the Depression years, however, and it was not until early 1932 that the newly-formed Bethpage Corporation took over the lease and operated the golf course as a public facility for a couple of seasons. Over 70,000 rounds of golf were played during 1932-1933. In the meantime, the park was growing in popularity. Picnic areas were created, and the riding stables, bridle paths, and tennis courts were improved and opened to the public. Yet there seemed little hope that the park would remain available to the public for very long.

But finally, on August 26, 1933, by an act of legislative magic enacted by Parks Commissioner Robert Moses, the Bethpage Park Authority was created and took title to the property. During 1934, construction of a new clubhouse, three new courses, and a polo field began as a Work Relief project, employing as many as 1,800 men at the height of the construction activity. Work was completed the following year.

Famed architect A.W. Tillinghast was engaged as consultant to help revamp the existing course (renamed the Green, or #1 course) and design the Blue (#2), Red (#3), and Black (#4) courses. It would prove to be his last design project, one he would leave midstream to accept a position with the PGA, traveling the country advising clubs how to reduce their golf course maintenance expenses.

Nonetheless, the Blue and Red courses were opened to the public in 1935. The Black Course took longer, though, and it was not until Memorial Day of the following year that the public got its first look at a course destined to become a legend in the New York area.

The Black Course was something special, almost as if the architect had been

ABOVE LEFT: AN ARTIST'S RENDERING OF THE NEW CLUBHOUSE. *(Golf Illustrated)*

ABOVE: A.W. TILLINGHAST. *(Golf)*

OPPOSITE PAGE: DIAGRAM OF THE ORIGINAL 72-HOLE COMPLEX AT BETHPAGE. *(Bethpage State Park)*

PLAN OF DEVELOPMENT FOR
BETHPAGE STATE PARK
FARMINGDALE LONG ISLAND
SCALE OF FEET

Long Island State Park Commission
Babylon Long Island New York

184)

Top: A hole on the Green Course. *(Golf Illustrated)*

Bottom: The 18th green on the Red course in 1935. *(Bethpage State Park)*

Top: The seventh hole on the Blue Course in 1935 is now the 14th hole on the Yellow Course. *(Bethpage State Park)*

Bottom: The 14th hole on the Yellow Course in 1958. Note the changes in the greenside bunkering. *(Bethpage State Park)*

given the freedom to let his creative juices run wild one last time. Tillinghast himself gives considerable credit to Joseph Burbeck, the state engineer who oversaw the project from start to finish.

> *"Now it was Burbeck's idea to develop one of these layouts along lines which were to be severe to a marked degree. It was his ambition to have something which might compare with Pine Valley as a great test, and although my continual travels over the country in the PGA work have prevented me from seeing play over Bethpage's Black since its opening, I am rather inclined to believe from reports from some of the best players that it is showing plenty of teeth.*
>
> *"Yet thousands of 'weak sisters' undoubtedly will flock there insisting on at least one tussle with the Black Leopard, just to show that they can 'take it.' If they had to play under such punishing conditions, week in and out, they probably would chuck their clubs in the lake and take to pitching horseshoes for recreation."*

Tillinghast's expression at Bethpage Black took him back to his roots as a young architect, for there is a striking resemblance between Bethpage Black and Pine Valley, that penultimate example of penal architecture designed by Tillinghast's long-time friend, George Crump.

When first shown the Bethpage acreage, Tillinghast noted its similarity to the site in southern New Jersey on which Pine Valley had been built. To quote him from an editorial comment appended to an article in the April 1934 edition of *Golf Illustrated*, of which he was the editor:

THE PAR–3 EIGHTH HOLE ON THE BLACK COURSE DURING THE 1938 EXHIBITION. *(Bethpage State Park)*

> *"The terrain presents infinite variety. Never quite flat but gently undulating, it grades to impressive ruggedness which is never permitted to suggest arduous playing conditions. It is strongly remindful of the Pine Valley land, that strange freak of rolling country in otherwise flat south Jersey. The character of many of the fairways, too, is similar to that of the famous Pine Valley in their isolation one from the others."*

And while the Black course is not quite as severe in its hazards as Pine Valley, to the average publinx player hitting from the middle tees, it is every bit as foreboding and unforgiving, seldom allowing a mishit shot to go unpunished. Each hole presents a unique and demanding challenge, and paints a vivid impression likely to stick in the golfer's memory for quite some time.

In that 1934 *Golf Illustrated* editorial quoted above, Tillinghast expressed a particular fondness for two holes on the Red Course:

> *"Some of the holes are almost entirely natural, and it is likely that two of these, 4 and 5 of No. 3 Course, will be particularly appreciated. The first of these is a one-shotter of about 180 yards, while the other is a remarkable three-shotter of natural perfection."*

And for the fourth hole on Black:

> *"When this is played from the full length of the teeing ground it should prove one of the most exacting three-shotters I know of anywhere. In locating and designing the green, which can only be gained by a most precise approach from the right, I must confess that I was a trifle scared myself when I looked back and regarded the hazardous route that must be taken by a stinging second shot to get into position to attack this green."*

(187

The new clubhouse, a rambling colonial-style building approached via a tree-lined road that ends with a small circular drive paved with Belgian blocks, was unveiled on August 10, 1935. Noted clubhouse architect Clifford C. Wendehack served as a consultant in its design.

The Red and Blue courses were quickly recognized as superb tests of golf, although not in the same league as the Black Course. Together, the two hosted the 1936 U.S. Public Links Championship, won by movie extra Paul Abbott.

Al Brosch, regarded as Long Island's best home-grown professional, was a graduate of Farmingdale High School. He got his start in golf as Benjamin Yoakum's private caddie at Lenox Hills, and became Bethpage's pro soon after the facility opened. Brosch won 10 Long Island Opens and eight Long Island PGA titles over the years,

The Blue Course underwent a major facelift in 1958 when a fifth course, the Yellow (originally called "White"), was added to the park's facilities. Eleven, perhaps 12, holes on the original Blue Course became part of the new Yellow and revised Blue courses, while totally new holes were built and incorporated into both layouts. Architect Alfred Tull supervised the revision, and the two courses opened for play on May 30, 1958.

Perhaps the most famous exhibition ever held at Bethpage took place on September 29, 1940, and matched Sam Snead against Byron Nelson. Snead won that day with a superb 68 but, according to legend, things didn't always go that smoothly for "The Slammer" at Bethpage. On one occasion, Snead is said to have walked off the Black in disgust, calling it an "unfair test of golf." Supposedly Snead's tantrum was the result of hitting his second shot over the green at the fourth hole, a cruel fate with which Black regulars can sympathize.

OPPOSITE PAGE, TOP: SAM SNEAD,
PAUL RUNYAN, JIMMY HINES OF
LAKEVILLE, AND AL BROSCH
BEFORE A 1938 MATCH ON THE
BLACK COURSE. *(Bethpage State Park)*

OPPOSITE PAGE, BOTTOM: GOLFERS
ARRIVING AT BETHPAGE DURING THE
DEPRESSION. *(Bethpage State Park)*

EVEN IN 1940, FROM THIS SCORECARD, THE
BLACK COURSE WAS A MONUMENTAL TEST.
(Jim Tingley)

23

Golf in a Nor'easter: The 1936 U.S. Amateur

The 1936 U.S. Amateur, held at the Garden City Golf Club in mid-September, collided head-on with the tail of a hurricane, something Long Islanders call a "nor'easter." The storm struck on September 18 during the semifinals, and seriously affected the play and outcome of the matches that day, and the finals the next day.

The storm's gale-force winds, with velocities as high as 50 miles per hour, flattened the press tent and dramatically impacted club selection. The torrential rains "came down in sheets" during the afternoon and left the course (and greens) flooded. The competition continued despite the conditions, and at times the players had to "putt" with their niblicks over the puddles on the greens. At one point, it was feared that the finals would be postponed for one day, but that did not happen. The conditions—the weather and the course—were ideal for good golf.

In one semifinal match, the ultimate winner, Johnny Fischer, a 24-year-old law student from the University of Cincinnati, ousted Johnny Goodman, the 1933 U.S. Open winner who would eventually capture the Amateur in 1937. According to the *New York Times*:

> *"From a competitive standpoint, the match between Fischer and Goodman was a far more spectacular one, for here was a pair of youngsters, the two outstanding American golfers of the present day, who battled each other tooth and nail over the entire route, playing great golf while doing it.*

THE FOUR SEMIFINALISTS (L TO R): JOCK MCLEAN, GEORGE VOIGT, JOHNNY GOODMAN, JOHNNY FISCHER. (*American Golfer*)

THE PRESS TENT AFTER THE NOR'EASTER.
(Garden City Golf Club)

(191

"It was a match that was kept in suspense from the moment they started out in the morning until late in the afternoon when the great little Nebraskan missed two drives. The critical one came at the seventeenth hole, the thirty-fifth of the match. One down playing that one, Goodman's tee shot caught the bunker in the center of the fairway ... the ball was buried in the sand, only a small part of it showing. All he could do was hack at it, and it failed to come out. As it hit the face of the bunker, it dropped back into the sand, carrying all his cherished hopes and ambitions with it."

What actually happened was that the grip of Goodman's driver became so damp that he lost control of the club, and topped his last three drives, losing all three holes with 6s. Fischer won the match 2&1; neither player would have broken 80 in the difficult conditions they faced during the afternoon round.

The following description (from the *New York Times*) of Goodman's final putt on the 17th hole provides insight into what the golfers faced that miserable day:

"After considerable difficulty finding a spot on the green that would give him a chance at the hole, Goodman putted with an iron and left his ball short as a patch of water checked its run."

In the other match, Jock McLean, a 24-year-old whiskey salesman from Glasgow, Scotland, used a three-quarters swing with an exaggerated follow-through to take the measure of 44-year-old George Voigt, a Long Islander who never did win the major title his outstanding game once promised. Voigt literally couldn't stand up in the strong winds. McLean won the match 8&7, and became only the fourth foreigner to reach the finals in our national championship—only Harold Hilton, in 1911 at Apawamis, was able to take the trophy overseas.

One almost fatal by-product of the semifinals was an injury to Fischer, who strained a ligament in his left ankle fighting the gale winds. In a performance seldom surpassed for sheer courage and doggedness, Fischer had the ankle taped the morning of the finals, then retaped before the afternoon round, hoping that his fast yet fluid swing would accommodate the transfer of his weight forward to the injured ankle.

Nonetheless, Fischer top-hooked almost every drive while wincing in pain. He literally played the finals on one leg—and courage. According to the *New York Times:*

"The injury was aggravated this morning when he slipped playing out of a

bunker on the thirteenth hole and gave it another wrench. That might easily have been the reason for his wretched golf in the morning and for the first few holes in the afternoon. Not only was he either topping tee shots or hitting them more crookedly than he has ever done before, but he was chipping badly and missing putt after putt to give McLean several holes he didn't deserve to win.

"Fischer was disinclined to talk about his lame left ankle. 'I had to favor it, on my drives especially,' said Johnny, 'but I got so excited toward the end there was no feeling in the foot at the finish.'"

Not surprisingly, McLean took advantage of his rival's injury and grabbed a three-hole lead after 23 holes had been completed. At that point, the man who had wielded a hot putter all week long suddenly began to three-putt—five times between the sixth and 13th holes—but nevertheless retained a one-hole advantage. Fischer dodged a bullet at the 16th hole by laying McLean a stymie, denying him a winning two-putt par. After halving the 17th hole with birdies, they came to the 18th tee. John Kiernan, in his "Sports of the Times" column, tells the story of the final match:

"This was a pitch of 166 yards across a pond to a green pretty well guarded by traps. Fischer went straight for the pin on the left side of the green. He had to gamble on getting close to the pin or going over into the deep trap beyond. McLean sensibly played it a wee bit safer. His shot was nearer the center of the green for direction, but ran further than he intended.

"The Scot had a long downhill putt. He saw that Johnny was about twelve feet away facing a sidehill putt. So Jock dribbled his putt to within a foot or so of the cup and then stretched himself on the green with a sigh of relief. That would about clinch it. He could see himself being welcomed back to Glasgow with the big gold cup under his arm, the first golfer from the British Isles to win the United States Amateur Championship in a quarter of a century. He was the man who had vindicated British golf in the wake of so many defeats at the hands of so many United States sharpshooters.

"Hoot awa', mon. The McLean was ance mair chief of a great clan. Then Johnny Fischer coolly sighted his sidehill putt and rolled it smoothly into the cup for a birdie 2 that squared the match.

"How Jock McLean managed to get up off the ground this observer will never know. The click of that putt as it hit the bottom of the cup must have been a horrible sound to his startled ears."

It was now McLean's turn to make an error, running his approach through the green on the short first hole, and into a bunker, Fischer hit the green and sank a 20-footer for a birdie that won the championship.

The unfortunate role that the stymie played in the outcome of this championship match underlined the fact that the stymie had outlived its usefulness as a fair component of the Rules of golf. It was abolished by the USGA soon thereafter. The *New York Times* described the stymie and its impact on the outcome:

> *"The hole that paved the way for Fischer's sensational victory was the thirty-fourth, where McLean, fifteen inches from the cup for a 4, had not the slightest chance to hole out when Fischer laid him that stymie. The only thing he could possibly hope to do was to push his ball over Fischer's and get it into the hole on the fly. He tried that and almost lost the hole, the ball sliding almost three and a half feet beyond the hole after it landed.*
>
> *"That was as tough a break as any one has ever had in the championship. But for that, McLean would be the titleholder tonight."*

194)

THE **AMERICAN GOLFER**

TE EDITORS

Harry Cooper
Bernard Darwin
George T. Dunlap, Jr.
Willie Macfarlane
Francis Ouimet

OPPOSITE PAGE, TOP: USGA PRESIDENT
JOHN G. JACKSON OF DEEPDALE PRESENTS
THE TROPHY TO FISCHER. *(American Golfer)*

OPPOSITE PAGE, BOTTOM: THE PUTT ON #18
THAT SENT THE MATCH INTO EXTRA HOLES.
(American Golfer)

RIGHT: JOHNNY FISCHER IS CARRIED OFF
THE COURSE FOLLOWING HIS VICTORY IN
THE 1936 U.S. AMATEUR. *(American Golfer)*

24

The World's Fair PGA

In 1939, the national PGA organization wished to stage its championship in the New York area at a site near the World's Fair. The tournament was scheduled for the second week of July, the week after the Palm Beach Round Robin was to be contested at nearby Fresh Meadow. The PGA's first choice was Pomonok, a club that preferred to shun the tournament spotlight. Begrudgingly, the members granted permission.

The tournament almost didn't get off the ground, though. When the entry of 1936 PGA champion Denny Shute arrived late, and PGA officials refused to allow him to play, the players threatened to boycott the event. Ultimately, the players won the showdown; Shute was eventually eliminated in the third round and the PGA averted a media nightmare.

Ben Hogan was one of four golfers to card 138 scores to lead the qualifying rounds. Ultimate winner Henry Picard was close behind at 140, and the year's U.S. Open champion, Byron Nelson, joined him in the finals. Picard saved his best golf for the finals, as Fred Corcoran reported in the *PGA Magazine:*

THE POMONOK CLUBHOUSE. *(PGA Magazine)*

"It was not until his match with Nelson, however, that Henry displayed the outstanding nerve, poise, under-pressure gaminess, and prowess of which he is capable when roused to the height of his best championship effort. It was in this seething 37-hole struggle that he turned on his greatest blast of under-par heat. His

medal aggregate for these last two rounds of 68-67=135 attests to the flashy scoring pace he reserved for Lord Byron, and capping it all as a champion would, he wound up the affair with an extra-hole birdie three."

Picard was 1-down after 33 holes and trapped at the 34th, with Nelson safely on the green. Picard saved his half there with a clutch explosion to 12 feet and a clutch putt. At the 35th he left his 15-foot attempt for a birdie on the lip of the cup, and remained 1-down.

Picard almost reached the green on the short (300 yards) uphill finishing hole, while Nelson's drive in the middle of the fairway left him with a tricky approach. Nelson played a safe shot onto the green, and then Picard chipped to within six feet of the hole, laying Nelson a partial stymie, Nelson played his putt around Picard's ball and left it next to the cup for a par, but Picard holed his putt to even the match.

Corcoran's words describe the bizarre finish to the match:

"At the 37th, which proved conclusive,—a testing two-shotter measuring 350 yards—Picard's drive along the right side of the fairway collided with a moving

(197

THE 17TH GREEN WITH 18TH HOLE AND CLUB-
HOUSE IN THE BACKGROUND. *(PGA Magazine)*

truck in the crowd and stopped underneath it. In moving the truck, one of its wheels ran over the ball, embedding it in the soft turf. Picard was allowed a lift in accordance with the rules of golf as the ball had come to rest and was embedded by an agency outside the match. Nelson's tee shot was down the left side of the fairway, and his second stopped within six feet of the hole. Picard then played a pitch shot that rolled ten feet beyond the cup. After studying the line quite carefully, he stroked the ball into the hole for a birdie three. Nelson then was faced with the task of holing a tricky six-foot putt to keep the match even. He stroked the ball for the cup and almost at the hole, the ball rolled off line, giving Picard the hole and the match."

Picard won the princely sum of $1,000 for his victory, giving him $8,177 for the season, best on the Tour. It is interesting to note that the truck that ran over Picard's ball was a newsreel truck, and the film taken that day has been preserved. The Long Island television network (Channel 12) has shown that film occasionally in recent years.

Sadly, Pomonok barely survived another 10 years after the 1939 PGA, becoming an early victim of the exodus of the masses from the city into the suburbs. Fortunately, quite a bit is known about the club's origins and the golf course that was worthy of a national championship. Pomonok traces its roots to Flushing, and

PGA President George Jacobus (center) presenting the trophy to Henry Picard (left), with Byron Nelson looking on. *(PGA Magazine)*

to one of the first golf clubs on Long Island. It began in 1886 as the Flushing Athletic Club, which leased an 83-acre site in the "quaint and picturesque" village of Flushing. It was just a short walk north of Northern Boulevard along Whitestone Avenue, not far from what is now the business district of town, between 149th Street, Willets Point Blvd., and Bayside Avenue.

The club had sufficient acreage for a short nine-hole course built by Tom Bendelow in March of 1896. The major hazards on the course were stone walls and numerous "cop and sand pit" bunkers. The feature hole on the course was the 530-yard ninth hole that "stretched out like the crack o'doom." Walter Travis played some of his first rounds of golf at Flushing. With the lease on its property scheduled to expire in 1919, the club found itself at a crossroads. The majority of the membership favored finding a new site and building an 18-hole course there. But there were some who were sentimentally attached to the original site. And so the club split, with the larger contingent moving on to form the Pomonok Country Club in 1920. Those who remained reorganized as The Old Country Club and eventually expanded their course to 18 holes. The Old Country Club proved quite popular during the 1920s, but failed to survive the Depression.

Pomonok was named for a tribe of native Americans that once inhabited the area. The club was located near the intersection of Kissena Boulevard and Horace Harding Boulevard, overlooking from the north what is now the Long Island Expressway, just to the east of the Queens College campus. Devereux Emmet designed the course, which was regarded as one of the most interesting courses in the East. It rolled over hilly terrain and featured exceptionally large greens. The course had the proverbial "million traps," each one strategically placed, and several of the greens, including four of the final six, were almost completely encircled by sand. Among the more interesting holes were the third, a 235-yard par 3 with a deep bunker 25 yards ahead of the partially-sand-encircled green; the 12th, a 575-yard par 5 that played uphill at the end to a green featuring a three-foot high horseshoe-shaped tier at the back; and the 17th, a 108-yarder played to a plateau green set in a complete circle of sand.

Pomonok was famous for its girl caddies during the 1920s. The members, many of whom purchased lighter bags, carried fewer clubs...and gave up swearing, appreciated their proficiency.

After the war the club found itself surrounded by housing developments. In 1949 the decision was made to disband the club and sell its property to real estate developers. Eventually, Parsons Boulevard was extended through the property, indeed over the very site of the Pomonok clubhouse.

25

The Postwar Boom: People and Highways

The face of Long Island changed dramatically following World War II. The exodus of the masses to the suburbs, and the accompanying highway construction to facilitate commuter travel, also had an impact on Long Island's golfscape. Some clubs, especially those in eastern Queens, were crowded out of their homes. Some closed their doors forever, others simply moved out to Nassau County.

Fresh Meadow may, or may not, have been the first to read the handwriting on the wall, but it was the first to react. The realities of advancing civilization began arriving on the club's doorstep in 1945, bringing with them the threat of significantly increased real estate taxes required to build the schools and improve the roads and utilities the club's new neighbors would need. Fresh Meadow's leaders had to address the question of whether the club was still viable in its Queens location. Rather, they found that a move would be in the club's best interests, and on February 25, 1946, the club voted to sell its property in Flushing and purchase the financially-troubled Lakeville Club in Lake Success. And the great Tillinghast course soon became the site for a 3,000-unit housing development.

The Lakeville Club by this time already had a rather complicated tale to tell. In 1923, Nathan Jonas, one of Fresh Meadow's most influential members, purchased 171 acres of rolling, heavily-wooded land in Lakeville, and converted it into a country club for the enjoyment of his friends in the theatrical and motion picture world, men such as Irving Berlin, Eddie Cantor, and Oscar Hammerstein. Also belonging to the club were actor Ed Wynn, Ring Lardner, sportswriter Grantland Rice, and the governor of New York, Al Smith.

The firm of Colt & Alison produced an outstanding course on the grounds, one that brought Lakeville prominence as "one of the most beautiful and exclusive clubs in America." The Depression seriously eroded Lakeville's membership, and the club, which had been born with the proverbial silver spoon in its mouth, eventually fell into the hands of financial institutions. During the war years, the club was leased to the nearby Glen Oaks Club, whose grounds across the street from the security-sensitive Sperry-Gyroscope Corporation were taken over by the U.S. Navy. After the war, Glen Oaks returned to its original site, and the Lakeville Club was sold to Fresh Meadow.

The aforementioned Glen Oaks Club was organized in 1924 on land purchased from the William K. Vanderbilt estate in Lake Success, south of the lake, with the old Motor Parkway forming its southeastern border. Included was the Vanderbilt Mansion, high on a hilltop, which became the clubhouse. Enter the Northern State Parkway, which was constructed in 1927, its right-of-way cutting through club property. Some 40 acres were condemned for the highway, and another 18 acres to the north of the road, including the clubhouse site, were isolated from the remainder of club grounds. This necessitated two major changes: a redesigned golf course and a new clubhouse.

Once returned to its original site in 1946, Glen Oaks began to feel the pressure of suburban sprawl. The Glen Oaks Village complex was built beyond the western border in 1949, and in 1955 the club welcomed a new neighbor to its south, Long Island Jewish Hospital. By the late 1960s the need for more extensive facilities was apparent, and so the club sold its property on the Nassau-Queens border (the North Shore Towers complex was built on the site, retaining enough acreage to house a relatively short 18-hole golf course called the Towers Country Club). At the same time, the club purchased a 250-acre Winthrop property in Old Westbury, where a new 27-hole golf course, designed by Joe Finger, was built.

As Nassau County became a major suburban "bedroom of New York," the need for a superhighway became apparent. Hence, the Long Island Expressway, which plundered anything, and everything, in its path. The first course to fall was Oakland, the second oldest golf club in Queens. It was located in Bayside, high in the hills overlooking Little Neck Bay, a few miles to the east of Pomonok. Oakland was founded in 1896, and was Walter Travis's home base prior to 1900. Its membership roster was a virtual "Who's Who of New York Society," including among

(201

With the original Oakland clubhouse sitting high on the hill, Harry Vardon tees off, with Walter Travis (right) watching (circa 1900). (American Golfer)

others H.P. Whitney, W.K. Vanderbilt, and Bernard Baruch.

Oakland's second clubhouse became known affectionately as "Golfer's Paradise," and one day would serve as the administration building for Queensboro Community College, which now occupies a portion of the club's property. Oakland was twice cursed, actually—the Clearview Expressway also passed through its old grounds.

Next in line was the exclusive Deepdale Golf Club, whose course sprawled northward from the shores of Lake Success into the path of the new highway. Deepdale was founded in the 1920s by William K. Vanderbilt Jr. who decided to convert some of the rolling acres around his summer estate into a very private golf course. Indeed, Vanderbilt's course was one of just a handful that Charles B. Macdonald gave his personal attention to after 1917.

When the roadway for the Long Island Expressway cut across the northern part of the golf course in 1954, Deepdale moved to its present location slightly to the east and on the northern side of the highway, where architect L.S. "Dick" Wilson built a challenging new course that cascaded down from the hillside to the service road for the Expressway. Deepdale's original Spanish-style stucco clubhouse

A GOLFING SCENE AT OAKLAND.

(Golf Illustrated)

DIAGRAM OF
OAKLAND GOLF
CLUB LINKS
LOCATED AT
BAYSIDE, L.I.

541 YARDS — 6
311 YARDS — 5
4
263 YARDS
13
464 YARDS — 12
585 YARDS — 14
510 YARDS — 3
16
413
316 YARDS
17
325 YARDS
2
163 YARDS
15
1
228 YARDS
POND
218 YARDS
18
331 YARDS — 7
11
385
8
140 YARDS
10
344 YARDS
368 YARDS
9
TREES
CLUB HOUSE

(203

ABOVE: DIAGRAM OF THE OAKLAND COURSE
IN 1915. *(New York Telegram)*

LOOKING ACROSS LAKE SUCCESS TOWARD
THE 18TH HOLE ON THE ORIGINAL
DEEPDALE COURSE. *(American Golfer)*

remains to this day as home base for the village-operated Lake Success Country Club, which took over the property in 1954. The Lake Success club had the old golf course completely revised to fit the restricted acreage. Just the last two holes from the original Macdonald design remain, playing as the present seventh and ninth holes. Also preserved is the wall mural in the dining room depicting the entire 18-hole Macdonald layout.

A few years later, in 1962, Deepdale welcomed a new neighbor to its east (also north of the Long Island Expressway), the transplanted North Hills Country Club and its new Robert Trent Jones-designed golf course. North Hills was forced to move from its former home in Douglaston, just south of the Expressway, by rising New York City real estate taxes. That property was sold partly to Cathedral College, but mostly to the city. Long Island golf architect Frank Duane refashioned its old course, after some loss of land, into the city-operated Douglaston course. The original course in Douglaston was designed and built by the father-son team of William Tucker Sr. and Jr. who also were known for building the field at Yankee Stadium.

North Hills started life as the Belleclaire Country Club of Bayside, which was established in 1919 just to the west of the Oakland Golf Club between Horace Harding Boulevard, Bell Boulevard, and Rocky Hill Road. The club's property was sold for real estate development in 1927, and a nucleus of 126 members moved on to found North Hills later that same year. Those who stayed behind reorganized as Old Belleclaire, which did not survive the Depression.

According to a photograph and caption appearing in *Golf Illustrated* in 1925, Belleclaire staged a 9-hole "match" between a golfer, a baseball player, an angler, and an archer, each using the implements of his own sport. Lou Gehrig won the contest, edging Leo Diegel by one "stroke." Details of the rules and scoring system used did not accompany the photo. The best-known hole at Belleclaire was the 18th, which was considered one of the most picturesque water holes on Long Island. It was a 150-yard par 3 with a pond extending from immediately in front of the tee all the way to the edge of the green.

In the early 1950s, Parks Commissioner Robert Moses condemned the Meadow Brook Hunt Club's property so that a parkway could be built connecting the mid-Nassau region with the beaches on the south shore of Long Island. In honor of the club it displaced, that roadway was called the Meadowbrook Parkway.

In 1953, ground was broken at the club's new home in Jericho, land where the club's hunters once pursued their pastime. Noted architect L.S. "Dick" Wilson was contracted to build a new course of championship proportions, concurrently with

(205

The Belleclaire match between golfer
Leo Diegel, baseball star Lou Gehrig of
the Yankees, an angler, and an archer.
(Golf Illustrated)

his work at Deepdale. Wilson had the new Meadow Brook ready for play in 1955. It immediately drew rave reviews, with some observers touting it as the best course in the United States. Certainly, the greens were the country's largest then, and may still be today.

The eighth is Meadow Brook's centerpiece, a 615-yard par 5 that doglegs left, then right. No less an authority than Byron Nelson called it the best extra-long par 5 in the country. Nelson's opinion was based on the various hazards the hole presents, above and beyond its enormous length. Three bunkers guard the first bend, yet the drive must flirt dangerously close to them so that the second shot can clear the tree line and bunker that protect the second dogleg. The green has been reached in two shots only three times, twice in casual play (George Burns and Randy Cavanaugh with help of a tailwind) and once in competition by Jimmy Wright in the 1974 Met PGA Championship without any aid of the wind.

26

A Second Life For The Gold Coast Mansions

The glitter of the Gold Coast Era coincided with the Roaring Twenties, and dimmed with the Depression. Not only did the excitement of the nightly social life disappear, but over time many of the mansions that witnessed the gala parties were abandoned and fell into disrepair. This is the story of several of those estates that found a second life as golf and country clubs.

The first is Oheka, the estate of Otto Herman Kahn, a man of enormous wealth, charm, and generosity. Yet the German-born banker, financier, railroad baron, philanthropist, and patron of the arts always seemed to be on the outside, looking in. For Otto Kahn was Jewish, at a time when it was not fashionable for Christians and Jews to intermingle socially. Kahn took up residence in Manhattan in 1913, and quickly came to be known as "The King of New York." He sponsored many struggling actors and theatrical groups, and his $2 million helped establish the Metropolitan Opera.

In 1914, Kahn paid more than $1 million to purchase a 443-acre tract of land in Cold Spring Harbor. The result was "Oheka" (a name derived from the first letters of his name), the second largest private residence in the United States (only Biltmore in Asheville, North Carolina, was larger). Oheka was built on the highest point of Long Island, a man-made mountain that took two years to "grow" and provide a beautiful vista of Long Island Sound. The 127-room mansion, encompassing 109,000 square feet, featured a ballroom with a 60-foot ceiling and a grand dining

hall that could seat up to 250 guests. Designed by the noted architect William Adams Delano, Oheka was completed in 1919.

Kahn, his wife, and five children moved into Oheka in 1919, just in time for the Roaring Twenties. The Long Island Railroad built its Cold Spring Harbor station near Oheka to accommodate Kahn's numerous guests. His parties were frequent and elegant. One became a memorable part of the "Gold Coast" legend, the result of the anti-Semitism Kahn faced all his life. He had been excluded from the greatest of all North Shore parties, the one given by Clarence Mackay to honor the Prince of Wales, and so decided to "get even." He let it be known that a person of the highest nobility would be a guest at Oheka, and that he planned to honor him with a gala party. Everyone who was anyone vied for invitations, four "grand dames" going so far as to have their husbands deliver introductory speeches for the unrevealed guest of honor. After the last of these had concluded, in marched a chimpanzee, nattily clad in a tuxedo, to take the seat of honor!

OPPOSITE PAGE: OTTO KAHN.
(Golf Illustrated)

ABOVE: OHEKA, THE OTTO KAHN ESTATE, NOW COLD SPRING COUNTRY CLUB. *(Nassau County Museum at Long Island Studies Institute)*

(207

After being denied membership at a prominent local club, Kahn decided to build a private course on his estate. To this end, he engaged Seth Raynor to build a championship course complete with replicas of famous British holes in the Macdonald-Raynor tradition. Thus was born the Oheka Country Club. As legend tells us, Kahn would watch his guests and local professionals play, note where their drives tended to land, and overnight a bunker would appear on that spot!

Otto Kahn died of a massive heart attack in 1934 at age 67. Oheka has since experienced a troubled and uncertain existence. Not so the golf course. In 1947, a group of 15 men, many of them former members of the defunct Willow Brook Country Club in Lynbrook, banded together as the Cold Spring Country Club and purchased the golf course. The course has undergone one major change, when Robert Trent Jones built the present fifth and sixth holes, replacing two short par 4s that ran to and from the mansion.

Next came the Pine Hollow Country Club, formed in 1955 when a small syndicate purchased the 133-acre estate of Consuelo Vanderbilt Balsan, a great-granddaughter of Cornelius Vanderbilt, intending to convert it into a golfing utopia, a luxurious private club. It was one of the first of the great estates to be fully air-conditioned, and was adorned with marble fireplaces, sculptured gold bronze dolphins for sink faucets, and had a direct phone line to Europe. On the grounds were a swimming pool, tennis courts, and formal gardens. The syndicate engaged William Mitchell to build a championship golf course, the first of several he would design on Long Island. It would soon host the first PGA Tour event ever held on Long Island.

The story of the Old Westbury Golf & Country Club goes back prior to the turn of the century when William C. Whitney purchased the property, which was bordered on the north by Northern Boulevard, and engaged the architectural firm of McKinney & (Stanford) White to design and build his estate, which was completed in 1887. When the senior Whitney died in 1904, the estate passed on to his son Harry Payne Whitney, and "The Manse" became a favorite gathering place for the elite of turfdom and society. One of the leading polo players of his day, Whitney housed his own string of polo ponies on the grounds, and maintained living quarters for his polo-playing guests in an adjacent building. At the same time, the Whitney racing stable enjoyed its halcyon era, racing eleven champions, including (among others) Equipoise, Top Flight, and Regret, the latter a filly that won the 1915 Kentucky Derby.

H.P. Whitney died in 1930, and after his widow passed away in 1942, their son Cornelius Vanderbilt "Sonny" Whitney inherited the estate. Sonny immediately demolished the old mansion, the remains of which are now buried beneath the lake fronting the final green of the "All Woods" nine. That same year (1942), he built the mansion that has become the Old Westbury clubhouse. The Dutch Colonial structure included 30 rooms, a wine cellar, and a swimming pool, with hi-fi music piped into every room. Whitney and his wife, the former Eleanor Searle, lived on the family estate until 1958, when they divorced. In 1960 Whitney sold the 530-acre estate through an intermediary who quickly turned around and sold 200 acres, including the mansion house, the tennis house, the polo buildings, the stables, and the tower, to the newly formed Old Westbury Golf & Country Club. Much of the remaining acreage became the New York Institute of Technology.

Old Westbury was created as a nonsectarian country club, a noble attempt to overcome racial and religious prejudice that was noted in the Congressional Record and featured in a story in Newsweek. The 27-hole Old Westbury golf course, designed by William Mitchell. opened for play on July 4, 1962.

Like Old Westbury, the Mill River Club was formed to foster brotherhood. Its founder, William S. Roach, set out with the explicit purpose of being different, or diverse. Mill River was conceived as a "truly balanced, non-sectarian club."

Roach set his plans in motion in 1964 after purchasing Appledore, the former "Gold Coast" estate of Henry and Eleanor Davison located one mile north of Northern Boulevard, with Planting Fields Arboretum immediately to the north and the campus of SUNY Old Westbury to the west. Davison died in 1961 and his widow, faced with the prospect of selling her 126-acre home to real estate developers and seeing it subdivided, happily accepted Roach's offer. Mrs. Davison felt that she could live with the fact that her grounds would be maintained as a beautiful golf course and particularly that her Normandy Tudor mansion would be preserved as a clubhouse. For his golf course, Roach turned to a relative unknown named Gerald Roby, who had spent his career in golf course architecture working with William Mitchell. Roby did the Mill River job for his old friend Roach, then retired. The new club and golf course were ready for their grand opening on May 29, 1965. Mill River also was cited in the Congressional Record for its non-sectarian policies.

Straddling Northern Boulevard in Muttontown were nearly identical mansions owned by a pair of sisters and their husbands. Both found new life as country clubs. The one to the south became Charter Oaks, later called Fox Run, which is now defunct. To the north lay The Chimneys, the 44-room red brick Georgian mansion of Howard Brokaw, who had made his fortune manufacturing U.S. Army uniforms during World War I. The house possessed 13 chimneys servicing 26 fireplaces, hence its name. The property eventually was purchased by the newly-formed Muttontown Club, which unveiled its Alfred Tull-designed golf course in 1962.

James Burden gained his wealth from the iron business, and converted a dairy farm into his estate which he called Woodside. He lived in a brick and stone Georgian manor designed by William Adams Delano, where he entertained such house guests as President Franklin D. Roosevelt and the Prince of Wales. Woodside was sold to the Woodcrest Country Club, which unveiled its William Mitchell-designed golf course in 1963.

BELOW: APPLEDORE, NOW MILL RIVER CLUB. *(Mill River Club)*

BOTTOM: WOODSIDE, THE JAMES BURDEN MANSION THAT IS NOW WOODCREST COUNTRY CLUB. *(Nassau County Museum at Long Island Studies Institute)*

27

The Professional Tours Visit

Prior to World War II, the Metropolitan Open Championship was an annual stop on what then constituted the "tour." Indeed, along with the U.S. Open, PGA Championship, Western Open, and North & South Open, it was considered one of the "majors" among the tour events. The event rotated between clubs on Long Island, in New Jersey and Westchester, and occasionally in Connecticut or Staten Island. It was played 10 times on Long Island between the years 1913-1939. The Met Open continues to be contested annually, every three years on Long Island.

Elmer Ward, president of the Palm Beach Company, a clothing manufacturer that was one of golf's first corporate sponsors, conceived the Palm Beach Round Robin in 1938. The inaugural edition that year was played in Cincinnati, where the clothes were made. All contestants were expected to wear Palm Beach slacks during the tournament. The Round Robin was considered a hybrid event on the Tour, because its format restricted the field to just 15 (later 16) of the season's leading players and its dates coincided with the British Open, an open week on the Tour schedule. The Palm Beach had a unique, albeit complicated, scoring system. Originally. the 15 players competed in threesomes over seven rounds, with each playing both his rivals simultaneously at match play. Consequently, each contestant met each of the other 14 players, and the overall winner was determined by the total count of "pluses" and "minuses" (holes won or lost) accumulated.

The first New York area Round Robin was played on Long Island, at Fresh

OLIN DUTRA, WINNER OF THE 1932 MET OPEN AT LIDO. (*American Golfer*)

Meadow, in 1939. The $5,000 purse was one of the largest offered on the Tour that year. "Light Horse" Harry Cooper won the $1,000 first prize over a field that included Sam Snead, Ben Hogan, Walter Hagen, and Craig Wood, although the 74 he shot in the seventh and final round almost cost him his entire 14-point lead. He won by just two points.

The 1940 renewal was a promoter's dream, with Ben Hogan and Sam Snead finishing first and second. Paul Runyan won in 1941, the third consecutive year the event was held at Fresh Meadow.

After a hiatus during World War II, the Round Robin returned in 1946 at Winged Foot. The format was changed in 1948 when the field of 16 played just five rounds in foursomes, their medal scores determining their points for each match. The Palm Beach returned to Long Island in 1953 at Meadow Brook, providing that club with its last hurrah before the Meadowbrook Parkway was built through the golf course. Cary Middlecoff won at Meadow Brook in 1953, and Sam Snead was an overwhelming winner in 1954 with 62 points to his nearest rival's 26. At Deepdale in 1955, Snead won his fourth (of five) Round Robin, and established a new course record 65 in the final round (he missed an 18-inch putt on the 18th hole).

In late June of 1958, Pine Hollow hosted the Pepsi-Boys Club Open, the first sanctioned PGA Tour event held on Long Island. With a purse of $60,000, underwritten entirely by Pepsi (for one year only), it was the richest event on that year's Tour calendar, with the proceeds benefiting the Boys Club of New York.

Arnold Palmer won the tournament in rather unusual style for him. The Masters champ led all the way, with rounds of 66-69-67-71=273, 11 under par. His first-round score established a new record for the course. The key moments for Palmer were an eagle two on the third hole and hitting the 575-yard 13th hole with a drive and 4-wood. George Bayer drove the ninth green, only to three-putt.

U.S. Open champion Tommy Bolt created a stir when he withdrew from the tournament in a fit of temper after five-putting the ninth green. According to the *New York Times*:

"The champion had scored a 42 for nine holes, including a 7

(211

The Met Open 1908-1940

YEAR	SITE	WINNER
1913	Salisbury Links	Alex Smith
1916	Garden City Golf	Walter Hagen
1919	North Shore	Walter Hagen
1922	Lido	Marty O'Loughlin
1924	Engineers	Mike Brady
1926	Salisbury CC	Macdonald Smith
1929	Lido	Bill Mehlhorn
1932	Lido	Olin Dutra
1935	Lakeville	Henry Picard
1938	Fresh Meadow	Jimmy Hines

Palm Beach Round Robin

1939	Fresh Meadow	Harry Cooper
1940	Fresh Meadow	Ben Hogan
1941	Fresh Meadow	Paul Runyan
1953	Meadow Brook	Cary Middlecoff
1954	Meadow Brook	Sam Snead
1955	Deepdale	Sam Snead

at the par-4 ninth. He missed a putt for a birdie 3 there, then jabbed and knocked the ball back and forth back-handed until he holed out."

Bolt was serving a year's probation at the time, and had walked out on the Piping Rock Pro-Am earlier in the week after playing five holes, claiming that he was weary. He was fined $500 for his actions, which were considered detrimental to golf. Jay Hebert finished second behind Palmer, with Don Fairfield third and Sam Snead in a tie for fourth. Fairfield drew attention for his play during the second round in the following article:

> *"Fairfield had his own way of cracking par. He was on the wrong fairway purposely at four holes. 'A short cut,' he said, 'I had a lot of 40- and 50-footers that went in,' he added."*

The first edition of the LPGA Tour's Western Union International Classic was held at North Hills in 1978. Judy Rankin shot a nine-under-par 283 to win, while pretournament favorite Nancy Lopez stumbled at the start, four-putting the treacherous second green. The final four editions of the Western Union were held at Meadow Brook between 1979 and 1982. As the fourth round started in 1979, three players—Judy Rankin, Donna Caponi, and Beth Daniel—were tied at one under par. Daniel, a rookie on the Tour following a highly impressive amateur career, birdied three of the first five holes in quest of her first professional victory—before heavy rain and gusty wind postponed the party. Although several players had already finished their rounds, the final round was postponed and replayed the next day.

Daniel started almost as well the next day, with two birdies on the first four holes, only to give it all back on the par-3 sixth hole where her tee shot came to rest against the back rim of a bunker. At this point she was even with Judy Rankin, who was playing behind her. Daniel lost the tournament on the 10th and 11th holes with a three-putt par and a bogey, then Rankin gave herself a cushion with a birdie 4 on the double-dogleg 17th. Her final-round 70 gave her a two-shot victory, her first since winning the inaugural edition of the WUI in 1978.

Sally Little was in total command in 1980. Tied for the lead after each of the first two rounds, and leading by three strokes going into the final round, she survived a near-nightmare on the first hole with "one of the greatest shots I'll ever play in my life." The *New York Times* provides the details:

SAM SNEAD TEES OFF DURING THE 1953 PALM BEACH ROUND ROBIN TOURNAMENT. HE WOULD WIN THE EVENT IN THE TWO SUCCEEDING YEARS AT MEADOW BROOK. *(R.W. Miller Library)*

"Miss Little saved herself from serious trouble on the first hole, where her third shot landed in a left bunker. Her attempt to blast out sent the ball completely over the green and behind the bunker to the right of the green. That left her with a difficult shot to the pin, which was tucked up against the right bunker and far below her feet. But with a magnificent light-touch sand wedge off hardpan, she dropped the ball over the bunker to the green, a foot from the pin, and took a bogey 6."

A strong breeze picked up on the back nine, making the tight pin placements almost unapproachable, and Little responded, playing the links-like 10th through 13th holes one under par, then placed a 5-wood within 18 inches on the par-3 15th hole to assume a seven-stroke lead. Although stumbling to a double bogey-bogey finish, she shot 284 for a four-shot victory over Amy Alcott and Daniel.

Donna Caponi had a five-shot lead over Julie Stanger heading for the final nine in 1981, only to find trouble on the short, dogleg-left 14th hole, where she missed the fairway for the only time in the tournament. According to the *New York Times*:

(213

"Miss Caponi hit her drive into deep grass next to the bunker on a steep hill just over 100 yards from the green. She then hit a nine-iron while standing in the sand-bunker, and her ball ended up in another greenside bunker. She barely got out of that, chipped and needed two putts."

Western Union Classic		
1978	North Hills	Judy Rankin
1979	Meadow Brook	Judy Rankin
1980	Meadow Brook	Sally Little
1981	Meadow Brook	Donna Caponi
1982	Meadow Brook	Beth Daniel

When Stanger birdied that same hole, Caponi's lead was down to two shots, but she shrugged off the miscue and parred the final four holes to ensure her victory.

Beth Daniel turned in a 12-under par score of 276 in 1982 to make amends for 1979.

The total prize money for the event was $100,000 in 1979, then $125,000 the final three years.

The Senior Tour arrived at Meadow Brook in June of 1987 for the inaugural Northville Invitational. The tournament's name was changed to the Northville Long Island Classic in 1989. Northville continued its sponsorship through 1998, and in 1999 the tournament's title was changed to the Lightpath Long Island Classic, named for the telecommunications arm of Cablevision Systems Corporation.

Gary Player and Bruce Crampton tied after 72 holes in the first Northville, with scores of 278, 10 under par. Player won the play-off on the second extra hole, canning a 30-foot birdie putt. The first year was the only year the tournament was played over 72 holes. The present 54-hole format was adopted in 1988. The seniors

LEFT: GARY PLAYER'S WINNING PUTT IN 1998. *(Long Island Classic)*

OPPOSITE PAGE: LEE TREVINO WITH THE LONG ISLAND CLASSIC TROPHY IN 1995. *(Long Island Classic)*

Northville / Lightpath Long Island Classic	
1987	Gary Player
1988	Don Bies
1989	Butch Baird
1990	George Archer
1991	George Archer
1992	George Archer
1993	Ray Floyd
1994	Lee Trevino
1995	Lee Trevino
1996	John Bland
1997	Dana Quigley
1998	Gary Player
1999	Bruce Fleisher
2000	Bruce Fleisher
2001	Bobby Wadkins

had nothing but praise for Meadow Brook. Billy Casper, twice U.S. Open champion, called it "one of the greatest courses I've ever played," one that "could house a National Open easily." Another former Open winner, Gene Littler, termed it "a good, old-fashioned golf course." And Chi Chi Rodriguez remarked, "This is about the toughest course I've ever seen for seniors." With the pins placed in their championship positions on Sunday, only a handful of players were able to better par.

At the 1987 Northville, Butch Baird bet $50 to George Bayer's $10 that the unsuspecting Bayer couldn't two-putt from eight feet above the cup on the 18th green. Bayer knocked his putt 30 feet past the hole and off the green! In 1988, both Bobby Nichols and Ben Smith scored double eagles, the only instance of that feat in Senior PGA Tour history. Both carded 2s on the same hole, the 472-yard par-5 third hole.

The 1989 Northville will be remembered for its asterisk. Because of heavy rains in the days preceding the tournament, two greens (the ninth and 14th) were ruled unplayable. Consequently the golfers played just 16 holes each day—except the final day when a 17th hole was needed to settle a four-way tie among Butch Baird, Frank Beard, Don Bies, and Orville Moody, all of whom completed 48 holes at nine-under-par. Baird won the play-off with a 42-inch birdie putt after Beard

missed from the same distance.

When Lee Trevino won the 1995 Classic, it marked his 25th victory on the Senior Tour, placing him first on the all-time list of winners among the seniors. Scoring records were set during the 2000 Classic. Bruce Fleisher took advantage of a rain-softened course to establish a new course record 63 while en route to a tournament record 63-66-69=198 for 54 holes. Jim Dent equaled Fleisher's record with a second-round 63. In 2001, Bobby Wadkins won his Senior Tour debut at the Lightpath, shooting a final-round 68 that included a holed wedge shot for a double-eagle 2 at the third hole. Wadkins joined three others atop the leader board with a downhill 20-foot putt at the 16th hole, then won the tournament with a 10-foot downhill putt at the 18th hole. Ironically, Wadkins had not won in 712 starts on the PGA Tour.

Attendance at the Long Island Classic peaked at over 82,000 in 1994. Prize money has risen from $300,000 in 1987 ($100,000 to the winner) to $1,700,000 in 2001. Since 1989, the Classic has raised more than $2 million for Schneider Children's Hospital.

28

The Recent Shinnecock Opens

After an absence of 54 years, the U.S. Open returned to Long Island in 1986. The "host" was Shinnecock Hills, giving the world its first extended view of the course.

Shinnecock Hills' "modern" course was built in 1931, after Suffolk County decided to extend Route 27 (Sunrise Highway) through the Hamptons area. The proposed route cut right through the old course. The club purchased land north of the old course, and hired the prominent architectural team of Toomey & Flynn to design a completely new course. Built under the supervision of young Dick Wilson during 1928-1931, with a work crew that once again included several Shinnecock Indians, the course opened for play on July 1, 1931. A few holes from the old course were kept as part of the new course, most notably the "Redan" seventh, which was added by Charles Blair Macdonald in 1916. The course was called "the nearest thing in America to a British linksland course." While this may have been true in its earlier days, the course has now matured, and many of its holes more closely resemble those at Sunningdale near London than the seaside links of Scotland, England, or Ireland.

Located two miles from the Atlantic, and even closer to Peconic Bay to the north, Shinnecock Hills is usually buffeted by strong winds, with the prevailing breeze coming from the southwest off the Atlantic. The sandy terrain is dotted with nearly 150 bunkers, although on most holes these do not front the greens, giving the golfer the option of playing a run-up shot under the wind. Most of the putting surfaces are small, and many feature severe fall-offs to the sides or rear.

Above all else, Shinnecock Hills is a strong test of driving skill. The longer hitters must carry crests in the fairway and find the flat zones in the course's undulating, often turbulent, terrain. For the average player, just reaching the island fairways can be a challenge. Most tee shots must carry a sizable expanse of thick rough and bunkers. Many of the tees on the longer holes are elevated, offering the player a panoramic view of the hazards he must contend with en route to the green. Many of the holes appear to be straightaway at first glance, but must be played as a slight dogleg because the fairway twists and turns through the natural hazards, most notable of which are the fairway bunkers. Only five holes have a pronounced change of direction from tee to green. Finally, there is the rough—thick, clumpy, reed-like, often knee-high, capable of altering the path of the clubhead—lurking just off the often-narrow fairways, placing an even greater premium on accuracy off the tee. The course is, at one and the same time, an outstanding example of both the penal and strategic schools of golf course architecture.

A Glimpse at the Course

The long par-4 sixth hole (456 yards) is a rugged test, especially for the average player. The drive must carry a vast expanse of mounds, bunkers, and high rough that hide the fairway from view at the tee. The tree-lined fairway curves to the right, then bends around a pond some 50-75 yards short of the green. The average player most likely will be forced to play to the left (or short) of the pond, then must approach directly over the only greenside bunker. During the final two rounds of the 1986 Open, this hole, which plays against the prevailing wind, proved the most difficult on the course, the field averaging 4.37 strokes.

Once called the "Pond Hole," the sixth was the centerpiece of the new Shinnecock course when it opened in 1931. Dunes extended from tee to green along the right, but there was an "oasis of fairway" on that side that offered the better players the chance of getting home in two if they dared a 200-yard plus drive over a "mass of tumbling dunes" that preceded the target. It was this same characteristic that made the "Channel Hole" at Lido so famous.

The severe examination of golfing skills at Shinnecock Hills begins in earnest at the ninth tee, and continues throughout the back nine. The ninth hole bends left around a large hill (the hole's name, Ben Nevis, refers to a famous hill in Scotland), and the longer hitters must cut the corner to avoid driving through the fairway. From the drive zone the fairway rolls through a series of dramatic, wavelike undulations before reaching the foot of the elevated green. The embankment leading up to

the green is covered with rough and dotted with four bunkers. The green sits on a plateau in front of the clubhouse, well above the fairway—and seemingly unprotected!

The 11th is a superb little par 3 of 158 yards that requires a do-or-die shot to a tiny. heavily-bunkered, severely-contoured green. Four bunkers, set some 15 feet below the putting surface, guard the front and right side of the green. The putting surface features a mound at the left front, and falls off to the right and rear. A chip from beyond or to the left of the green easily may roll right through the putting surface. *Golf* magazine rated this hole among the 100 best in the country in 1986.

From its highly-elevated tee near former professional Charlie Thom's cottage, the 14th plays down into a valley, then up a tree-lined fairway that narrows as it approaches the green. The drive must be accurate, avoiding bunkers left and right at the bottom of the hill, and the second shot must be threaded through a very narrow entrance to a green set beyond four bunkers. Another of *Golf* magazine's best 100 holes in the country,

The 16th is a straightaway par 5 of 542 yards that doglegs twice around its fairway bunkering. The trap in the right rough of the drive zone appears dead center from the tee, forcing the drive to the left. From there the hole drops into a swale and curves around a nest of five bunkers on the left, with which the average player must contend on his second shot, especially when playing against the prevailing wind. The putting surface is protected up front and to the sides by five bunkers, and is separated from the fairway by a collar of rough, leaving little chance of rolling the ball onto the green.

Shinnecock Hills' finishing hole is a strong par 4 that doglegs twice to the left. The hole is tree-less, set in full view of the clubhouse, albeit in the shadows of the ninth. The tee shot must be played with a slight draw to avoid running through the fairway. The approach must carry an elbow of rough and traps, which creates the second dogleg, to reach a green that is protected by three bunkers.

Opposite page: The Pond Hole (#6) from the tee in 1930. *(Golf Illustrated)*

Top: Approach to the 15th hole in 1930. *(Golf Illustrated)*

Middle: The par-5 16th hole in 1930. *(Golf Illustrated)*

Bottom: The par-3 17th, then the eighth, in 1930. *(Golf Illustrated)*

Opposite page: The Pond Hole from behind the green looking at the water hazard. *(L.C. Lambrecht)*

Below: Raymond Floyd in 1986. *(United States Golf Association)*

The 1986 Open

The 1986 Open started with a flourish. A nor'easter, bringing rain, 20-30 mile per hour wind and temperatures in the high 40s, hit the area on Thursday, producing weather conditions that would have been considered awful by British Open standards. Bob Tway's even-par 70 led the field, but only 47 of the 156 contestants were able to shoot 75 or better.

The weather improved considerably for the last three rounds, and the scores dropped accordingly. After Saturday's third round, 14 players were clustered within four strokes of the lead. The 13th hole proved pivotal when Greg Norman flew the green with his approach from deep rough, and his pitch back from thick shrubbery ran through the putting surface, leading to a double-bogey 6. When fellow competitor Lee Trevino birdied after nearly holing his approach, Norman's three-stroke advantage had evaporated. Norman did regroup, and regained the lead after three rounds.

The final day belonged to Raymond Floyd, though. At 43, he became the oldest player to win the Open championship. His 75-68-70-66=279 left him the only player under par, and his 111 putts established a new Open record. He won $115,000.

Victory did not come easily, though, for it was not until the 14th hole that Floyd grabbed the lead for the first time. When the leaders reached the turn, nine players were deadlocked at one over par. Floyd started his charge with a downhill 18-foot birdie putt at the short 11th hole. Floyd was playing with the late Payne Stewart, who took the lead with a birdie at the 12th hole, only to bogey the 13th hole while Floyd birdied from four feet to get on even terms. Stewart also bogeyed the 14th hole to give Floyd the lead, one that Floyd padded with a 10-foot birdie putt on the 16th hole.

Floyd's subpar finish exceeded even his own hopes, as Dave Anderson reported in his *New York Times* column the following day:

> *"Don't do anything foolish....on the last nine holes of the U.S. Open, everybody comes back. There are more bogeys on the last nine holes of the U.S. Open than in any other tournament in God's creation."*

Mark Calcavecchia, Lanny Wadkins, and Chip Beck all shot their final round on Sunday in 65 strokes, establishing a new competitive course record for Shinnecock Hills. The latter pair then had to wait more than an hour to learn that their exploits had, in the final analysis, vaulted them into a tie for second place, two strokes behind Floyd.

The 1995 Open

One of the most memorable shots in U.S. Open history was played right here on Long Island. It was the 4-wood that Corey Pavin hit to the 18th green at Shinnecock Hills in 1995. Pavin's shot, a low draw that bounced short of the green and rolled right at the pin, finishing just 5 feet from the hole, didn't win the Open. Rather, it was an emphatic exclamation point. He missed the birdie putt, in fact, but already had a one-shot lead going to the final hole. Ultimately, he won by two strokes with a 72-hole score of even par 280.

Pavin entered the final round three strokes in arrears, trailing the likes of Greg Norman, Tom Lehman, Phil Mickelson, and Bob Tway, who had fought bravely through the gusty wind in Saturday's third round. Norman and Lehman led after three rounds at 1-under, one stroke better than the latter pair. Lehman charged into contention on Saturday with a brilliant 67, but bogeyed four of five holes Sunday, starting with the eighth, then sealed his fate with a double-bogey at the 16th. Norman hit just 13 greens over the weekend, but scrambled well on Saturday to stay in contention. Not so on Sunday, though, when crucial putts on the 12th and 13th holes rolled over the front lip of the hole. A bogey on the 17th in response to Pavin's shot to the 18th ended Norman's chance to win.

Bob Tway hit more greens than anyone else in the tournament, but his putter failed him. He bogeyed the last three holes when birdies were needed. Phil Mickelson started with a 68, but added two strokes per round to fall out of contention. Pavin, meanwhile, birdied the ninth, 12th, and 15th holes to take the lead. Just as important were two "saves" from five feet, one at the seventh hole, before he got rolling, the other at the 17th to preserve his lead. On the latter hole, he hit his 6-iron over the green and through the fringe, then came up short on his first putt.

After hitting his monumental 4-wood to the 18th, Pavin, in his own words:

> *"When I saw it come off the club face, I knew I hit a good shot, and it was low and it was starting to hit the right-center of the green drawing right at the pin, and I couldn't resist; I had to run up the hill and watch it. I wanted to see the ball land and see what it did."*

What it did was to secure Pavin's place in golf history as the winner of a Shinnecock Open.

222)

COREY PAVIN IN 1995. *(United States Golf Association)*

29

New Kids on the Block

For some two decades, there was little change to Long Island's golfing facilities, both public and private. That changed dramatically during the 1990s when Long Island's public course golfers were treated to a growth in outstanding facilities unheard of since the original four-course Bethpage complex was created in the mid 1930s. A number of highly acclaimed upscale courses have opened, designed by prominent architects, giving publinxers a taste of country club golf on a daily fee basis. At the same time, five outstanding new private clubs have been (or will soon be) born, one already nationally ranked and tested in championship competition.

Oyster Bay

The Town of Oyster Bay which opened its Tom Fazio-designed Oyster Bay Town Course in Woodbury in 1989 provided the impetus for change. Soon thereafter, *Golf* magazine ranked the course among the country's Top 50 public layouts. The grounds at Oyster Bay have a "Gold Coast" history. The course lies on "Woodlands," a 121-acre estate just north of the Jericho Turnpike that was purchased in 1928 by Andrew Mellon and given to his daughter Alicia as a wedding gift. She and her husband, U.S. Ambassador to France David Bruce, used it as a summer retreat for many years. Architect William Adams Delano, who had served on the White House Architectural Committee, designed the 38-room, two-story Italian-style mansion.

It features a pro shop, men's and women's locker rooms, a grill room, and three dining rooms upstairs, each a converted bedroom. The grounds included numerous century-old trees, many of which were preserved for the golf course.

The original course design team consisted of Tom Fazio and his uncle, George Fazio, who died during the construction process. The Fazios called the site the best piece of property they ever had to work with. After George's death, the original routing of the course was almost completely discarded, and the eventual routing can be attributed to Tom.

Although the golf course opens up somewhat on the back nine, for the most part it is rather narrow and quite hilly in spots. Most of the greens are undulating, with an assortment of tiers, mounds, and ridges creating numerous interesting pin placements and tricky putting angles. Other memorable features of the course, and a Fazio trademark, are the long, sinewy, beautifully-sculpted bunker complexes along the fairways or fronting the greens.

The most talked-about hole at Oyster Bay is the fourth, although the final three holes deserve equal billing, combining to form one of the toughest finishes on Long Island. The fourth plays down into a hidden fairway, then turns 30 degrees to the right beyond the landing area and marches straight uphill to a green some 50 feet above the fairway. There is a large bunker complex along the right side of the fairway between the drive zone and green. The putting surface is set amidst mounds, and there are bunkers flanking the toughest pin placement on the upper left tier.

(225

Colonial Springs

With one exception, subsequent new facilities have inherited far less in terms of natural surroundings or elegant old buildings. Most of them have had to shape relatively barren, featureless terrain into interesting golf courses, often of the links style, and build new clubhouse facilities from the ground up.

The first of these to be unveiled was Colonial Springs in East Farmingdale, which opened in May 1995. The facility is the creation of Stephen Locke, who acquired 225 acres from the adjacent Pinelawn Cemetery property for the purpose, then engaged award-winning architect Arthur Hills to design three nines (The Pines, The Lake, and The Valley), any two of which in combination play to about 6,800 yards from the championship tees. The course was Hills's first in the Northeast. Hills converted land that was flat as a pancake into a natural feeling course that meanders through rolling terrain. The focal point of the layout is the 11-acre man-made

OYSTER BAY #18 *(Tony Wimpfheimer)*

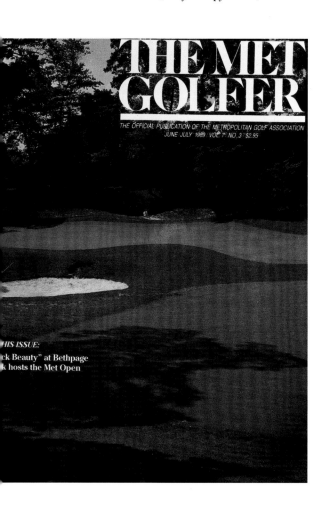

lake that is a major factor on the finishing holes on all three nines, hugging the left side of the left dogleg closer on the Lake nine and the right side of the Valley nine finisher from tee to green, and crosses from the right in front of the home green on the Pines nine.

One of the truly exceptional new holes on Long Island is the "Valley hole," the seventh on the Valley nine, a moderate-sized par 5 with a distinct Scottish flavor. The hole rolls through its own man-made valley, with a bunker tucked into the terrain left of the drive zone. Halfway, the trees disappear and the sides of the valley, seeded with fescue, become more evident. The severely undulating green is preceded right, then left, by bunkers.

Harbor Links

The Port Washington sand pit became a new publinx in 1998, called Harbor Links. This prime geological site certainly has as much historical significance as any other golf acreage on Long Island. For it was from the Port Washington sand pits that immigrants took 200 million tons of sand by boat to Manhattan to help build the city's skyscrapers, bridges, and subways.

The sand pit setting, overlooking Hempstead Harbor, is perhaps the most unusual home for a golf course on Long Island, a fact that architect Michael Hurdzan has used to great visual and strategic advantage. The course is built on a reclaimed sand mine, and a high bluff overlooks the western hemisphere of the property. The links style course, which stretches to 6,927 yards from the back tees, has a distinct western (some say moonlike) flavor. Perhaps the highlight of the course comes on the front nine, where both the fifth and sixth holes feature divided fairways. The significantly higher left side of the fifth fairway, if attained, provides a level view of the green. On the sixth, the right side occupies higher terrain on the straight line to the green, although closely flanked by trouble on the right.

Long Island National

In July 1999, Long Island National opened, thereby becoming the first Robert Trent Jones Jr. designed course on Long Island, nicely complementing his father's Montauk Downs and his brother Rees's Atlantic. The course, which is operated by American Golf, is located northeast of Riverhead in Long Island's wine country.

Long Island National is a dramatic example of what maximum architecture can

OPPOSITE PAGE: THE VALLEY HOLE (#7) AT COLONIAL SPRINGS. *(Kristin Quirin)*

PAGE 228: THE SPLIT FAIRWAY ON THE SIXTH HOLE AT HARBOR LINKS.*(James Krajicek)*

PAGE 229: LONG ISLAND NATIONAL, FROM BEHIND THE SECOND GREEN. *(James Krajicek)*

do with minimum land. The property was formerly the 152-acre potato farm of Adam Gatz, who had farmed the land since 1956. After Gatz retired in 1986, he and son Bill decided to convert the flat, featureless farmland into a golf course, although neither was an avid golfer. Enter Jones, whose crew shaped the deep layer of sand into natural appearing wind-swept dunes that seem to have been there forever. The fairways roll and tumble between the dunes, which are covered by high fescue grass. Jones calls the course "an amalgam of British and American golf."

Long Island National plays to 6,838 yards from the back tees. The first five holes have a distinctly Scottish feel, with the second and third holes sharing a common fairway at one point, St. Andrews style. The par-5 fourth hole "falls off a cliff" into a 15-foot-deep basin at the far reaches of the drive zone, eventually climbing back up to a dramatic two-tiered green. The course comes back to its Scottish beginnings for the final four holes. The 15th and 17th share a rolling 18,000 square-foot double green that is 100 yards deep.

TallGrass

TallGrass was the vision of Leonard Delalio Sr., whose family owned sod farms in Suffolk County. When one such farm, a 152-acre tract in Shoreham that was totally flat and featureless became nonproductive, Delalio decided to convert it into something beautiful—a golf course—rather than sell it for development into home sites.

To that end, Delalio engaged up-and-coming architect Gil Hanse, whose proposal for the property was by far the most appealing Delalio had seen. Hanse completely reshaped the land, creating elevation changes, including a man-made canyon (through which three holes play), hauled in tons of sand to create the network of waste bunkers that meander throughout the course, and planted the fescue grasses that gave the course its name. Hanse took two years to build the course, which opened in July 2000. *Golf Digest* has nominated TallGrass the best new public course of 2001.

Although not quite 6,600 yards from the tips, TallGrass is truly a gem of a thinking man's course. Avoiding the course's numerous hazards is the golfer's primary consideration. Among the par 3s are a "Redan" (#9) and a "Short" (#14), both staples on Macdonald-Raynor courses. The "Canyon" hole (#11) plays from an elevated tee into the canyon; its fairway is an island between waste bunkers that extend from tee to green.

The third hole is a 411-yard par 4 whose fairway tilts right to left toward a large

TALLGRASS, #3. *(Phil Arnold/Golfscape Photography)*

waste bunker that dominates the left side of the hole from 150 yards in—and snatches a good number of unwary long hitters. The green is elevated, with two bunkers well below the left side. The fifth hole plays only 375 yards, but the driver stays in the bag. A sandy barranca crosses the fairway 250 yards from the tee, and some well-placed tall grass borders the landing zone. Once across the barranca, the hole plays uphill to a deceptively bunkered green. In between, the par-3 fourth plays across some wild terrain reminiscent of Pine Valley—sand, wild grasses, and mounds.

Links at Shirley

When Mel Mindich was an engineering student in college, he chose designing a golf course as his senior project. Today the Scarsdale real estate developer/avid golfer has brought that dream to fruition as the Links at Shirley, which opened in May of 2000. Mindich purchased the 213-acre site, which is 1,000 yards from the ocean, in 1995. He envisioned an 18-hole golf course and a separate development of homes. When the latter proved impractical, a lighted nine-hole par-3 course replaced it. He engaged young Jeff Myers, who apprenticed under Gary Player, to convert the flat, waterless terrain dotted with scrub pine and oak trees, into a rolling linkslike course. Designed with an eye toward speed of play, the Links at Shirley was nominated by *Golf Digest* in its "Best New Public Course" category for 2001.

The sixth is the hardest driving hole at Shirley. The tee shot must reach the crest of a dramatic rise in the fairway so that the green can be seen on the approach, which is typically played downwind to a shallow green set precariously behind a deep pot bunker. The sixth green is part of a double green shared with the eighth hole, a shortish par-4 with a long, cavernous waste bunker perilously close along the right side. The par-3 seventh is played across a similar waste bunker.

Mindich calls the 17th the "Irish hole." It is a long bunkerless par-4 played into the wind, with water in front of the tee and grassy dunes to either side of the landing area reaching up to toss an errant drive back into play. Trees frame the hole on both sides. The par-5 13th adds a touch of Scotland, with a large "Spectacles" bunker crossing the fairway just inside 300 yards from the back tees, and a Redan-like green demanding a soft touch on the approach. The par-3 12th has the Pine Valley flavor, with a huge waste bunker extending tee to green.

LINKS AT SHIRLEY'S PAR 3 SEVENTH. (*James Krajicek*)

Stonebridge Golf Links Country Club

Stonebridge is the recreation of the old Hauppauge Country Club, which opened its doors in 1960. It is also the first course designed by George Bahto, who has parlayed his longtime interest in the golf courses of Macdonald, Raynor, and Banks into parallel second careers as author and golf course architect.

Industrialist Carl Lizza purchased Hauppauge in the late 1980s. Within a decade, Lizza conceived a metamorphosis of the 135-acre site, one that would include a brand new golf course and clubhouse and 105 home sites woven among the new golf holes. The facility was renamed for the four stone bridges that were to be built across the water hazard at the new fourth hole (to date, only one has been built).

Stonebridge's new 25,000 square foot clubhouse includes a pro shop, ZZ's Grill, a catering room seating 175 people, with a members' lounge and cocktail lounge on the second floor.

Bahto's golf course recreates features found on the great British golf courses, many of which were first introduced in this country at the National Golf Links. Stonebridge has five par 3s, including a watery, left-to-right Redan (#4), a Biarritz (#7) with a landing area and swale preceding the green, a Short (#15) with a deep horseshoe crater in the middle of the green, and a cleverly-bunkered Eden (#17).

There are few, if any, courses on Long Island with green complexes comparable to Stonebridge. Some of the more challenging are the Road hole (#5) green, which curves gracefully around a frontal pot bunker and at times leaves the golfer with an impossible two-putt; the Punchbowl (#12) green set above and around a Lion's Mouth bunker with similar impossible putting angles; and the three-tiered 18th green, where the left and right sides of the dance floor are raised and a valley runs through the middle.

The approach on the 16th hole must finish on the correct side of the hog's back that runs vertically through the center of the green, while the tee shot on the short par-4 sixth hole must deal with a principal's nose bunker in the center of the drive zone. The tighter left side of the fairway offers the better approach angle to a green that tilts significantly right to left.

The Village Club of Sands Point

The Guggenheim estate in Sands Point, overlooking Hempstead Harbor, has had a storied, albeit varied, existence over the years. It started life as host to Gold Coast

THE HORSESHOE-SHAPED BOWL IN THE 15TH GREEN AT STONEBRIDGE. *(James Krajicek)*

(235

society during the 1920s, was transformed into a corporate resort for IBM, and recently became a facility for residents of Sands Point. The estate was built by Isaac Guggenheim, then purchased by his brother Solomon in 1922 following the former's death. In 1924, Solomon, founder of the Guggenheim Museum in Manhattan, engaged Scottish golf professional William Mackie to lay out a nine-hole golf course on the property. The course was called Trillora. In 1953, IBM chairman Thomas Watson purchased the estate as a country club for IBM's New York area employees. The Beach House was built in 1954.

The property was sold to the Village of Sands Point in 1994, and since 1997 has been operated by the Village for its resident members. During the years 1999-2000, architect Tom Doak transformed the course into a completely new 18-hole layout. The course now includes two of Long Island's strongest par 4s and a stunning new par 3 on the harbor. The ninth is a left-dogleg that tumbles downhill to a green perched atop a knoll, with a phalanx of beautifully-sculpted bunkers well below its left side. The par-3 14th is set in a forest of old trees up above the water. It calls for a do-or-die shot over a vegetation-filled gully to reach the green. The cart ride from tee to green is perhaps Long Island's most exhilarating, culminating next to the beach club.

The tee shot at the 15th could be the most demanding on Long Island. The shot is hit through a chute in the trees, and the terrain on the left side of the hole falls down from well above the fairway, which tilts to the right toward the water hazard that comes into play in the drive zone and continues along the right side of the narrow fairway.

Great Rock

The most recent to open (on July 4, 2001), Great Rock in Wading River, has far more trees and elevation changes than the others, and takes full aesthetic advantage of the numerous rocks and boulders on the grounds – some are actually in play! The "great rock" itself sits boldly behind the tenth green.

Great Rock is the second public course built in recent years by the business partnership of Arthur and Mark Calace (father and son) and Tom Costello and local golf architect William "Buddy" Johnson (the first being Mill Pond, which opened in 1999). Johnson converted the 137 forested acres into a totally natural golf course that follows the often dramatic changes in elevation to great visual effect. Unlike its neighboring links courses, Great Rock's fairways are all lined with mature trees.

VILLAGE CLUB AT SANDS POINT, 14TH HOLE. *(Kristin Quirin)*

(237

Perhaps the signature hole at Great Rock is the medium-length par-4 eighth, which curves to the right, then plays abruptly uphill at the end to an elevated green, fronted by a deep bunker and framed behind by a manmade wall of boulders.

Just as picturesque are the par-5 seventh, which tumbles downhill through the drive zone, curves left, then climbs back uphill and to the right, with bunkers right, then left threatening the average player on his second shot; and the left-dogleg 17th, a par 4 that climbs steeply uphill on the approach shot.

Others

Several other top quality upscale public courses have opened in recent years, and merit mention here. Cherry Creek in Riverhead features a par-6 finishing hole and will soon add a second 18. Calverton Links has recently added a second nine that features one of Long Island's most challenging dance floors. Mill Pond in Medford has three nines, and one hole with a tree standing in the middle of the fairway.

These new courses join such standbys as Pine Hills, Rock Hill, Swan Lake, Middle Island, Spring Lake, Crab Meadow, Island's End, Sunken Meadow, and the Suffolk County courses at Bergen Point, Indian Island, and West Sayville to give Long Islanders a wide variety of excellent public courses.

GREAT ROCK'S PAR 3 FIFTH HOLE. (*James Krajicek*)

PAGE 241: THE THIRD AT EAST HAMPTON, A CRENSHAW-COORE DESIGN, REMINDS THE GOLFER OF PINE VALLEY. (*L.C. Lambrecht*)

Atlantic Golf Club

Long Island's private sector has had five additions in recent years, two of which, Friar's Head, a Ben Crenshaw-Bill Coore design just north of Riverhead overlooking the Sound, and Laurel Links, a Kelly Blake Moran design just east of Riverhead on the North Fork overlooking Peconic Bay, are scheduled to open in 2002.

The East Hampton Golf Club in Amagansett, a Crenshaw-Coore design that opened in 2001, features a front nine that reminds one of Pine Valley and a back side that has more of a linksland flavor.

The Bridge, a Rees Jones design on the site of the old Bridgehampton Raceway, was scheduled to open early in 2002. The course features dramatic elevation changes atypical of East End courses, and stunning views of Peconic Bay,

The forerunner of the new clubs is the Atlantic Golf Club, also in Bridgehampton, which already is ranked among the country's Top 100 by *Golf Digest*. Atlantic is the brainchild of Lowell Schulman, a Westchester builder and golf devotee who saw the need for another private club in the Hamptons and was able to overcome the social and ecological concerns of the summer residents who had vigorously resisted new developments, housing or otherwise. For newcomers to the East End, obtaining membership in a private club is nearly impossible.

Schulman made the commitment to developing a first-class club in August of 1988 and immediately found an ideal site, a 203-acre farm north of Bridgehampton. Its glacial topography, ridges and swales, wetlands, and a number of deep kettle ponds, with a distant view of the ocean four miles away, excited him. He quickly summoned architect Rees Jones, a traditionalist like Schulman, who quickly confirmed the latter's opinion that a world-class golf course could be built on the land—indeed, that many of the holes were already there, waiting to be found.

Atlantic opened for regular play in 1992—and to rave reviews, winning *Golf Digest*'s "Best New Private Course" award. Atlantic hosted the Met Open in 1995 and the U.S. Senior Amateur Championship in 1997. The clubhouse, a Jaque Robertson design in the traditional Long Island shingled style with deep porches and dormers, opened a year later.

The golf course at Atlantic can be described as "linkslike." Most of the holes are framed by an endless array of knobs, mounds, and moguls, creating bowl-like settings. The greens are framed by mounding and moguls to accentuate the target, and for the most part feature subtle rolls rather than bold contours. Most of the greens are protected by large bunkers that take away half the entrance, creating a "dogleg" effect on the approaches, protect most of the greens. From the appropriate side of the fairway, though, the bump and run approach under the wind can usually be employed.

The 13th hole is Atlantic's conversation piece, a par 5 that calls for a drive of 200 yards over a forested gully, then quickly turns to the left around four bunkers. The green is set above a large, deep bunker across its left front.

The 90-degree right-dogleg 14th hole calls for extreme precision off the tee with out-of-bounds along the left side of the drive zone and two large bunker complexes set in deep rough to the right of the turn of the tumbling fairway. The approach to the green must carry a stretch of rough and negotiate a narrow entrance between rough and mounds left and a huge bunker to the right.

The fifth is an imposing par 4, Atlantic's most demanding driving hole. It curves gradually to the right, with a long, sinewy bunker guarding the angled entrance to the fairway, which is framed by high mounding along its left side and preceded by a long carry over rough. The back-to-front green is lightly bunkered, but by the time the average golfer gets there, into the prevailing breeze, he has earned the respite.

242)

LEFT: THE DOWNHILL 13TH AT THE BRIDGE,
WHICH OFFERS DRAMATIC VIEWS OF
PECONIC BAY. THE COURSE WAS DESIGNED
BY REES JONES AND OPENED IN 2002. *(L.C.
Lambrecht)*

RIGHT: THE OPENING HOLE AT ATLANTIC
GOLF CLUB, ALSO A REES JONES DESIGN. IT
HOSTED THE 1997 U.S. SENIOR AMATEUR
CHAMPIONSHIP. *(L.C. Lambrecht)*

30

From Ragged Monster to the Open

In November of 1996 the United States Golf Association announced that the 2002 U.S. Open would be played on the Black Course at Bethpage State Park. It would be an historic event, the first U.S. Open ever to be played on a truly public golf course. The USGA believes that it will also be the biggest Open in history, and anticipates the sale of 42,500 admission tickets daily. It quickly recruited 4,500 volunteers from the local community, most of them public golfers, to help run the event. This will, indeed, be "Every Man's" Open.

It would be no simple task to convert this heavily utilized public facility into a U.S. Open site, but the New York State Parks Department, headed by Bernadette Castro, was ready for the challenge. A new 4,000 square foot golf shop was opened in the spring of 1999, costing $1.5 million. Another $4 million of private funds was used to overhaul the clubhouse. The locker rooms were renovated, a new restaurant and sports bar were built. New brick paths were built around the clubhouse, and new cart paths installed on the other four courses (carts are not allowed on the Black Course). According to General Manager Dave Catalano, the coming of the Open simply accelerated the state's long-range plan for Bethpage.

The Black Course, obviously, has been the principal focus, and course superintendent Craig Currier and his crew have done a magnificent job bringing a somewhat ragged public golf course up to the conditioning standards of some of the country's greatest private courses. The USGA provided $3 million to make the transformation possible, and golf architect Rees Jones, a second-generation "Open Doctor," offered his services as a favor to the state. Jones's task was to restore the course to its original Tillinghast design, and his main focus was on the many massive bunkers that give the course its character—and reputation. He also removed some trees that had grown beyond Tillinghast's strategic plan, repaired some worn grasses around the greens, but didn't alter the greens themselves. Many Bethpage regulars wonder how those greens will stand up to the best golfers in the world, given their very mild contours. The greens are quite small in size, and severely bunkered, and many predict there will be as many "sandies" and one-putt "saves" as there will be birdies.

This is not the first restoration the Black Course has undergone in recent years. When New York State took over the operation in 1975, maintenance budgets were slashed drastically, and the condition of all five Bethpage courses suffered. The Black Course fell into disfavor with the national evaluators, and even was dropped from Golf Digest's ranking of the 50 best public courses in the country.

A change for the better came in 1982 when the Black Course underwent a six-month, $100,000 refurbishing. Bunkers were restored to their original shape and filled with new sand. A few new bunkers were added, and 3,000 young trees were planted. The other four courses followed suit in succeeding years, and by the fall of 1987, it was the Black's turn again, the course being closed for further embellishment and fine-tuning.

In the last three decades the Black course has been the site of several major regional championships, before and after the renovations. In 1972 Jimmy Wright put on one of his virtuoso performances, winning the New York State PGA by 11 strokes with a four-round total of 281, three under par. During that same tournament, Mal Galletta, Jr.'s 65 established the competitive course record. During the 1980s the reborn Black Course hosted the Metropolitan PGA Championship and the Long Island PGA Championship (twice).

At the same time, the Red Course became the permanent home for the Long Island Open, with the winning score often approaching 200 for three rounds—remarkable golf over what Bethpage regulars regard as a truly challenging Tillinghast gem.

The Met Open made its first-ever appearance on a public course in 1989, at Bethpage Black. What resulted was a blanket finish, with defending champ Bobby Heins edging amateur George Zahringer III of Deepdale in a three-hole aggregate play-off after the pair had tied at 210, with Bruce Zabriski and Piping Rock's Jim Albus one stroke in arrears. Zahringer led through most of the tournament with rounds of 67-69-74, but called a three-putt par at the 13th hole, followed by two bogeys, the turning point. Heins birdied the last hole from four feet to force the play-off, then won when Zahringer bogeyed the first and 17th holes.

Both players were impressed with the Black. Heins commented:

"I just love this course. It has everything that I saw in Scotland and Ireland and some distinctly American touches as well. It's one of the best."

And Zahringer, who was playing the course for the first time, called it:

"the best layout I've ever seen, public or private. There is a uniqueness at every hole. And it's gorgeous. You could certainly play any national event here, without question."

Heins (73-67-70=210) and Zabriski (70-72-69=211) returned to the Black Course for the 1990 New York State Open, but the real story centered around Doug Miller, assistant pro at Pine Hollow. Miller fired an opening round 66, one over the course record, despite a two-stroke penalty for "loss of caddie." After a three-hour rain delay, Miller's caddie was a few minutes late returning to the third tee, causing a delay in play. The penalty proved quite costly in retrospect, when Miller missed a five-footer on the final green to finish one stroke behind Heins at 211.

Since 1996, the New York State Open has made Bethpage Black its home course, and all six winners have represented Long Island clubs. The list of winners includes Rick Hartmann then of Fresh Meadow, Mark Brown of Tam O'Shanter, John Nieporte of North Hills, and P.J. Cowan, a three-time winner representing at different times Montauk Downs and Eisenhower Park.

As a final preview for the 2002 U.S. Open, the Met Open returned to the Black Course in August 2001, and the course played at 7,289 yards (3,539-3,750 — par 70) for the championship. Once again, history was made, and records were challenged.

The record-seeker was Rick Hartman of Atlantic, who fired a course-record-equaling 65 in the second round to assume a four-stroke lead at 69-65=134. But it was amateur Johnson Wagner who rewrote the history books. Just two weeks prior, the 21-year-old senior at Virginia Tech shed a cloak of anonymity by winning the Met Amateur. At Bethpage, he fired a third-round 66 to erase a six-stroke deficit and win by three over Hartman, who finished with a 75. Wagner thereby became the fifth amateur to win the Met Open, and the second to win both the Met Open and Met Amateur in the same season.

OPPOSITE PAGE: BETHPAGE 1ST – THE VIEW TO THE GREEN FOR THE PLAYER'S SECOND SHOT TO THE OPENING HOLE AT BETHPAGE BLACK, WITH THE HOLE PLAYING 430 YARDS. *(L.C. Lambrecht)*

PAGE 248: BETHPAGE 2ND – THE HOLE PLAYS ONLY 387 YARDS BUT HERE, LOOKING FROM BEHIND THE GREEN TO THE FAIRWAY, THE PLAYER'S APPROACH SHOT MUST BE PLAYED UPHILL ABOUT 40 YARDS TO A BLIND GREEN. *(L.C. Lambrecht)*

PAGE 249: BETHPAGE 3RD – A SOLID PAR 3 OF 210 YARDS REQUIRES PLAYERS TO PLAY TO THE FRONT RIGHT OF THE GREEN, WITH THE MOST DIFFICULT HOLE LOCATION TUCKED ON THE LEFT SIDE BEHIND THE GREENSIDE BUNKERS. *(L.C. Lambrecht)*

PAGE 250: BETHPAGE 4TH – A SPECTACULAR PAR-5 AS THE DRIVE IS PLAYED TO A RISING FAIRWAY. *(L.C. Lambrecht)*

PAGE 251: BETHPAGE 4TH – THE SECOND SHOT MUST BE PLAYED OVER A MASSIVE BUNKER TO AN ELEVATED FAIRWAY WITH THE GREEN IN THE DISTANCE ALSO ELEVATED AND WELL PROTECTED BY ANOTHER SET OF HUGE BUNKERS. *(L.C. Lambrecht)*

The Black Course, Hole by Hole

From its championship markers, the Black can be stretched to 7,295 yards with a par of 70, long enough to challenge even the best Tour players. But the course plays tougher than that because the greens, as a rule, are relatively small and tightly bunkered. Consequently, the Black provides a stern test of long-iron play, not to mention accuracy from the tee to find the ideal position on the tree-lined fairways from which to attack the flag on the approach shot.

If any one feature gives the course its character, though, it is the bunkering. No less than eight greens are so tightly protected that the golfer has virtually no entrance to work with, almost no chance to roll a shot onto the carpet, and consequently very little room for error. Three holes call for heroic drives over massive bunkers if the player wishes to have any kind of shot at the green. Add to this, thick rough dotted with bunkers and mounds—rough that would not seem out of place at Shinnecock Hills, the National, or Garden City Golf—and you have a severe test of U.S. Open quality masquerading as a public course. A sign at the first tee warns the unwary of the course's difficulty. Most of the lesser-skilled Bethpage regulars routinely play one of the other courses.

Hole #1 – Par 4, 430 yards:

The Black's opener starts from an elevated tee behind the clubhouse and plays to a relatively flat fairway that bends sharply to the right in the drive zone. Tall trees at the corner starting 230 yards from the tee dictate a drive to the left center of the fairway. The small green slopes toward its left front and is flanked by four sizable bunkers, three of these to the right.

Hole #2 – Par 4, 387 yards:

The second is a short par 4 that curves to the left through a tree-lined valley. Most long hitters will have to lay up off the tee, possibly with an iron, and will then face a semiblind approach to a tabletop green. One large bunker set 15 feet below the putting surface protects the left side of the green, but the approach shot more likely will have to fly over a series of bunkers across the right front.

Hole #3 – Par 3, 210 yards:

The third is a small par 3 played over a deep rough-filled "crater" to an elongated green. The front of the putting surface is bunkered, and a second trap to the left of the green gets its fair share of activity.

Hole #4 – Par 5, 522 yards:

The fourth is a classic short par-5 hole. From the new tee cut back into the woods, the drive is played

BETHPAGE 2ND

BETHPAGE 3RD

BETHPAGE 4TH

Bethpage 4th

THIS PAGE AND OPPOSITE: BETHPAGE 5TH

to a rising fairway, and must favor the left side to set up a reasonable chance of reaching the green in two. A nest of four bunkers edges out into the fairway from the left rough, poised to catch the slightest mistake in that direction on the tee shot. From that point the undulating fairway bends slightly to the left before reaching a huge cross bunker that is some 25 yards long and whose steep face takes the hole to a significantly higher level. The bunker is 150 yards from the green, and poses a definite threat—if only psychological—to the average player on his second shot. To reach the green in two requires a long iron or wood shot that floats in, feather-soft, over a huge, high-lipped frontal bunker, a danger that is rather mild compared to the hazards beyond the green—a steep drop into an old quarry that is filled with sand and rough, from which few are able to escape with their par intact. The more conservative player may choose to lay up short of the green to the far right side of the fairway, a position from which a short pitch to a relatively open green can be played. This hole was an engineering wonder, carved out of a glacial hogback totally devoid of top soil.

Hole #5 – Par 4, 455 yards:

The fifth hole is one of the great par 4s in the country, according to *Golf* magazine's 1986 survey. The tee is elevated, and the drive must carry a small rough-infested hill and a huge bunker set at a diagonal to the tee. The player can bite off as much of the bunker as he pleases, but unless he decides to "go for it all," a carry of at least 230 yards, he is not likely to have a reasonable shot at the green. The hole bends slightly to the left—a dogleg more evident when the drive is played to the left—and rises some 30 feet in its last 50 yards to a saucer-like green totally surrounded by rough and three huge bunkers. The fifth is rated the number 1 handicap hole on the Black.

Hole #6 – Par 4, 411 yards:

The sixth is another superb two-shotter. The drive is played over a steep ridge to a fairway that bends around two meandering bunkers set in mounds at the left corner, but which actually are on the direct line to the green. Many long hitters will attempt to carry these bunkers, but have a small target because the fairway dips quite sharply not far beyond them. The average hitter choosing to play to the right off the tee must contend with a hidden bunker lurking just off the fairway. The approach is played downhill to a green nearly surrounded by four bunkers.

Hole #7 – Par 4, 484 yards:

The seventh hole bends sharply to the right in the drive zone, with a line of trees quite close at the corner. The tee shot is further complicated by a massive bunker some 150 yards long set diagonally to the fairway, once again tempting the player to bite off as much as he dares. At its far right corner

PAGE 252: BETHPAGE 5TH, THE BUNKER HERE IS SET AT A DIAGONAL TO THE TEE AND THE PLAYERS WILL BE AT RISK DEPENDING UPON HOW MUCH OF THE BUNKER THEY CUT OFF. THE SECOND SHOT IS TO AN UPHILL GREEN, 30 FEET ABOVE THE FAIRWAY. *(L.C. Lambrecht)*

PAGE 253: BETHPAGE 5TH GREEN – FROM BEHIND THE GREEN, ONE CAN SEE THE DIFFICULTY WITH CARRYING THE SHOT ALL THE WAY TO THE GREEN OF THE MONSTROUS 455 YARD UPHILL PAR 4. *(L.C. Lambrecht)*

OPPOSITE PAGE: BETHPAGE 6TH – A BEAUTIFUL SETTING FOR THE SECOND SHOT INTO THIS DOWNHILL PAR-4. SHORT RIGHT AND LONG CAN BE DEADLY. *(L.C. Lambrecht)*

BETHPAGE 6TH

256)

BETHPAGE 7TH

the carry is well over 220 yards from the championship tee. Once the fairway is reached, the hole is fairly routine, proceeding along its tree-lined path to a green bunkered at its front corners, the trap at the right having a rather severe lip. A pair of fairway bunkers along the way, one to either side, may catch an errant second shot.

Hole #8 – Par 3, 220 yards:
The eighth hole is a nice adaptation of the 14th at Pine Valley. From a tee 90 feet above the green, the player must traverse an unkempt stretch of severe rough and two artificial ponds— one in front of the green, the other to the left—before reaching the safety of a putting surface that tilts from back to front. A shallow bunker behind the green catches many an overclubbed tee shot, while a steep hillock to the right can be used to bank a shot onto the green.

Hole #9 – Par 4, 420 yards:
The ninth plays from an elevated tee across some severe rough to a fairway crossed diagonally in the drive zone by a deep swale. The hole bends left at this point, with the forest line close on both sides, especially at the corner of the dogleg. The drive must carry to the top of the rise, beyond the swale, or the approach will be blind and played from a sidehill lie. Rough and three large bunkers tightly guard the green up front. The high lip of the middle bunker conceals the putting surface from view on the approach.

Hole #10 – Par 4, 489 yards:
From the tee, the 10th hole looks rather innocuous—long but relatively straight and flat. But miss the fairway to either side and you'll be in a mixture of deep rough, mounds, and bunkers more indigenous to Garden City Golf Club. The fairway falls into a deep swale just before the green, creating an "elevated" putting surface that is protected by large bunkers at its front corners.

Hole #11 – Par 4, 444 yards:
The 11th is more of the same. The penal rough, mounds, and bunkers extend from tee to green along both sides of the fairway. The drive is blind, played over a corner of the rough from a tee set below fairway level, behind the swale. The green, which pitches sharply from back to front in true Tillinghast style, is protected by extremely long bunkers on either side. These extend well out into the fairway and will catch the average player's hook or slice that falls short of its target.

(257

OPPOSITE PAGE: BETHPAGE 7TH – A LONGISH PAR-4 OF 484 YARDS, THE SECOND SHOT BECOMES EASIER AFTER A DIFFICULT DRIVE. *(L.C. Lambrecht)*

PAGE 258: BETHPAGE 8TH – A BIG ELEVATION DROP CREATES CLUB SELECTION DIFFICULTY FOR THE PLAYER ON THIS LENGTHY 220-YARD PAR-3. *(L.C. Lambrecht)*

PAGE 259: BETHPAGE 9TH – THREE LARGE BUNKERS AND DEEP ROUGH WILL PREVENT AN ERRANT SHOT FROM BOUNCING INTO THE GREEN OF THIS 420-YARD HOLE THAT COMPLETES THE FRONT NINE. *(L.C. Lambrecht)*

PAGE 260: BETHPAGE 10TH – ONE OF THE LONGEST PAR-4'S IN OPEN HISTORY, NUMEROUS BUNKERS ALONG BOTH SIDES WILL CATCH AND PUNISH ERRANT SHOTS. *(L.C. Lambrecht)*

PAGE 261: BETHPAGE 11TH – A PARTIALLY BLIND TEE SHOT CREATES JUST ONE OF MANY OBSTACLES THAT PLAYERS WILL FACE ON THIS 444-YARDER. *(L.C. Lambrecht)*

BETHPAGE 8TH

BETHPAGE 9TH

BETHPAGE 10TH

BETHPAGE 11TH

Hole #12 – Par 4, 489 yards:

The tee shot on the 12th is possibly the most demanding on the course. From the championship markers, the hole is a sharp left dogleg, with tall trees on the left standing watch at the corner. However, it is a huge double-tiered cross bunker in the drive zone that gives the 12th its character, requiring a shot of some 240 yards to clear. Play short of that bunker, or to its right, and the hole becomes a par 5. The problems don't end in the fairway. The green is protected by three large, deep, high-lipped bunkers set amidst mounds and thick rough, and the two-tiered putting surface pitches toward the left front, a true Tillinghast green.

Hole #13 – Par 5, 566 yards:

The 13th is a long, relatively narrow par 5 cut through the forest. The tee shot must carry some 200 yards of rough to reach the fairway, and must favor the left center to avoid a tall oak at the corner of the slight bend to the right. The second shot—especially for the average player—must deal with a huge, deep bunker that juts out into the fairway from the left some 150 yards from the green. The bunker helps form a second dogleg—this one slightly to the left—and together with trees close in on the right, leaves only a dangerously narrow landing area in the fairway. The final approach shot has been made more difficult with the addition of a relatively flat crossbunker some 20 yards short of the green. Another bunker below the right front of the green gathers up many weak shots that follow the natural fall of the terrain at this point. The putting surface is relatively small and is contoured toward the left front.

Hole #14 – Par 3, 165 yards:

The 14th is a tricky little par 3 played over a deep rough-filled gully to an elevated green protected by three steep bunkers at its right front corner. The putting surface has a pronounced right-to-left pitch.

Hole #15 – Par 4, 477 yards:

The 15th hole is a backbreaker, a long par 4 that rises 50 feet over its last 35 yards to a small two-tiered green that is tightly guarded by three bunkers and surrounded by trees. The fairway ripples in the drive zone, where it bends slightly to the left. The player will not be able to see the lower portion of the flagstick to determine actual position of the hole due to the elevation change from fairway to green. Because of its change in elevation, the hole plays more like 500-510 yards.

Hole #16 – Par 4, 487 yards:

The 16th plays from a tee situated above the 15th green to a deceptively wide-open fairway crossed by a dry ditch. The drive must favor the left side, however, to open up the approach, which must be

OPPOSITE PAGE: BETHPAGE 12TH - DIFFICULT CROSS BUNKERING WILL TEST THE DRIVING ABILITY OF PLAYERS ON THIS 489-YARD, PAR-4, BACKBREAKER. *(L.C. Lambrecht)*

PAGE 264: BETHPAGE 13TH - AT 566 YARDS, THE LONGEST HOLE ON THE COURSE REQUIRES NEGOTIATING A NUMBER OF TREES BOTH LEFT AND RIGHT FOR THE PLAYER TO HAVE A GOOD CHANCE AT BIRDIE. ONCE AGAIN, THE GREEN IS WELL PROTECTED BY BUNKERS. *(L.C. Lambrecht)*

PAGE 265: BETHPAGE 14TH – THE SHORTEST HOLE ON THE COURSE AT 165 YARDS, THREE LARGE BUNKERS PROTECT THIS PAR 3 AND THE GREEN HAS SEVERE RIGHT TO LEFT PITCH. *(L.C. Lambrecht)*

PAGE 266: BETHPAGE 15TH – PERHAPS THE MOST DEMANDING OF ALL HOLES, THIS 477-YARD, PAR-4 HOLE GOES UPHILL 50 FEET IN THE FINAL 35 YARDS AND IS TIGHTLY GUARDED BY BUNKERS WITH A SMALL, TWO-TIERED SLOPING GREEN THAT WILL TEST THE NERVES OF ANY PLAYER (NOTE THE FIRST CUT OF ROUGH ON THE RIGHT SIDE). *(L.C. Lambrecht)*

PAGE 267: BETHPAGE 16TH – A DECEPTIVELY WIDE-OPEN FAIRWAY GREETS THE PLAYER ON THIS DOWNHILL PAR-4 OF 487 YARDS AND FINISHES WITH A GREEN WELL PROTECTED BY BUNKERS. *(L.C. Lambrecht)*

BETHPAGE 12TH

264)

BETHPAGE 13TH

BETHPAGE 14TH

266)

BETHPAGE 15TH

BETHPAGE 16TH

BETHPAGE 17TH

BETHPAGE 17TH

threaded between four greenside bunkers, three of which are to the right. It is the front bunker on that side that gives the hole its character, edging out into the entrance to the green, demanding that a very precise long-iron approach be played, quite possibly with a slight fade.

Hole #17 – Par 3, 213 yards:

The 17th is an imposing par 3, one of the most challenging one-shotters on Long Island. The long-iron tee shot must carry a pair of massive frontal bunkers whose high lips conceal a shallow, figure-eight-shaped green that is set slightly on a diagonal to the tee. The left portion of the green is tiered slightly higher than the right, and has more depth. The right side has a narrow entrance, but an over-clubbed shot in that direction will find the rear bunker. Two more traps, one on either side of the green, pose a serious threat only to the misdirected shot. In design, this hole is not unlike the famous 17th at Pebble Beach, give or take an ocean.

Hole #18 – Par 4, 420 yards:

The 18th hole has recently been converted by Rees Jones from a disappointingly weak finisher to a real challenger. It plays from an elevated tee to an elevated green set in a natural amphitheater behind the clubhouse. The drive zone is narrowed progressively by a series of bunkers to either side, only 20 yards wide at the farthest point of the bunkers 270 yards from the tee. The green is protected by huge, high-lipped bunkers at its front corners, and two more behind. The final dance floor tilts severely back-to-front.

PAGE 268: BETHPAGE 17TH – FROM THE TEE, THE BUNKERS CREATE A VISION OF DESERT WITH SAND VIRTUALLY SURROUNDING THE 213-YARD, PAR 3. *(L.C. Lambrecht)*

PAGE 269: BETHPAGE 17TH, AT 213 YARDS, THIS PAR 3 WILL OFFER MANY PUNISHING RESULTS TO ERRANT SHOTS, BE IT THE ARRAY OF BUNKERS OR THE TALL GRASS IN FRONT. *(L.C. Lambrecht)*

OPPOSITE PAGE: BETHPAGE 18TH — U.S. OPEN "DOCTOR" REES JONES STRENGTH-ENED THIS HOLE THAT NOW PLAYS AT 420 YARDS WITH THE SECOND SHOT UPHILL TO A SLOPING BACK TO FRONT GREEN. *(L.C. Lambrecht)*

BETHPAGE 18TH

BETHPAGE 5TH

Epilogue

As the world awaits "Every Man's Open" at Bethpage Black, Long Islanders can look across their golfscape and be proud…and grateful. Visitors who attend the 2002 Open and find the time to tee it up themselves will find an outstanding array of courses, both public and private, classic and modern. And they will leave convinced, as Charles Blair Macdonald was, that Long Island does provide the ideal terrain for a variety of golfing experiences of the highest quality.

Golf on Long Island has never been better. The reasons why can be summarized in two words: restoration and resurgence.

Golf course renovation has been a national focus for the past decade, and Long Island is certainly in the vanguard. Restoration is the primary element of renovation these days, and Long Island's classic courses have never looked better.

Long Island's public courses have followed suit. Bethpage Black is now truly awesome, its conditioning rivaling that of the very best private clubs.

(273

OPPOSITE PAGE: BETHPAGE 5TH

(L.C. Lambrecht)